S0-FJO-408

DECISION MAKING IN SOVIET POLITICS

This book is about the way in which the Soviets reach their decisions. Based on research by other sovietologists and by himself, the author focuses on the conditions which allow specialists and societal groups to influence decision making. In *Decision Making in Soviet Politics* John Löwenhardt analyzes the decision-making processes in ten issues from different policy areas. He shows that agenda building is a crucial phase in Soviet decision-making processes. Specialists frequently succeed in placing issues on the political agenda and sometimes they manage to frustrate the policy demands of the men in the Kremlin. As a result, the decisions that are finally reached often have the character of compromises between different groups of specialists and Party leaders.

John Löwenhardt lectures and does research at the Institute for Eastern European Studies, University of Amsterdam. His publications include *The Soviet Politburo*.

Decision Making in Soviet Politics

by

JOHN LÖWENHARDT

St. Martin's Press
New York

 For information, write:
St. Martin's Press, Inc., 175 Fifth Avenue, New York, NY 10010
Printed in Hong Kong
First published in the United States of America in 1981

ISBN 0–312–19013–1

Library of Congress Cataloging in Publication Data

Löwenhardt, John.
Decision-making in Soviet politics.

Bibliography: p.
Includes index.
1. Soviet Union–Politics and government–1953-
–Decision making. 2. Public administration–Soviet
Union–Decision making. I. Title.
JN6531.L68 1981 354.4707′25 81-4703
ISBN 0–312–19013–1 AACR2

For my father
in memory of Mimi de Leeuw

Contents

List of Figures and Tables

Preface

Some years ago Jerry Hough, the enfant terrible of American sovietology, wrote that a dissertation should preferably not retain its original organization and conceptual framework from its inception to its completion. If it did, the student would not have learned enough to cause a reconceptualization. The history of my dissertation confirms his thesis that writing a dissertation is a learning experience. At the beginning of my stay at Columbia University's Russian Institute (1973-1974) I studied decision making in Soviet science policy. At that time I did not yet have a concrete idea about how to organize the book. Later I had the good fortune to meet the historian Loren Graham, with whom I had a number of stimulating talks. He advised me to delve into the issue of the 1961 reorganization of the USSR Academy of Sciences, and I used the rest of the year to complete a case study on this subject. Once I returned to Holland, I was confronted with the problem of finding a theoretical framework for the presentation and interpretation of my findings, a framework which would link up my work with that of others who study Soviet politics. The existence in books and journals of several dozen case studies of Soviet decision making, case studies which had often been written independent of each other, made me decide to use them as the basis for empirical generalizations which were to be tested by my own case study. At first this led to a rather odd separation of theory from fact reporting, but thanks to the advice of Hans Daudt the arrangement of this book has much improved.

My study of the Academy of Sciences reorganization is based on printed sources. I have tried to arrange interviews with those Soviet scientists who were directly involved in decision making, but in spite of the 'spirit of détente' of the late 1970s the Soviet authorities have not seen fit to allow me a few straightforward interviews on a rather harmless subject. Thanks to these authorities, however, I came to meet a scientist who had lived through the reorganization and was willing to talk with me. In August 1979 Alexander Lerner, a Jewish cyberneticist who has been waiting for permission to emigrate since 1971, was refused registration at the International Political Science Association's XI World Congress in Moscow. This serious violation of academic freedom by the Soviet authorities in cooperation with IPSA executives naturally drew the attention of Dutch political scientists, and thus I came to know dr. Lerner. I am very grateful to Alexander Iakovlevich for his interview and hope that he will soon be able to continue his scientific work in Israel.

My greatest debt is to my teacher, Jan Willem Bezemer, whose exciting lectures on Soviet history and politics made me decide to major in sovietology in the first place, who did his best to convince me that it would be much better for me to choose a profession with some chance for employment, and who, once I had persisted, encouraged, helped and corrected me whenever he could. He, together with Hans Daudt, read the manuscript of this book. Parts of it were read by Loren Graham and by Ger van den Berg of Leyden University's Documentation Center on East European Law, whereas Diane Everts-Doolan corrected my ramshackle English. She should not be held responsible for the fact that my English is not as smooth as that of a native speaker. To all of them I am indebted for their valuable suggestions. The Netherlands Organization for the Advancement of Pure Research (ZWO) provided me with the means for my stay at the Russian Institute in New York.

Finally, it is a pleasure to record my thanks to the ever cheerful Niko Heijnis, who typed most of the manuscript, to Inge Angevaare and Fenna Westerdiep for the enthusiasm with which they worked on the lay-out, and to my colleagues at the Institute for Eastern European Studies for providing me with ample time for research and writing.

January 1981 *JOHN LÖWENHARDT*

Introduction

The central objective of this book is to generate empirical generalizations that may serve as theoretical propositions on decision making and group influence in Soviet politics. For several reasons, a complete and all-encompassing theory of decision making in the Soviet Union is not the aim. First, a theory of decision making, in my opinion, is not valid unless it is an empirical theory, i.e. a system of logically related, empirically testable, lawlike propositions.[1] Such a theory is a human construct based on empirically observed phenomena. A political theory not based on the observable world would be a normative theory and would fall in the category of political philosophy. I believe that our understanding of decision making in Soviet politics is not advanced by excercises in political philosophy. Second, I am well aware of the limitations of the scientific inquiry of Soviet political processes. What we can discover of the goings-on in Soviet political institutions will always remain limited, especially if compared with democratic systems. The construction of a theory would require the availability of many more empirical data than are potentially at our disposal. This is not to say that we are not making any progress; it is a pleasing fact that more and more studies of Soviet decision making are partially based on interviews with the persons involved. A third reason is that a theory of decision making in Soviet politics would have to be able to explain the variations in decision-making practice over a period of more than sixty years and at a number of different levels: national, republican, provincial and local. On the one hand we know from numerous sources that the way in which decisions were reached in 1928 was different from 1919, and that the practices of Stalin in 1948 differed from those of Khrushchev in 1958 or Brezhnev in 1978. We know that the political styles were different, but we do not know all the details of these differences. On the other hand only very few in-depth studies of republican, provincial or local decision making have been written up to now.[2] A theory covering the complete sixty year period and all possible levels of decision making would have to involve both a developmental and a 'geographical' component and would thereby become forbiddingly complex. An attempt to build such a theory on empirical foundations is premature. In this book I will limit myself to decision making at the national level in the immediate post-Stalin period, roughly the 1950s and 1960s.

The relationship between theory building and empirical research is not a simple one, leading, for example, in a straight inductive line from the gathering of empirical data to the ultimate activity of theory construction. The processes of theory building and empirical research, on which it should be based, cannot so easily be separated. In the words of the French political scientist Maurice Duverger, one cannot do effective research without good theory, but effective research is also a prerequisite for good theory.[3] Through theory we know where to look for significant data, what to investigate and which hypotheses to test.

As far as Soviet decision making is concerned, a certain amount of empirical data is available in the form of case studies of decisions, groups and institutions. These data are raw and unshaped. In the process of their uncovering, the scientists have often used impromptu conceptual frameworks, sometimes consciously, sometimes unconsciously. Very little <u>cumulative</u> research, using one more or less well developed theoretical framework, has been done. The empirical generalizations that I hope to present will be based on case studies of ten decisions. I will re-interpret the outcomes of these case studies with the use of a conceptual framework based on general agenda-building and decision-making theories <u>and</u> on the specifics of Soviet decision making as revealed in these case studies. Thus I aim to develop theoretically significant empirical generalizations that may guide other scientists towards significant questions to ask, and towards their application on other decisions taken during different periods of Soviet political history. At the same time, the study is comparitive, but only in the sense that it makes use of an approach originally developed in the context of American politics.

The case studies on Soviet decision making and the role and influence of specialists that have been performed in the past, have come to different conclusions, ranging from negative - no influence on policy outcome - to positive. In his recent book on the role of criminologists in criminal policy making, Peter Solomon has summarized these conclusions by grouping them into four 'images of the Soviet policy-making process'.[4] These images differ according to the role played by persons outside the political leadership. In the first image, outsiders have virtually no influence on policy formation and decisions can be explained almost exclusively in terms of factional conflicts among the Party leaders. This view is to be found in the works of, a.o., Conquest, Ploss, Linden and Tatu.[5] The second image, to be distilled from works of Brzezinski & Huntington, Barghoorn and Meyer, concedes that outsiders do, in some small measure, influence policy decisions. But their influence depends on an invitation by some faction of the leadership and is concentrated in the latest stages of decision making, primarily in the mobilization of support for decisions already reached. As a rule they do not create an issue or initiate a policy discussion.[6] A third image holds that specialists and officials outside the political leadership, acting as individuals or as groups, do indeed influence the formation of policies by presenting the leaders with policy alternatives. In this view, the influence of these participants is limited only by the leadership's power to ignore or overrule their advice. This image summarizes the conclusions reached in quite a few case studies written in the late 1960s and early 1970s, such as those by Barry, Juviler, Graham, Stewart and Schwartz & Keech.[7] The fourth and final view is a variant of the third image, from which it differs in that it stresses comparitive conclusions. In this image constraints upon the influence of outside participants are not typical for the Soviet policy-making process, but are similar to the constraints that face actors in democratic decision making. A typical representative of this view is Jerry Hough.[8]

On the basis of his research, Solomon concludes that during the middle and late 1960s criminologists had considerable influence upon some decisions and had 'made a moderate impact upon the face of Soviet criminal policy as a whole.'[9] In addition, according to Solomon, most of the constraints upon their capacity to influence criminal policy, were similar to the limitations affecting specialists in the American and British policy-making process. Therefore his conclusion is that the results of his research confirm the fourth image of the Soviet policy-making process, at least as far as the role of criminologists in criminal policy-making is concerned. The question then is whether this is a peculiarity of criminal policy. On the basis of research performed by others, Solomon finds it safe to conclude that 'between 1956 and 1970 the participation of specialists broadened in a good number of areas in Soviet policy making and that specialists influence probably grew in most of these as well.'[10] He finally states that as of the beginning of the 1970s the Soviet policy-making process resembles Jerry Hough's model of institutional pluralism.[11]

In this book I do not aim at comparative conclusions. I believe that it is too early for such conclusions, for much more cumulative research on Soviet decision making is to be done. But this criticism should not conceal the fact that if we limit ourselves to Solomon's findings as far as the influence of criminologists on Soviet criminal policy-making is concerned, his book is of great value. It conveniently summarizes the different images of the decision-making process. We may try to find out whether Solomon was correct in suggesting that specialists also participated in areas other than criminal policy. It just may be that the third image is not typical for all areas of decision making and that in some particular area specialists enjoy only limited influence on the political leadership. Moreover, even though Solomon's analytic framework is rather simplistic and his test of influence - 'changing the probability of a given outcome'[12] - is approximate, he nevertheless has supplied us with a wealth of data supporting the conclusion that during the 1960s Soviet criminologists did indeed to a considerable extent influence criminal policy making. If one aims at the accumulation of relevant data, as I do in this book, such findings are only welcome.

We are still far removed from a theory of decision making in the Soviet Union, not to speak of a theory of decision making in general. Even if the degree of secrecy surrounding Soviet politics would be significantly reduced, Party archives would be thrown open and memoirs freely published, such a theory would still be a long way ahead. However, those engaged in political research should realize that a theory will not be forthcoming unless we work towards it. Theories, after all, are more of a process than an end result. They are never 'finished', but always subject to change caused by the uncovering of unexplained-for data and possibly the falsification of one of its propositions. Theory building is a creative process which should proceed concurrently with the empirical research of political phenomena.

The empirical material used in this study is limited in a number of different ways. These limits at the same time outline the limitations of the empirical generalizations to be drawn from the data.

First, I am exclusively concerned with Soviet domestic policy. Foreign policy is off-limits here, not so much because decision making on foreign policy issues is expected to be fundamentally different from decision making on domestic issues, but because it is much less open to research. It is more difficult to investigate the Soviet decision-making process when foreign policy issues are concerned, partly because the merits of the different foreign policy proposals are not usually discussed in the press, as they often are in the case of domestic issues. Nevertheless I have decided to include one issue with both domestic and foreign-policy aspects, viz. the demand for large-scale emigration of Jews to Israel as expressed in the 1967-1971 period. Of all ten cases studied in this book, this was the only issue in which Western publics were to some considerable extent interested, and in which this interest may have played a role in the considerations of Soviet decision-makers. Its analysis is hoped to be illuminating for the differing treatment by the decision-makers of 'orthodox' and 'unorthodox' dissent.[13] This book focusses on orthodox dissent, i.e. on agenda building and decision making in issues where the parties basically accept the Soviet system and its values. Their demands, criticism and proposals do not imply a fundamental change of the system; on the contrary, they are thought to be instrumental to the system. Nevertheless, the inclusion of an issue with aspects of unorthodox dissent is expected to be useful, for it may direct our attention toward peculiarities which might otherwise be overlooked.

Second, I am primarily concerned with the period between the death of Joseph Stalin and the deposition of Nikita Khrushchev, 1953-1964. This is because this period is the most intensively investigated as far as decision making is concerned. Not surprisingly, it is also the period when decision-making processes were relatively well visible, through such things as the publication of Central Committee Plenum Reports and the unrestrained political style of Party leader Nikita Khrushchev.

Third, though one of my primary concerns is to investigate the influence of diverse political groups in the decision-making process, it is the decision which is in the focus of my analysis, not the group. Others have built their books around a number of separate groups, most notably Gordon Skilling and Franklyn Griffiths in their volume on *Interest Groups in Soviet Politics*.[14] I feel that one of the main drawbacks of this approach is the difficulty of proceeding from the establishment of the group status of different bureaucracies and professions to the establishment of their influence in decision making. If the security police or the military or the industrial managers may be considerd an interest group in terms of certain defining characteristics, this in itself does not prove that they influence decision making in their policy area. To establish such influence relationships, one will have to engage in the in-depth study of individual decision-making processes. When doing so, the focus shifts from the group to the decision, and the group-aspect is de-emphasized. One may find - as did Peter Solomon - that in specific cases influence was, indeed, wielded, though it may not be so obvious that is was wielded by a determined operating, well-organized interest group.

Fourth, this study is not concerned with routine decisions, such as the annual fixation of planning directives. Only decisions which constitute a policy change and which were precedented by more or less hotly debated issues, will qualify for inclusion in this study.

Fifth and finally, a prerequisite for the inclusion of a decision in this study is that it has been the subject of serious study by qualified sovietologists. This point needs some clarification. In the course of my study of Soviet decision making I decided to investigate one particular decision in-depth, the 1961 reorganization of the USSR Academy of Sciences. This decision had been the subject of an excellent study by Loren Graham, which had raised new questions in my mind.[15] In writing this case study - as reported in Chapter 4 - I have not been guided by a specific analytic framework. This has been done on purpose, the purpose being to present a historical report of the data on this issue which would be as complete as humanly possible. The report should not be clouded by too much interpretation of events. In this way, in my conception, two important requirements of scientific reporting could be met. First, colleagues wishing to judge my case study would be able to determine if indeed I have found all the data available. Second, the separation of factual reporting (Chapter 4) and political analysis (Chapter 5) would enable him to establish if the interpretation of specific facts and events has indeed been correct, and if no unjustified inferences have been made.

As was said above, a theory of decision making should be an empirical theory. This implies that the conceptial framework which is to be used in interpreting the facts such as reported in Chapter 4 should be based on empirical referents as much as possible. Such a conceptual framework should preferably not be invented in the abstract. It has therefore been my intention to develop such a framework both on the basis of Western theorizing on decision making (based on observed political phenomena) and on the basis of the store of knowledge we have of decision making in the Soviet Union. Quite a few case studies have been written on decisions taken during Khrushchev's years in power, but, as noted above, surprisingly little cumulative investigation has been performed. The students of Soviet decision-making have not often compared each others findings on the decision-making process. I have wanted to undertake such comparison, and to find out what is common, and what not. In doing so, I will generate both the conceptual framework with which to interpret my own case study, and the empirical generalizations which may be tested by applying them to that case study. In such a way, a set of theoretical propositions on decision making in the Societ Union, empirically based on past research, is checked and possibly revised with the help of my own research.

Of course this approach is beset by dangers, one of the most obvious being that I have to rely on the work done by others. What if they have overlooked significant events, crucial policy speeches or important newspaper articles? I have tried to insure myself against this danger by studying different studies of one and the same decision, hoping that what one scholar would have failed to see, someone else would have noticed. In addition, for most of the case studies I have been able to extend the source base available by using the comprehensive subject catalogues available at the University of Amsterdam's Institute for Eastern European Studies, as well as its rich collection of Soviet publications.[16]

The issues included in this study are the following:

1. Virgin lands campaign, 1953-1954
2. The Sovnarkhozy reform of 1957
3. Abolition of the Machine-Tractor Stations, 1951-1958
4. Family law reform, 1954-1968
5. Introduction of governmental tort liability, 1956-1961
6. Anti-parasite legislation, 1956-1965
7. Reform of primary-secondary education, 1952-1959
8. Opposing pollution of Lake Baikal, 1958-1978
9. Jewish emigration from the Soviet Union, 1967-1971
10. Reorganization of the USSR Academy of Sciences, 1954-1961

In Chapter 1 I will deal with the concepts that are central to the study of decision making - issues, decisions and policy, agendas - and present alternative models of agenda building and decision making. Chapter 2 will contain factual reports on the issues 1-9. Chapter 3 will be dedicated to the search for empirical generalizations on agenda building and decision making and will be based on the conceptual framework of Chapter 1 and the reports of Chapter 2. In Chapter 4 I will present my own case study of the reorganization of the USSR Academy of Sciences. The concluding Chapter 5 will show to what extent the generalizations of Chapter 3 were confirmed or modified by the results of my own research. In this way chapters with a more or less theoretical character will alternate with historically oriented chapters.

1 Conceptual Framework

Decision making involves issues, decisions, policy, agendas and actors. I will discuss these categories here, and proceed to present alternative models of agenda building and decision making.

Issues

Decisions are made over issues. If there were no issues, if this world was free of discord, it would be quite uninteresting to the political scientist. Decisions represent a phase in the process which transforms issues into policy; it is therefore only natural to start out with the concept _issue_. An issue is a conflict. Cobb and Elder have defined it as 'a conflict between two or more identifiable groups over procedural or substantive matters relating to the distribution of positions or resources.'[1] Strictly speaking an issue thus defined does not have to involve a political conflict. The 'matters' in this definition may be private, non-political, such as would be the case in a conflict between a consumers' union and a factory over air pollution or toxic toy paint, or between two factions of a voluntary association over the distribution of seats in its board. An issue is only interesting to us as far as it involves _public_, not private matters, i.e. public positions and resources. In non-communist systems it may be a problem to decide whether an issue is private or public, and to the parties involved it may cost much effort to transform a private issue such as toy-paint safety into a public issue. In the Soviet Union, however, marxism-leninism leaves almost nothing in the private realm, so that the problem of ensuring that a specific issue is regarded as a public matter and not something to be left to private arrangements, is hardly a problem at all.

Issues originate in different policy areas, depending on their subject matter. Some concern the production and deployment of new weapons, others the composition of the annual state budget ('guns or butter') or the right to leave one's country. The issues studies in this book are taken from different areas, all but one in the internal policy realm:

- Economic policy: agriculture/production (Virgin lands)
  industry/organization (Sovnarkhozy)
  agriculture/organization (MTS reform)
- Law and social policy (Family law reform; Tort liability; Anti-parasite legislation)
- Science and education policy (Educational reform; Academy of Sciences reform)
- Environmental protection policy (Lake Baikal).

The issue of Jewish emigration is a special type, involving both domestic and foreign policy. This distinction in different policy areas has not been presented to suggest a well-developed typology; I merely want to stress that the policy area may be of importance for the way in which the decision-making process develops. Whether this is in fact the case remains to be seen.

Issues may vary in scope. Whether citizens should have the right to take their government to court for harm caused by an improper official action is one possible issue, whether or not a country should collectivize its agriculture is quite another. The policy area, of course, is different, but so is the degree to which the issue involves value re-allocation. At any moment in time values are distributed in a society in a specific way, and issues stem from demands to re-allocate them. More refrigerators and fewer tanks, the right for Jews to emigrate or for any citizen to organize whatever association or political party he wants: the degree of proposed value re-allocation of the issue will differ. It may involve the whole population, or only specific groups. It may entail large income transfers or fixing a nominal fee. The degree to which an issue involves value re-allocation will be called its scope. This concept is difficult to operationalize since it involves so many aspects. Braybrooke & Lindblom have tried to do so, though they were concerned with a somewhat different concept: the size of changes effected by decisions. They feel confident that the subjective element of value appreciations can be overcome, 'for in any society there develops a strong tendency toward convergence in estimates of what changes are important or unimportant.'[2] Indeed, it is not so difficult to establish that the party system or relations between church and state will be considered as 'large' issues and school lunch programs as a 'small' issue, but using this crude method it is impossible to establish the relative distances between the scopes of different issues. The arrangement of a great number of issues on a continuum between 'small' and 'large' would require a quite sophisticated operationalization.

However, for the purpose of relating an issue's scope to the formal position of its initiator, the criterion provided by Braybrooke and Lindblom may suffice:

> We consider the introduction through public policy of what is considered to be a new and important element ... to be a large or non-incremental change. On the other hand, a somewhat greater or reduced use of an existing social technique or a somewhat higher or lower level of attainment of some existing values is a small or incremental change.[3]

The concept of incremental changes introduced here, is then split up in two types: repetitive changes, such as a change in grain procurement prices or enrollment quota's for the universities, and nonrepetitive changes. Soviet examples of the last type would be the introduction of a guaranteed monthly income for collective farmers or the right for them to carry passports. Non-incremental changes, i.e. large changes in important variables, are thought to be more frequent in the Soviet Union than in non-communist systems. Brzezinski and Huntington believe that

> On the whole, it can probably be said that Soviet history offers more examples of clear-cut selection, both domestically and in foreign po-

licy . Both the Stalin period and the post-Stalin phase have been punctuated by dramatic new programs and reforms. The collectivization, the Stalin-Hitler pact, the party-state reorganization of 1962, and the 'peaceful coexistence' doctrine all involved sharp turns. It is, however, likely that gradually, with the Soviet Union becoming a more developed society, it will become more difficult for the leaders to change course abruptly, at least in domestic affairs, without causing major economic and social dislocations.[4]

On the other hand, Braybrooke and Lindblom have stressed that the incremental nature of policy making is often disguised, 'more often in the Soviet Union than in the United States'[5], thereby suggesting that in the Soviet Union more decisions are incremental than meet the eye. Certainly economic planning has become an incremental affair after the large decisions of the 1920s; and after the collectivization of agriculture in the early 1930s - another large decision - changes in agricultural organization and production have been incremental, some repetitive, others not. The question is: are large decisions over large issues still being taken, or do incremental issues hide behind large decisions?

Above I have mentioned the concept of the initiator of an issue. I have also defined issue in terms of a conflict. Now how exactly are issues being created? Of course empirical research must provide the answer, but for the time being we may consider some logical possibilities. Logically, an issue is created if and when a person (to be called the initiator) or group, prompted by dissatisfaction with the existing distribution of values in society, criticizes this distribution and proposes or demands a re-allocation. The person or group may be anyone, in the Soviet context I would say: from the Party leader or the Politburo to an unknown Soviet citizen. Once the demand for re-allocation has been made there is conflict between the existing situation and the demand; the issue has been created. If a person more or less often succeeds in initiating issues, we may call him a political entrepreneur.

This conflict may not only vary greatly in scope and intensity, it may also be suppressed. A first possibility is that a Party Secretary wants to apply a rather drastic change in the current distribution of values and does not want to be hampered by opposition to his plans. In such case he nevertheless acts as a political entrepreneur. The Party Secretary may either succeed or fail in his attempt to suppress conflict. Failure may - at least logically - be brought about by powerful opposition in the Party Presidium or Secretariat, but also by opposition from below, for example from societal groups or governmental institutions. If this should be found to happen we may perhaps conclude to considerable influence of such groups on the allocation of values.

Alternatively, the status-quo may be challenged not from above but from below, by individual citizens or social groups. As long as their demands remain isolated and do not reach either the political top or the public, an issue may have been created but exists on a subterranean level and is ineffective. We know of many instruments available to the political leadership to protect itself from the spontaneous creation of issues by grassroots activists. Examples of such instruments are the state monopoly of the mass media and consequently the institutional affiliation of publications, the censorship system and Party control through primary Party organizations. Nevertheless, since such systems are not perfect, the logical possibility remains of public issues being created 'from below'. In the next chapters we will see if this logical possibility is ever realized.

Decisions and policy

A decision is a choice made by a person or collective for one of several alternative ways of acting. Since I am concerned with public issues, only decisions made by authorities are considered. Political decision making is the binding allocation of values for a society or parts of it, to paraphrase David Easton.[6] The authorities involved do not necessarily have to be <u>public</u> authorities in the sense of members of the administration, though often they are. In one-party states in particular, Party officials with no formal position outside the Party apparat qualify as well. Many of their decisions, of course, are formalized through the proper state channels, but even intra-Party decisions will often have such profound social consequences that the position of these authorities equals that of public authorities.

Obviously, decisions and policy are closely related concepts. Decisions often result in new or changed policy, whether such was aimed for, or not. On the other hand, there may be policy in the absence of decisions, i.e. policy may be made through so-called non-decisions.[7] In such case the existing situation is kept unchanged and demands for change are effectively suppressed. A policy may also be seen as the end-result of a number of consecutive decisions. However, policy is almost never the result of the neat and rational schemes that political scientists have designed for policy making. A policy, in the words of Charles Lindblom,

> ...is sometimes the outcome of a political compromise among policy makers, none of whom had in mind quite the problem to which the agreed policy is the solution. Sometimes policies spring from new opportunities, not from 'problems' at all. And sometimes policies are not decided upon but nevertheless 'happen'.[8]

Instead of selecting one particular policy area - such as agriculture or criminal policy-and analyzing Soviet policy in that area, I have chosen to compare policy <u>making</u> in limited issues from different areas. In each of these issues the focus is on the decision-making process preceding <u>one</u> particular decision. Depending on the issue, this decision may be seen as part of an ongoing policy-making process, or it may be seen as a fundamental change in policy. The decision to abolish the Machine-Tractor Stations, for example, may be considered as part of Khrushchevs agricultural policy, aiming at increased efficiency and productivity. Alternatively, it may be seen as a once-and-for-all, fundamental change as far as the ownership of means of (agricultural) production is concerned. The truth is that the decision was both. For these reasons it does not seem wise to speak of policy making. True, the result of the decisions studies here is that policies were made, changed or terminated, and these aspects will of course be quite visible in the case studies. True also, the case studies often span a period of quite a few years. However, the focus remains on isolated decisions.

If someone changes his behavior in anticipation of the expected reaction of someone or something else, influence is at work. The law of anticipated reactions, as it has been formulated by Carl Friedrich, implies that just about anything may exercize influence. Without being aware of it, the parent influences his child, who, fearing punishment, refrains from the mischief he was about to execute. The voter may influence a member of parliament even through they never met: in deciding how to vote on a specific issue, the representative weighs the possible reactions of 'his' voters. The tiny mosquito influences the sleeper, many times his size and strength, who may reluctantly decide not to sleep by the open window for fear of being harrassed during the night. Influence may be exercized by persons, groups, animals, objects, rules, norms, values and what have you. It is no surprise then that it may be exercized by an ideology as well.

The influence of ideology on decision making has been a recurrent theme in American political science literature since Peter Bachrach and Morton Baratz introduced the concept of 'nondecision' in the early 1960s. Nondecision making, they wrote,

> ...is a means by which demands for change in the existing allocation of benefits and privileges in the community can be suffocated before they are even voiced; or kept covert; or killed before they gain acces to the relevant decision-making arena.[9]

This leads us to one of the few advantages of studying Soviet politics: the fact that the nondecision-making process is more obvious and open to analysis than in democratic countries. In contrast to the United States, the Soviet Union has its officially formulated state ideology, prescribing which ends may be pursued, and which not; which means are allowed and which strategies should or should not be followed. In fact, though marxism-leninism allows for quite some freedom in the interpretation of the ends to be aimed at, the means and strategies to be used, many alternatives have explicitly been excluded. They have been exhaustively codified in the censors' so-called Talmud. It is not wise - courageous, yes; wise, no - for a Soviet citizen openly to demand such things as the introduction of competing political parties, private ownership of the means of production or the elimination of collectivized agriculture. It is not wise to insist on his right to criticize political leaders and to execute such right without taking precautions. Even if he wished to do so, he would not be able to proceed far beyond the small group, for he would be denied access to the means of communication, controlled and censored by the state. The only means available for publicly expressing demands which run counter to official ideology, are esoteric communications in seemingly harmless texts, and samizdat publications. Only in the second half of the 1960s had the fear for possible reprisals subsided enough for samizdat to become a wide-spread phenomenon.

Here I am concerned only with what the Societ citizen can do within the 'proper' channels. I am not interested in what Brzezinski and Huntington have called 'unorthodox dissent', which wants to provide an alternative to the existing political system or essential parts of it.[10] I am only concerned with orhodox dissent, which accepts the basic ideological and political premises of the ruling party and sets itself the task of improving the system. Of course, no sharp line can be drawn between orthodox and unorthodox dissent. The most interesting issues are situated in the area where orthodox and unorthodox dissent meet. A study of such issues might teach us how change of the system can be brought about from within.

Agendas

Improving on the work of Bachrach and Baratz, Roger Cobb, Charles Elder, Jennie-Keith Ross and Marc Ross have introduced the agenda-building approach.[11] They have stressed that the early phases of the decision-making process have long been ignored. For students of Soviet politics it is imperative to realize that this observation - made in the context of the study of American politics - is of great relevance as far as their own work is concerned. Analyses of Soviet decision making have often lacked an in-depth study of the question 'where do public policy issues come from', as several of the case studies used as sources in Chapter 2 may witness.[12] The question of how issues are being created and 'why some controversies or incipient issues come to command the attention and concern of the formal centers of decision-making, while others fail' has often been bypassed because the investigators thought that no information was available or did not want to go looking for it, or both.[13] With my study of the Academy of Sciences reform-researched and analyzed by Loren Graham many years before - I want to show that the early phases of the decision-making process may not be left out on punishment of an incomplete and incorrect picture.

A political agenda is a set of issues demanding binding decision making. Two types of agendas have been distinguished: the public agenda and the formal agenda. On the public agenda - originally termed systemic agenda by Cobb and Elder - are issues that are viewed by great sections of the public as falling within the range of legitimate concerns meriting the attention of the polity. These are the political controversies which, in the view of a sizable portion of the public, deserve attention and require action by the proper authorities. The formal agenda, in the definition of Cobb and the Rosses,'is the list of items which decision makers have formally accepted for serious consideration'.[14] Of course, at any moment there are many different but overlapping formal - as well as public - agendas in a country. In the Soviet Union one may distinguish the union agenda, consisting of all issues for which a decision by central Party and government agencies is demanded, and republican, provincial and local agendas. I am concerned only with the union agenda, which, in terms of the formal agenda, may be seen as the aggregate of the agendas of the Politburo, Secretariat, Council of Ministers, Supreme Soviet and union ministries and agencies. This is not to say that the question of how and under what conditions an issue may move from lower-level agendas to higher-level agendas and vice-versa, is not an extremely interesting one. Issues which have always been thought to have originated in the Politburo may turn out to have been 'born' on a low level, and to have been passed on for decision.

What is interesting about political agendas is not so much their make-up or typology, but the relationships among them, and between them and the environment. What is necessary in the Soviet Union for an issue to reach public agenda status? How do issues most succesfully reach such status? How are they transferred from public to formal agenda status, by what means and under what conditions? These are the central questions of agenda building. They will be elaborated upon later in this chapter in the course of a description of alternative models of agenda building.

First, however, it will be useful to operationalize the public agenda concept, having done the same for the Soviet formal agenda. Cobb and Elder have neglected to undertake such operationalization, thereby circumventing the question: at what exact moment in time has an issue reached the public agenda, and at what moment has it not yet attained that status? Of course, in the United States with its abundance of ways in which grievances may be aired, such would be quite difficult. As far as the Soviet Union is concerned, operationalization is easier, due to the fact that the public communications system is organized hierarchically and is under permanent - though by no means complete - control by Party and censorship. In addition to this reason, operationalization is simplified by the circumstance that radio and TV - which could be two of the most important vehicles for the mass agenda - are not part of the public agenda because they hardly ever report or analyze controversial items.[15]

How exactly do we operationalize the Soviet public agenda? Is an issue on the public agenda once it has received attention in *Pravda* or *Izvestia*? Or should one say alternatively that an issue is on the public agenda once censorship has cleared its printing in whatever minor or limited-circulation publication - a local paper or a pamphlet of which fifty copies have been allowed? I opt for the second criterion. Thus, as far as the Soviet Union is concerned, I define the public agenda as consisting of all issues that have been printed in publications which have been approved by the censor. The public agenda, of course, is subject to permanent change as issues are being decided, new issues arise and old ones re-emerge.

The public agenda is made up of countless sub-agendas which have been roughly schematized in Figure 1. The two main distinguishing criteria in this Figure are all-Union versus republican/local, and general versus specialized. This leaves us with four quadrants. The periodicals listed in this Figure are only a few of the most typical examples of each quadrant; the listing cannot be exhaustive. Books and pamphlets are not mentioned here specifically, though any type of publication may

Figure 1: THE SOVIET PUBLIC AGENDA AND ITS SUB-AGENDAS

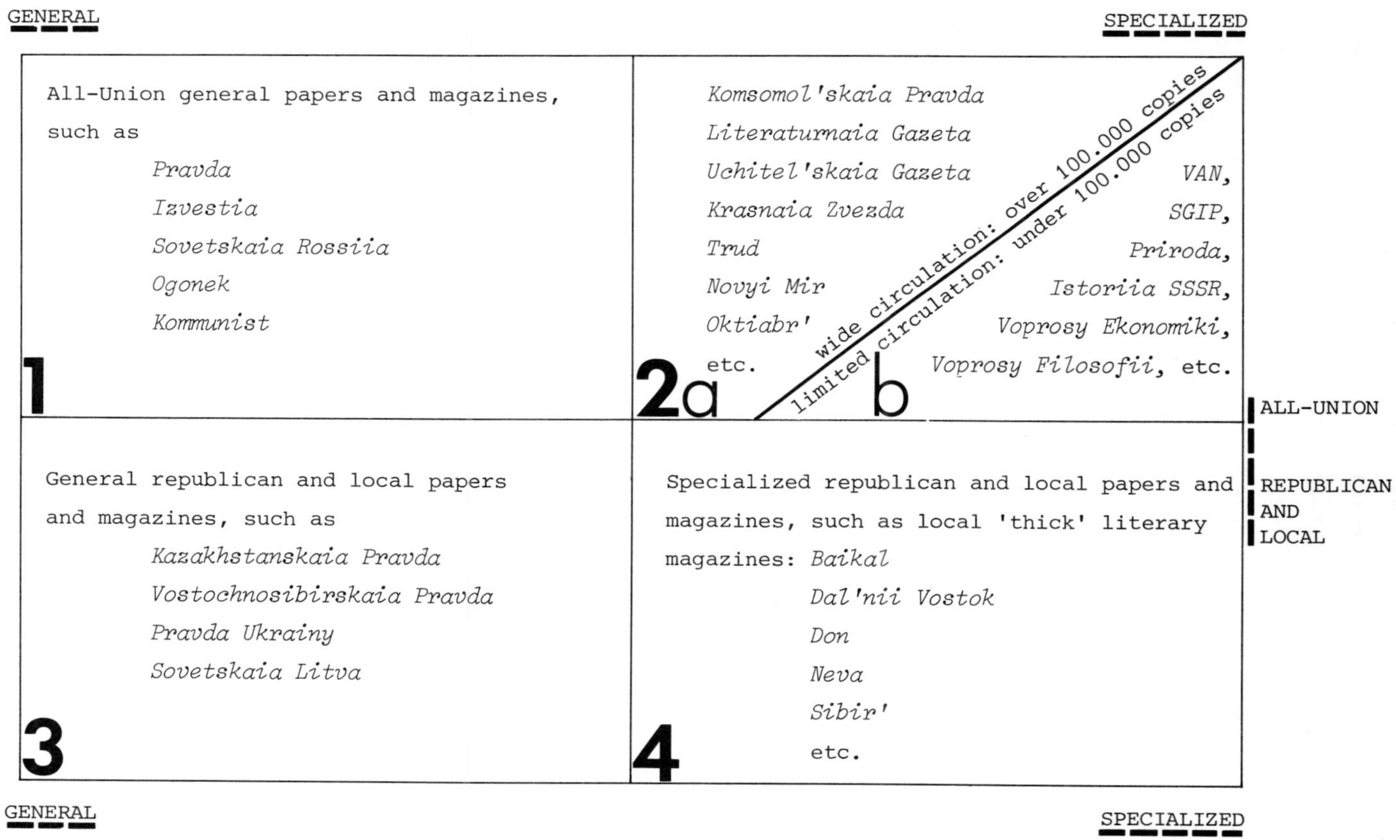

GENERAL	SPECIALIZED	
1 All-Union general papers and magazines, such as *Pravda* *Izvestia* *Sovetskaia Rossiia* *Ogonek* *Kommunist*	**2a** wide circulation: over 100.000 copies *Komsomol'skaia Pravda* *Literaturnaia Gazeta* *Uchitel'skaia Gazeta* *Krasnaia Zvezda* *Trud* *Novyi Mir* *Oktiabr'* etc. **b** limited circulation: under 100.000 copies *VAN*, *SGIP*, *Priroda*, *Istoriia SSSR*, *Voprosy Ekonomiki*, *Voprosy Filosofii*, etc.	ALL-UNION
3 General republican and local papers and magazines, such as *Kazakhstanskaia Pravda* *Vostochnosibirskaia Pravda* *Pravda Ukrainy* *Sovetskaia Litva*	**4** Specialized republican and local papers and magazines, such as local 'thick' literary magazines: *Baikal* *Dal'nii Vostok* *Don* *Neva* *Sibir'* etc.	REPUBLICAN AND LOCAL
GENERAL	SPECIALIZED	

be placed in the Figure, from an all-Union daily to a local book. In the first quadrant are the general national periodicals, such as general all-Union newspapers, weeklies and monthlies. They reach the mass public. The republican and local general papers and magazines of quadrant three reach smaller mass publics. Because of the great importance of the Russian republic, it would seem advisable to place RSFSR general periodicals in the first, instead of the third quadrant.

The second quadrant contains specialized all-Union publications. Here are the many sub-agendas of the all-Union agenda, in policy areas such as agriculture, education, environmental protection and so on and so forth. Some of these sub-agendas have their own mass-circulation newspaper, published by a ministry, Central Committee Secretariat department or mass organization: examples are _Komsomol'skaia Pravda_ (Komsomol, communist youth league), _Literaturnaia Gazeta_ (Writers' Union), _Krasnaia Zvezda_ (Ministry of Defence) and _Trud_ (Trade Unions). These papers reach millions of citizens. The thick literary magazines and specialized scientific journals are also in this quadrant; some, such as the literary monthlies, reach hundreds of thousands, others have a circulation of only a few thousand: _Ėkonomika i Matematicheskie Metody_ (Economics and Mathematical Methods), for example, which specializes in the modernization of economic planning, and the Academy of Sciences' Herald, _Vestnik Akademii Nauk_. Yet even these small publications are of all-Union character: they may only have a few thousand subscribers, but they are available throughout the Soviet Union in libraries and institutes. In this quadrant I have distinguished wide circulation publications (over 100.000 copies) from limited circulation publications (100.000 copies or less). This operation results in the distinction of no less than three classes of all-Union agendas:
the general mass agenda (quadrant 1), the specialized mass agendas (quadrant 2a) and the specialized agendas (quadrant 2b).

One of the questions which I will address is this: where and how may an issue enter the public agenda? How is the issue transferred from one sub-agenda (quadrant) to the other? Of course, much depends on the issue area and the issue's scope. A local issue is expected to be on a local agenda and may never reach the all-Union agenda. A Unionwide issue, on the other hand, may first be on an all-Union specialized agenda, entering, for example via the daily paper of some ministry or the journal of a research institute, or the issue may start out on a local general agenda, and only with great difficulty enter the general mass agenda. Alternatively, such an issue may be placed directly on the general mass agenda through publication of a controversy in *Pravda*, *Izvestia* or a similar periodical. Because of the affiliation of such publications with the topmost decision-making institutions, it may be assumed that if issues are being put on this agenda, they automatically qualify for the formal agenda as well. Once Soviet politicians allow the discussion of an issue in their most authoritative publications, they implicitly recognize that a decision on that issue must somehow be taken. Quadrant 1, therefore, represents a transitional stage between public and formal agenda.

Once an issue has reached the public agenda it is the subject of a public discussion. For a long time conventional wisdom in the West - supported by Soviet ideas on the function of the press - has been that such discussions are being initiated by the leadership in order to mobilize the population for a decision already taken, to demonstrate that the Soviet system is the supreme manifestation of democracy, or both. The populace, in this conception, may write letters, even critical letters, but the leadership manipulates the discussion and in the end publishes and accepts only those suggestions that it deems acceptable. Therefore the public discussions are no more than smoke screens meant to conceal the fact that the people have no power.

No doubt this view of public discussions applies to the mass discussions on the draft-constitutions of 1936 and 1977. However, the question is, is it correct to characterize the many and diverse discussions that have taken place since 1953 in this simple way? Were they really no more than empty propaganda devices? Philip Stewart has suggested that it makes great difference who initiates a policy discussion: the Politburo or lower-level institutions or groups.[16] He has thereby accepted that a lower-level agency may indeed initiate a discussion without prior consent of the Politburo, a presupposition that also underlies this book. In the case of initiation of a discussion by the Politburo - or some faction - he expects interest groups to have relatively little influence, compared with discussions where 'the leadership enters an ongoing policy discussion only after considerable individual and organizational support has coalesced around the specific proposals...'[17] His case study concerned the latter type of discussion and resulted in the finding of influence wielded by societal groupings over the top policy makers. Since Stewart studied only one case, his conclusion could not be comparative. In the next chapter I will apply his hypothesis to nine different cases, and we will see whether or not there is a difference between discussions initiated by the top leadership and discussions that were started on a low level.

Actors

The actors in the political process can be individuals, institutions or groups. The group approach of Soviet politics contends that interest groups play an important and at times influential role in the decision-making process.[18] Since this book has been influenced by products of that approach, it is no luxury to say a few words about groups and group influence.

Well-integrated studies of group influence in Soviet politics are scarce. The Skilling and Griffith volume has a lot to say about several groups, but little to prove as far as their influence on decision making is concerned. Through quantitative content analysis Milton Lodge has shown that certain Soviet elites are, indeed, to be considered as groups in the sociological sense, but he has failed to address the question of their influence.[19] Joel Schwartz and William Keech, on the other hand, have come very close to proving a case of group *influence*, but they in turn have neglected to address the question whether the influential scientists, educators and parents really acted as *groups*.

How, then, is a group to be defined? Milton Lodge has presented three conditions which must be present if elites are to meet the sociological requirements of a group:

1. They must view themselves as a distinct group (group self-consciousness);
2. they must be seen by others as groups (ascribed group status), and
3. the elite members must share a distinct set of beliefs and values, which distinguishes them from other elites.[20]

From his research he has concluded that his findings

> ...suggest that the elites are no longer transmission belts, are at a minimum potential interest groups, and by 1959-65 are perhaps active participants in the Soviet political system.[21]

Perhaps or perhaps not: that is the question, and the only way to find out is to investigate individual decisions. I believe that for purposes of political inquiry Lodge's criteria are not sufficient. His three requirements are necessary but not sufficient conditions for group status, at least if one wants to investigate group influence in decision-making processes. If we focus on such processes, two additional criteria have to be met:

4. interaction among group members, and
5. a conscious desire on the part of such members to influence decision makers.[22]

These five criteria distinguish groups - <u>political</u> groups - from aggregates; they are necessary and sufficient conditions for group status in politics. Scientists as a group may very well satisfy all five conditions: they often view themselves as a distinct group, are seen by others as a group and share common beliefs and values, such as the belief that the scientific method contributes to the ability to explain and predict, and the value of truth. Interaction with other scientists - either through the printing press or orally - is essential to the cultivation of science, and scientists often desire to influence decision makers.

However, for the study of agenda building and decision making, the category of 'scientists' is much too broad. As Gordon Skilling has remarked,

> Scientists, for example, might be classified according to various criteria: institutional affiliation (Academy of Sciences, universities, other institutions); regional level of activity (All-union, union-republic, provincial or local); official or nonofficial employment (party apparat, government department or nonofficial institutions); geographical location of employment... scientific field... function (pure scientists, technologists, governmental administra-

tors); rank or position (full or corresponding member of the Academy of Sciences, or research employee), and so on. In each case it would be a matter of research to determine whether and in what degree the institutional, regional, or other subgroup posesses distinctive views of its own, and whether and in what degree it shares common attitudes with other subgroups in the broader category of scientists. It would also have to be investigated how far each subgroup was divided ideologically into opinion groups with differing political attitudes and policy demands.[23]

For the purpose of studying decision-making processes in the Soviet Union one may distinguish three types of political groups with differing degrees of 'groupness': interest groups, opinion groups and policy coalitions. This distinction reflects an on-going discussion in interest group analysis; in the preface to his book on the British Medical Association, Eckstein mentions the 'old definitional controversy over what constitutes an "interest group"...'[24] In this controversy, according to him, three different constituents are distinguished: attitudes, objective characteristics (such as income, occupation) and common aims (regardless of attitudes or characteristics). Eckstein reserves the term interest group for groups 'which are likely collectively to pursue political aims just because they have objective characteristics in common.'[25] For groups that are not based on a common interest (flowing out of a common set of characteristics) he uses the term attitude groups. As Wootton has shown, this distinction between 'objective' interest groups and 'subjective' attitude groups is related to the distinction between 'selfish' groups that pursue their own (material) interest, and 'unselfish' groups that pursue the 'public' interest.[26] Both distinctions, however, seem rather artificial; they are not helpful for our purposes, for two reasons:
First, as was shown in the quotation from the Skilling article, the fact that interest group members have certain objective characteristics in common does not guarantee that their policy aims will be the same. Therefore, in our research we have to look for different opinion groups that may exist within one and the same interest group.
Second, such opinion groups may form alliances; these I will call poli-

cy coalitions. I certainly do not suppose that the policy aims of such coalitions are wholly 'unselfish' as against the 'selfish' goals of interest or opinion groups. In actual politics we see that an 'unselfish' interest is hard to detect since the proponents of 'selfish' interests are often tempted to present their interests as 'public' or 'national' interests. Any group that wants to influence the Soviet decision makers improves its chances of success by communicating its demands in terms of the 'public interest', whether these demands are indeed 'unselfish', or not. Therefore, I would agree with Skilling that 'whether the "interest" involved is a "selfish" one or a more general concern for the "public interest" is a matter for investigation in each case and cannot be assumed a priori.'[27]

Policy coalitions are not to be considered groups in the strict sense defined above. Since they are composed of representatives of different interest and opinion groups, they are expected to lack in Lodge's first two criteria of a group. The members of a policy coalition will have some beliefs and values in common, the more so since they aim for a common goal. They will also interact and most certainly desire to influence decision makers: that, after all, is the purpose of the coalition in the first place. One of the most important ways to do so is to build support for their demands through their publication in the press. The fact that all papers and periodicals in the Soviet Union are affiliated with some institution means that it will be possible for policy coalitions to find their 'own' mouth-pieces. Often specific periodicals are drawn into defending the policy positions of the institutions with which they are affiliated. In addition to interest and opinion groups and institutions, a policy coalition may therefore also involve the editorial board of some periodical.[28] Such coalitions must be thought of as ad hoc alliances for the purpose of promoting one or a few specific issues; therefore I have not called them policy groups, but policy coalitions instead. It is a matter of empirical verification to determine whether groups or such loose coalitions - or both - play a significant role in the decision-making process.

Two other possible sorts of actors are institutions and individuals. By institutions I mean the boards of formally constituted state and Partyorganizations of varying size, competence and authority. This term stands for such diverse organizations as the Party Central Committee (a body meeting only for a few days once in a few months[29]), or its Secretariat (i.e. the top of the Party bureaucracy, with over twenty departments and several thousand employees), the KGB collegium (the top of the secret police network), the Council of Ministers' Presidium or its equivalent in the Supreme Soviet, and the Politburo. This is where decisions are taken. As a matter of course I assume that such institutions are not necessarily monolithic or unanimous in their decision making, that they may be split over policy issues and that coalitions between like-minded factions from different institutions may develop.[30] Such factions or coalitions may want to enlist the support of a broader group for their policy position.[31] The difference between an institution and a group is that an institution is a formal decision-making arena, and a group is not. The actions of institutions consist of resolutions, policy proposals and decisions. Often these actions are communicated to the outside public in speeches or reports by the chairman or president of the institution.

Individuals may turn into political actors independent of their institutional or group affiliation if they possess some special quality. I have in mind prominent scientists, artists and other intellectuals who, because of their prominence, enjoy relatively easy access to the political agenda. Peter Kapitsa, for example, may be listened to not because he speaks for some organization or group, but simply because he enjoys great prestige and his opinion is appreciated as a valuable input for decision making.[32] Of course, the knack of influence wielding is to have prominent personalities speak for organizations, policy groups or coalitions. In such case it may turn out to be quite difficult for the outside observer to determine who exactly is voicing a demand: is it the individual, the organization or some opinion group from within that organization?

One of the problems of the study of Soviet politics is to establish what institution is, or is supposed to be the decision-making arena in any issue. Is the final battle over educational reform to take place in the Ministry of Education's collegium, in the corresponding Party Secretariat department, in the Council of Ministers' Presidium, or is the issue perhaps important enough to be discussed and decided in the

Politburo? Did the Politburo ever discuss the pollution of Lake Baikal, or was the issue left to be decided upon by lower institutions? Laws, of course, emerge from an interplay between institutions such as the Secretariat departments, ministries, Supreme Soviet legislative committees, the Supreme Soviet Presidium and, ultimately, the plenary meetings of the two Soviets. But is each and every draft law supposed to be put on the Politburo agenda first, and if not, which are and which are not? The rules for the determination of decision-making arenas are unknown or too general to allow for detailed answers to such questions. We will have to see what can be learned in this respect from case studies of individual decisions.

Agenda building and decision making

The origin of issues and their conversion into policy are processes that may happen in many different ways. For analytical purposes we will have to summarize these processes in a number of models. This paragraph will deal with the relationship between agenda-building and decision-making processes and will present a number of alternative decision-making models. It will open with an analysis of the 1958 educational reform that is based on the *communis opinio* of Western students of this reform. In the next chapter (pp. 64-70) I will show that this analysis is not beyond criticism.

Educational policy is an important instrument in the hands of a regime which wants to change society. It may be used to promote social mobility, improve the skills of the working force or mobilize great sections of the population. As far as the Soviet Union is concerned, many observers of the educational scene have noticed a break in educational policy in 1958, when Party Secretary Khrushchev applied fundamental changes in the school system. Academic training in primary-secondary and higher schools ranked high in the aspirations of Soviet citizens, not so much as a goal in itself but as a means for reaching others, such as high status and decent work. Since the number of vacancies in institutions of higher education was limited and enrollment in secondary schools had greatly increased after World War II, by the late

1950s competition for access to higher education had become fierce. Many candidates were denied admission to higher education, and since their dislike of physical labor was great, many of them refused to take up a steady job. They applied for admission to a university or institute year after year, at a time when industry badly needed them.

In April 1958 Nikita Khrushchev initiated the fundamental change in policy that he thought would alleviate these problems. At the Thirteenth Komsomol Congress he criticized the existing situation and said that 'all children entering school must prepare themselves for useful labor.'[33] In his speech the Party Secretary proclaimed that things must change, thereby placed the issue on the formal agenda, and in addition he indicated the direction of change. One of the major problems, of course, was to mobilize the social groups involved - scientists, teachers, parents, pupils - , win their support and change their attitudes and behavior. During the weeks and months to follow the congress the issue was discussed at meetings, conferences and in the press. Thus the issue of school reform was placed on the public agenda in order to mobilize the professional groups that would eventually have to implement them, and expand the issue to new groups in the population in an effort to gain their support. At the end of the year the final decision on the precise profile of school reform resulted from a struggle between Khrushchev and adversaries in the Party Presidium and Central Committee.

Even though the final decision was not taken before the first announcement of policy change was made, this example of decision making fits well with the models of Soviet politics that prevailed in sovietology during the 1950s and 1960s: the bureaucratic and directed-society models.[34] It also conforms to what Brzezinski and Huntington have called the 'trickle down' model of policy initiation, typical for the Soviet Union as against a 'bubble up' model for the United States.[35] In fact, many students of Soviet politics have stressed this aspect of decision making, and no wonder: after all the CPSU is supposed to be <u>the</u> motor for change in Soviet society.[36] Through its initiatives it is expected to mobilize the masses for the attainment of communism. The question is, is the Party really the only, or in any case the major, motor for change?

The model which was used in describing educational reform has been called the _mobilization model_ of agenda building by Cobb, Ross & Ross. This model 'describes the process of agenda building in situations where political leaders initiate a policy, but require the support of the mass public for its implementation.'[37] In the model, which is thought to be typical for directed societies, issues are placed on the formal agenda by decision makers and are soon expanded to the public agenda in order to generate the support of specific publics, necessary for their implementation. Sometimes the formal decision-making process has been completed by the time the issue - then a decision - is placed on the public agenda and new policy is authoritatively announced. In other cases, an ultimate decision has not yet been taken.

The phases of agenda building are the following:[38] _initiation_ of the issue, i.e. placing it on the formal agenda; _specification_ of the issue (defining and re-defining its content); _expansion_, i.e. interesting new groups in the population (publics) in the issue; and _entrance_ into the public agenda. Different strategies can be used to achieve entrance as quick and as easy as desired by the decision makers.

Is the mobilization model the only useful model for agenda building in the Soviet Union? If so, this would imply a degree of originality and control over censorship that I assume to be lacking in the Soviet leaders. Cobb, Ross & Ross have proposed two other models of agenda building, the _inside initiative model_ and the _outside initiative model_. In the _inside initiative model_ issues arise in institutions, and those who are responsible for their initiation do not seek expansion of the issue to the public agenda. 'Instead', the authors write,

> ...expansion is aimed at particular influential groups which can be important in the passage and implementation of the policy, while at the same time, the initiators try to _limit_ issue expansion to the public because they do not want the issue on the public agenda. Instead they seek a more 'private' decision within the government, and generally stand to be defeated when the issue is sufficiently expanded to include public groups that might be opposed to it.[39]

Initiation and specification by an agency, government department or group with close ties to the decision makers, is followed by limited expansion of the issue to selected groups, <u>not</u> to the general public. In this model entrance is the attainment of <u>formal</u> instead of public agenda status. Soviet politics knows many issues which the decision makers consider to be too delicate or dangerous to be put on the public agenda. If such issues would linger on the public agenda, they could easily create an explosive situation, threatening the decision makers' positions. To prevent this from happening they have created a powerful instrument: censorship. This system employs many thousands of censors throughout the country, who are guided by a thick volume listing, according to its title, 'information not to be published in the <u>open</u> press'[40], in other words: information and issues not to reach the public agenda. As the title of this so-called Talmud indicates, there is in the Soviet Union a small <u>closed</u> press as well, functioning as the 'public' agenda for closed decision making.[41]

The inside access model, as it has also been called, seems to be quite relevant for the study of Soviet decision making, which often proceeds behind closed doors. In fact, two of the four 'basic patterns for resolving political issues' in 'normal' Soviet politics inferred by Schwartz & Keech from the study of two decision-making processes, are congruent to the inside initiative model. These authors have distinguished between issues initiated and decided within the group of top leaders, and issues which are raised and resolved on lower decision-making levels such as ministries and Secretariat departments. In both cases there is no expansion of the issue to publics outside the decision-making arenas: in the words of Schwartz & Keech the 'scope of the conflict' is not broadened.[42] The problem with this model is that it is not easy for us to track down cases of closed decision making, for as long as entrance to the public agenda is succesfully prevented by censorship, it will be very difficult to study the decision-making process for lack of sources. Even if the ultimate decision taken behind closed doors is eventually published, we may have to resort to Kremlinological techniques if we want to learn what went on.

The third model of agenda building is the <u>outside initiative model</u>. It 'accounts for the process through which issues arise in nongovernmental groups and are then expanded sufficiently to reach, first, the public agenda and, finally, the formal agenda.'[43] This model may be seen as a formalization of the input side of David Easton's system theory, in which demands coming from the social environment are being aggregated and reach the political system via gate keepers (the censorship!) as inputs.[44] It is typical - though not exclusive - to the democratic political system with many independent points of access to the public agenda. Social, economic, religious, cultural or other groups, spurred by certain grievances or ideals, voice demands and thus try to initiate an issue. Their demands may be broad and general, and in need of specification. In order to induce decision makers to place the issue on the formal agenda - once it has reached the public agenda -, it may be necessary to involve new groups of the population with the issue by linking it with pre-existing ones; this is called expansion of the issue. Cobb and Elder have distinguished four sorts of publics involved in the expansion process, two specific publics and two mass publics. This concept - the public of a group - has been defined by David Truman, one of the founders of the interest-group approach of American politics, as 'an aggregate of individuals who are aware, or who can be made aware, of various possible consequences of the group's action...'[45] A public should not be identifield with a political group in the sense defined earlier in this chapter. It would therefore be unwise to designate - as Cobb and Elder have done - specific publics as groups.[46]

Mass publics are of course the general public (the least interested and informed) and the attentive public, i.e. those people who are most interested in and informed about public issues in general. Before an issue will reach such mass publics, it may have come to the attention of specific publics. The distinction Cobb and Elder make between 'identification groups' and 'attention groups' seems to be somewhat too analytic to be very useful for research. Instead, it is important to realize that within the 'attentive public' diverse political groups may operate on behalf of each of the contestants in the issue.

Entrance, the final stage of agenda building, is the movement of an issue form the public agenda to the formal agenda, i.e. the recognition by decision makers that the issue warrants serious consideration and deserves to be resolved. In the Soviet Union, where censorship allows the decision makers a degree of control over the public agenda unrivalled by democratic systems, once an issue has reached public agenda status it probably reaches the formal agenda more easily than in democratic systems. The reason for this would be that decision makers will be able to keep unwanted issues off the public agenda. A simple example may illustrate this point. The socialization of medicine has been on the American public agenda for quite some time, but never reached formal agenda status, except, perhaps, in the form of certain sub-issues.[47] Although they have been very much opposed to socialization, the medical interest groups have not been able to suppress the issue completely. In the Soviet Union, however, the abolition of state health care and a return to private medicine is considered to be such crucial issue that it would never be discussed in public *unless* the Party leadership had already decided to put over the helm completely. If so, the mobilization model of agenda building would be applicable.

However, Soviet censorship is a complicated system, involving many thousands of censors in different parts of the country. They act as the gate keepers of the public agenda. They screen papers, magazines and books which are being published by different institutions with different affiliations, interests and beliefs about what promotes the general interest: central government ministries and agencies, departments of the Secretariat, republican and local Party or state organs, trade unions and so on and so forth. The publishing 'business' - including censorship - involves so many links that strict hierarchical control of all printed matter is out of the question. Thus issues get a chance to penetrate the public agenda even without prior consent from Moscow. Such entrance to the public agenda is often provided by specialized, local or limited-circulation publications; an issue will of course not immediately or automatically reach *Pravda* status. In the next chapter we will see how exactly issues penetrate the public agenda, and how they enter the formal agenda.

As we have seen above, agenda building starts with initiation and ends with entrance. The intermediate phases are specification and expansion. The three agenda-building models differ from each other in the level of initiation and in the order in which issues reach the public and formal agendas. The question now arises, what is the relationship between agenda building and decision making. I believe that the agenda building process is a subdivision of decision making. However, agenda building does not necessarily precede the taking of decisions. In the mobilization model it follows upon the decision, and public discussion of the issue must be seen as part of the implementation process. In the outside initiative model, agenda building comes first. In the ideal-typical case initiation, specification and expansion ultimately result in the issue's transfer to the formal agenda, i.e. in the recognition that it warrants binding decision making. These four phases of agenda building can be said to embrace the first two phases of decision making: initiation and persuasion, to be followed by the decision and implementation phases.[48] At all times we should remember that if a demand for change has successfully passed through the four phases of agenda building and has been placed on the formal agenda, this is no guarantee at all for the eventual satisfaction of that demand. It may be that the decision does not meet the demand, it may also be that if the decision does meet the demand, implementation is such that in the end the demand has not been satisfied at all. I believe that the study of Soviet decision making should not be limited to the decision phase alone, but should also pay sufficient attention to both agenda building ánd implementation.

In reality, of course, decision-making and agenda-building processes are more complicated than the three models presented here suggest. Models, after all, are abstractions from reality. Any particular issue, when passing through the public and formal agendas, may show diverse combinations of the three models. As Cobb, Ross and Ross have remarked,

> An issue which reaches higher level decision makers via either inside access or outside initiative, for example, may in a second stage be transmitted by them, through mobilization or inside access efforts, to lower level agendas of local communities or associations. Many issues take the opposite route, from lower level to higher level agendas; and some groups try to put their concerns before several different sets of decision makers at the same time.[49]

In the next chapters I intend to demonstrate that this statement is pertinent to the analysis of decision-making processes in the Soviet polity.

2 Cases in Soviet Decision Making

The nine studies which are being presented in this chapter must not be seen as fully developed case studies comparable to my case study of the Academy of Sciences reform. Their function in this book is different: they are to serve as a data base for developing a theoretical framework with which to analyze the decision-making process on the issue of the Academy of Sciences' reorganization.

Each study is based on at least two secondary sources. I have done additional research if certain points in those sources remained obscure or if additional primary sources have become available since their publication. A short introduction precedes each study: it is meant to place the issue in perspective and to help the reader switch from one policy area to an altogether different one. In order to keep the studies within limited proportions, the arguments of the proponents of different policy positions will in most cases be summarized. As a consequence these studies do not offer the reader the texture and flavor which should accompany analyses of policy debates. The aim is to describe the decision-making process as such, leaving out the paraphernalia.

The case studies will be arranged according to their policy area. I will begin with three issues in economic policy, the reclamation of the Virgin Lands (1953-1954), the reform of industrial organization of 1957 and the abolition of Machine-Tractor Stations (1951-1958). These were among the main issues during the succession struggle following Stalin's death in 1953. Three issues in social policy will be dealt with next: the question of legal relations between natural father and illegitimate child (1954-1968), the introduction of governmental tort liability (1956-1961) and Khrushchev's attempt to fight anti-social behaviour through popular justice (1956-1965). The three final issues are taken from different policy areas. They are the polytechnization of secondary education (1952-1959), the fight against pollution of Lake Baikal (1958-1978) and the emigration of Jews from the Soviet Union (1967-1971).

ISSUES IN ECONOMIC POLICY

The Virgin Lands, 1953-1954

The history of the decision to plow and sow thirteen million hectares of semi-arid virgin land located partly in Northern Kazakhstan, has been the subject of a number of case studies. Sidney Ploss has studied the decision-making process primarily from a perspective of top-level leadership conflict within the context of post-Stalin agricultural policy.[1] In his book on the Virgin Land Program, Martin McCauley has presented a rather superficial picture of the genesis of the March, 1954 decision.[2] The best study by far was written by Richard Mills and published in the *Slavic Review* in 1970.[3] Mills takes a multi-level view of the decision-making process, so that his attention is directed towards the interaction of top-level conflicts with the interests of - and conflicts among - lower-level institutions and groups. Thus, his study has documented

> ...the complexity of the political forces involved: Khrushchev, the September plenum, the Kazakh delegation to the plenum, the Kazakh bureau, the Kazakh first and second secretaries, the Secretariat in Moscow, the Kazakh *obkom* secretaries, the USSR Ministry of Agriculture, the Altai *kraikom's* first secretary, the chairman of the Kazakh Council of Ministers, the interests represented at the successive conferences on agriculture, the members of the Presidium.[4]

My reconstructions of this complex decision-making process will be based on Mills' research.

The Virgin Lands program emerged as a result of the need to expand wheat production either by intensifying production on existing farms, or by expanding acreage, or both. This need was most urgently felt by Nikita Khrushchev, who was engaged in a leadership struggle with Georgii Malenkov and a conservative faction in the Party Presidium.

In August 1953, Malenkov proposed to bring about a rise in grain production by way of measures intensifying production. Khrushchev, speaking at the September Central Committee Plenum, suggested that next to intensifying agricultural production, extensive possibilities were present. He named a few areas suitable for such expansion, but did not mention Western Siberia or Kazakhstan. However, during the Plenum Khrushchev consulted several officials from this republic; in his memoirs he has written:

> I'd heard about great opportunities for growing grain in the far reaches of Kazakhstan, so during the Plenum I had a talk with the First Secretary of the Kazakh Communist Party, Comrade Shaiakhmetov. I asked him how much land in his republic was fit for cultivation and what sort of yield the Kazakhs had been getting from their farms. From his answers, I could tell that he wasn't being sincere with me. He was deliberately underestimating the possibilities for expansion. In other words, he was clearly trying to convince me that only a small portion of the Virgin Lands in Kazakhstan were arable. He said we might be able to expand cultivation by a little more than three million hectares...[5]

Thus Khrushchev has acknowledged that the original idea of developing the Virgin Lands was not his; he has taken the idea and has worked for its implementation. We do not know from whom Khrushchev had heard about the great opportunities of Kazakhstan, but we do know that it had been discussed in the Party before, in 1930. In 1978 Leonid Brezhnev has even credited Nikolai M. Tulaikov, the specialist on agriculture in dry regions, with the original idea.[6] In the late 1920s and early 1930s Tulaikov was director of the then famous All-Union Institute of Grain Culture in Saratov and one of the government's principal advisors on problems of agricultural techniques.[7] He organized several agricultural expeditions, one of them to Kazakhstan, and wrote reports to the Central Committee.[8] These reports, according to Brezhnev, were the basis for Iakovlev's speech at the Sixteenth Party Congress of 1930, in which the large-scale agricultural development of Kazakhstan was announced.[9] Nikolai Talaikov was arrested in 1937 and died in 1938. He was not rehabilitated until 1962.

Khrushchev's aide for agricultural affairs Andrei Shevchenko has written that during the September Plenum (1953) Khrushchev had talks with officials from Northern Kazakhstan about the possibilities of developing this region and establishing large sovkhozy there. As a result of these consultations Kazakhstan was included in the Central Committee resolution adopted at the end of the Plenum, in addition to the areas mentioned in Khrushchev's report.Immediately after the Plenum Khrushchev - now the First Party Secetary - organized a meeting with representatives of the USSR Ministry of Agriculture and the Kazakh delegation at the Plenum; a little later he met with the members of the Kazakh Central Committee bureau and the *obkom* secretaries from Kazakhstan that had been present at the Plenum. The Kazakh Party officials were instructed to work out plans for the development of the Virgin Lands.[10]

The Kazakh Party leadership, with Zhumabai Shaiakhmetov as First Secretary and I.I. Afonov as Second Secretary, was not overly enthusiastic about the extension of the cultivated area with many millions of hectares and discussed its drawbacks at a Central Committee Plenum late November in Alma Ata; it may actively have tried to obstruct Khrushchev's plans.[11] Therefore, during one of the meetings that he had with lower-level Party functionaries from the Kazakh republic, Khrushchev asked the assembled *obkom* secretaries 'What quantity of land would it be possible to cultivate in the republic if the project were given a nationwide scope?' He later reported that 'At first they shyly spoke of three million hectares; they then began talking about seven, and they finally pulled it up to thirteen million.'[12]

While his ideas on the massive development of the Virgin Lands were slowly emerging, Khrushchev tried to add pressure from below to his own pressure from above in order to get the Kazakh Party leadership to move. When by the middle of December 1953 it became obvious that this policy had failed, Khrushchev brought the conflict in the open. *Pravda* published two articles which, by implication, said that a large extension of cultivated farm land in Western Siberia and Kazakhstan was possible, and that Khrushchev had the support of lower Party officials but was obstructed by the Kazakh Party leadership.[13] During the same month agronomists discussed the feasibility and costs of Khrushchev's plans

at a national conference, and a government commission was established and instructed to work out a program for the development of the Virgin Lands.[14] Khrushchev again sent for representatives from Kazakhstan and gave them concrete instructions. On January 22, 1954, he finally submitted his proposals to the Party Presidium in the form of a Memorandum on 'Ways of Solving the Grain Problem'.

The crucial feature of Khrushchev's memo was his proposal to expand the grain area during 1954-1955 with no less than 13 million hectares in the Volga region, Urals, Siberia and Kazakhstan. Of the total newly cultivated area, 8.7 million hectares would have to be developed by kolkhozy, and 4.3 million by state farms. Khrushchev did not indicate how big a share would fall to the Virgin Lands of Northern Kazakhstan. Richard Mills has claimed that in view of the fact that a program for extension of arable land by 2.3 million hectares during 1954 was already in progress under the current Five Year Plan, and possibly an additional 2.3 million in 1955, Khrushchev's proposal represented a radical expansion of current plans, _not_ a fresh start in a direction not tried before.

Immediately after this proposal had been made - and probably been opposed by members of the Presidium - Khrushchev took the offensive. He rallied for support among national Party and government officials and specialists, and removed the Kazakh opposition. Shaiakhmetov and Afonov were summoned to appear on January 30 at a session of the Central Committee Secretariat in Moscow, and were dismissed. They were replaced by P.K. Ponomarenko as First Secretary and L.I. Brezhnev as Second Secretary.[15] Khrushchev's plans were the main theme of discussion at four conferences on agriculture, organized at the end of January and early February.[16] The different policy positions which were being voiced here, were not aired in the press before, on February 7, the Presidium had partially given in to Khrushchev's Memorandum; at that date it accepted that at least 4.3 million hectares of Virgin Land were to be plowed by state farms in 1954. From the fact that I.A. Benediktov's speech, in which he named the exact amount of Virgin Lands to be plowed up by kolkhozy, was published on February 11, Mills has concluded that by that date Khrushchev's opponents in the Presidium had agreed to an extension of the agricultural area by 13 million hectares.[17]

The fact that Khrushchev had to overcome opposition in the Party Presidium is well established - the question is how widespread that opposition was and which persons were most active in opposing the First Secretary. Sidney Ploss has identified four 'dissenters' among the nine voting members: Molotov, Kaganovich, Malenkov and Bulganin.[18] Mills however, is certain of only the opposition of the first two, and perhaps Saburov. Malenkov's opposition according to him, has been minimal.[19]

The Seventh Congress of the Kazakh Communist Party which convened between 16 and 18 February, announced what Moscow had decided to be Kazakhstan's share in the national Virgin Lands program: 6.3 million hectares.[20] The elaboration and formalization of the decisions which had been taken during the previous month took place at the Central Committee Plenum of February 23 - March 2. At the opening of the Plenum, during the days when the first group of young volunteers was leaving Moscow for the Virgin Lands, Khrushchev held his fifth major speech on the Virgin Lands since the presentation of his Memorandum. He proposed that 2.3 million hectares of Virgin Land be plowed and sowed with grain in 1954 and the rest, 10.7 million hectares, in 1955. This goal was incorporated in the Central Committee resolution adopted on March 2 (published in <u>Pravda</u>, March 6) and in the joint Central Committee - USSR Council of Ministers decree published on March 28. The target for Kazakhstan (6.3 million hectares) was announced in the national press on March 25.

With this, the first phase in the development of the Virgin Lands came to an end. The implementation of these decisions was no easy matter and subject to ups and downs. Obstruction occurred frequently, but in the end Khrushchev's Virgin Lands campaign has proved to be a success many years after his demise.

The Sovnarkhozy Reform, 1957

The reform of industrial organization in the spring of 1957 was one of Khrushchev's most radical measures. The decision-making process - if one may call it so - leading up to the adoption on May 10 of a law completely overhauling industrial administration, was so short that it almost resembled a flash of lightning. At the same time the changes were very profound: over 140 industrial branch ministries were abolished (10 union ministries, 15 union-republic ministries and the corresponding republican ministries) and the country's industrial establishments were subordinated to regional economic councils (sovnarkhozy) instead. Thus the organization of industrial administration was abrubtly changed from centralized-functional into decentralized-general. Finally, the reorganization, involving a major reshuffling of leading economic administrators, was railroaded through the Central Committee and the Supreme Soviet over the opposition of a number of Khrushchev's colleagues in the Party Presidium. It is no surprise that the sovnarkhozy-reform became the immediate cause for their abortive attempt to remove Nikita Khrushchev from the political scene.

At the December 1956 Central Committee Plenum Khrushchev had suffered - in the words of Robert Conquest - a 'partial defeat', for in less than a year after its start his Sixth Five-Year Plan had proved to be overly ambitious.[21] More important still, the task of revising the Plan was not entrusted to the State Planning Committee Gosplan, but to the State Economic Commission, which became the second most powerful body on economic policy after the Party Presidium. Mikhail Pervukhin, member of the Presidium since 1952, was made its chairman. He had passed through a succesful career in the top ministerial bureaucracy since 1939.

A reversal of this trend towards centralization took place at the Central Committee Plenum of February 1957. In its resolution of February 14 the Plenum ignored the economic setbacks of 1956 and the critisism which had been expressed at the previous Plenum. In an effort to deflect attention from the critisism expressed in previous months, Khrushchev had attacked the industrial branch ministries, and his attack was reflected in the document where it said that 'the negative influence of the departmentalism of ministries in their approach of the solution of the major problems of economic development is a serious shortcoming...' since it leads to 'the weakening and disturbance of normal territorial relations between companies of different industrial branches that are situated in one and the same economic region...' The resolution concluded that 'the center of gravity of operational industrial administration' must be transferred to economic regions.[22] The Party Presidium and the USSR Council of Ministers were ordered to draw up concrete proposals and to present them to the USSR Supreme Soviet. Pervukhin's State Economic Commission was to be reorganized and contracted, and the role of _Gosplan_ was once again to increase.

It is not known how the other members of the Party Presidium reacted to Khrushchev's proposals before or during the February Plenum. However, Conquest has deduced that of the eleven members Malenkov, Molotov, Kaganovich, Pervukhin and Saburov were probably opposed to the proposed decentralization and that Voroshilov and Bulganin may have hesitated or been neutral.[23] Khrushchev's theses for the legislative proposal that he was to present to the next Supreme Soviet session were published at the end of March. They were accompanied by a summons for a nationwide discussion. His central thesis was that with the introduction of regional economic councils the union and republican industrial branch ministries would become superfluous and, by implication, would have to be abolished.[24] Khrushchev did not state explicitly that _all_ ministries would have to be abolished. Neither did he name a specific number of future _sovnarkhozy_, but only indicated that they would have to coincide with oblasti, krais and republics, naming Sverdlovsk, Cheliabinsk and Magadan oblasti and the Bashkir and Iakut ASSR's as proper examples of a possible _sovnarkhoz_-territory. He further elaborated on the internal organization and powers of the future _sovnarkhozy_ and on their relations with other state organizations. Khrushchev promised that the reorganization would 'immeasurably raise the responsabilities of the Party organs in the republics, krais and oblasti...' In present conditions, he wrote, local Party organizations were sometimes prevented from actively influencing the activities of companies, but the _sovnarkhozy_ would give them more rights and possibilities to influence the execution of the state plans.[25]

During the nationwide discussion that ensued in April, out of a total of 64 republic and oblast Party secretaries that responded in print, 51 (80%), requested a separate _sovnarkhoz_ for their own area, thereby endorsing the idea of the reform.[26] This signified a strong support for Khrushchev's proposal among local Party officials; this support cannot be explained away as the result of the bias of Soviet censorship, for articles in which state officials protested against Khrushchev's plan were printed as well.[27] What was absent, and quite significantly absent at that, was the reaction of the other Presidium members. With the exception of Kirichenko they ignored the issue: no one endorsed or even reacted upon Khrushchev's theses.

The law accepted by the USSR Supreme Soviet on May 10, 1957, did not itself institute the exact outline of the new economic regions and their sovnarkhozy; such was left to be done by the supreme soviets and councils of ministers of the republics.[28] The law abolished a great number of ministries, but Khrushchev stressed that '...as a result of the thorough exchange of opinions (during the nationwide discussion) it was considered necessary to retain a number of union ministries', such as those of the defense industry.[29] July 1 was set as the date for the completion of this large-scale transformation of industrial administration. Khrushchev's opponents in the Presidium did not want to wait for that date and within a few weeks the First Party Secretary was confronted with their demand that he resign from office.

The Abolition of the MTS, 1951-1958

As Soviet peasants were forced in the late 1920s and early 1930s to collectivize, the question of how to service them with tractive power became pressing. In the years of the Great Industrialization Debate and since, there had been discussions on the question of who should own agricultural machinery and who should not, and there had been experiments as well. But even for some time after Stalin's Politburo had taken the decision to industrialize the country and collectivize and mechanize agriculture, it had no clear idea how the mechnization of agriculture should be realized. It was eventually through the agitation of a young agronomist, A.M. Markevich, that so-called tractor columns were organized and promoted, and the idea for state-owned and state-operated Machine-Tractor Stations was launched. A Machine-Tractor Station (MTS), in his opinion, was to service the surrounding peasants with agricultural machinery and assist in the collectivization effort as well.

After Stalin's Politburo had decided for total collectivization early in 1930, the idea of creating one centralized MTS system for Soviet agriculture gained acceptance. At the end of that year a massive program for MTS construction was announced, and by the end of 1933 almost sixty percent of the total sown area of the kolkhozes was served by the MTS, of which there were nearly three thousand.[30]

In the decades to follow the Machine-Tractor Station developed into the major institution for centralized economic and political control over the collectivized peasants of the Soviet Union, the 'central institutional bulwark of the Soviet collective farm system', as Robert Miller has called it. The MTS became the center from which the activities in a number of surrounding kolkhozes were controlled. In return for payment in kind, it supplied them with tractors and combines for plowing, sowing, harvesting and many other activities. Both its activities and the annual production of the kolkhozes were planned from above; the payments in kind it received from the kolkhozes constituted a considerable share of total state procurements of grain. The MTS were supposed to operate on a <u>khozraschet</u>-basis, i.e. to make profits and become financially independent. The fees they charged would have to suffice for depreciation payments, wages and investments. A transfer of the MTS to full khozraschet status was, however, never seriously pushed.

In the MTS deputy directors for political affairs and, in times of crisis, political departments (<u>politotdely</u>) took care of Party control over agricultural management. In the course of the 28 years the MTS-system existed, its organization and mode of operation was subject to several reorganizations, as were the MTS-relations with kolkhozes, the rayon Party committee and the state. The issue of whether they should be maintained at all arose in the early 1950s.

In a March 1951 article in <u>Voprosy Ėkonomiki</u> the economist V.G. Venzher proposed to promote the role of the kolkhozes in the modernization and mechanization of agriculture.[31] Over a period of several years Venzher and others had conducted a number of semi-secret experiments in Krasnodar Krai with the transfer of agricultural machinery to the kolkhozes.[32] In November of 1951 a discussion erupted around the draft for a new textbook on political economy. In the course of this discussion professor Venzher and his wife A.V. Sanina wrote Party Secretary Stalin a number of letters in which they proposed to abolish the MTS and sell the machinery to the kolkhozy. In one of their letters they argued that

> It is wrong to believe that collective-farm investments must be used chiefly for the cultural needs of the village, while the greater bulk of the investments for the needs of agricultural production must continue to be borne by the state. Would it not be more correct to relieve the state of this burden, seeing that the collective farms are fully capable of taking it entirely upon themselves?[33]

Stalin was insensitive to their arguments; he considered them incorrect and the abolition of the MTS dangerous. The issue was duly publicized in his Economic Problems of Socialism in the USSR, thus signalling that there was considerable support for the Venzher-Sanina proposal. With Stalin's rejection of it, the MTS abolition was out of the question.

The thinking of Nikita Khrushchev about agriculture differed fundamentally from the way Stalin had approached the countryside. Robert Miller has observed that

> For Stalin the primary goal of policy toward the village, in addition, of course, to providing the basic food and fiber needs of the economy, was the maintenance of social and political control. Economic abundance and efficiency of agricultural production were clearly secondary, if desirable at all. For Khrushchev, on the other hand, the primary goals were economic abundance and efficiency, while social and political controls, although still seen as necessary, were not valued as much as ends in themselves...
> Khrushchev differed essentially from Stalin in the extent to which he was willing to pay for social and political control at the expense of economic development.[34]

After the death of Stalin a complex set of interrelated developments resulted in the abolition of the MTS in 1958. These developments took place at different levels of the Soviet economy and polity, and influenced each other. The Soviet peasantry was gradually rehabilitated and awarded a minimum of trust. First, through the unification of small kolkhozy, the kolkhoz became a unit of greater economic weight. The status of its chairman rose, and the quality of kolkhoz leadership improved through the increase in Party membership and the influx of young kolkhoz chairmen from the cities. A symptom of the raised self-consiousness of kolkhoz leadership and increased friction with MTS directors was that in July 1956, when Minister of Agriculture Benediktov had called a meeting of kolkhoz chairmen to discuss current agricultural questions, he was met by the participants with the yell 'We've had enough of the MTS!'[35] Second, after August 1955, MTS agronomists and animal specialists who worked on the kolkhozy and were supposed to supply them with technical advice, were transferred to the payroll of the kolkhozy. Thus the MTS lost part of their power over the kolkhozy. Third, when Khrushchev found out that no one really knew the cost of the grain that the state received from the MTS, he ordered that a number of studies be done. After these studies had revealed a lack of financial order in the MTS, it was decided that they would now really be transferred to <u>khozraschet</u>-basis: the state would eventually stop subsidizing the MTS and the stations would have to become financially independent. Fourth, several experiments in alternative MTS-kolkhoz relationships were initiated from below and tolerated from above. In February 1956 <u>Kommunist</u> published a request by two kolkhoz chairmen for permission to purchase a few tractors to be used for transportation purposes.[36] According to Miller, permission was quietly granted and many kolkhozes began building small tractors.[37] The experiment proved a big succes in terms of efficiency of the use of the tractors if compared with MTS tractors. In the years 1955-1957 there were several experiments with combined MTS-kolkhoz tractor-field brigades and the unification of a MTS and a kolkhoz under one director.

The exchange of opinion and of experimentation results took place in a series of conferences at the Central Committee Secretariat, the USSR Ministry of Agriculture and the Academy of Agricultural Sciences in 1956 and 1957. There are several indications suggesting that in the first months of 1957 Khrushchev made up his mind in favor of abolition of the MTS.[38] There are also indications suggesting that he encountered serious opposition in the Party Presidium and in the Secretariat, especially by what later came to be called the anti-Party group.[39] After he had succeeded in eliminating this opposition with the help of the Central Committee and in consolidating his position in the Party Secretariat, Khrushchev took over the initiative for the abolition of the MTS, but he did so carefully. In November the monthly Oktiabr' published an article by the Ukrainian journalist Ivan Vinnichenko, who, according to Miller, had in the past been associated with Khrushchev. He referred to a conversation he had had with the economists Venzher and Sanina on the ideological acceptability of the sale of MTS machinery to the kolkhozes, discussed the pros and cons of the experiments that had taken place and legitimized the issue for public discussion. Opposition against the plan soon appeared in articles in the journals Voprosy Ėkonomiki, Machine-Tractor Station, Oktiabr' itself and the Herald of Moscow State University.[40] Then on December 26, at the Ukrainian Central Committee Plenum, Khrushchev explicitly called for the abolition of the MTS so that the land and the equipment would be in the hands of one single boss. This speech was not published at the time, but the Khrushchev position soon came into the open. On January 22 1958, at a conference of agricultural workers in Minsk, he presented a catalogue of arguments against the maintenance of the MTS and proposed to sell the MTS machinery to the kolkhozy in order to raise the efficiency of agricultural production. The MTS were to be transformed into repair and trading stations. Khrushchev indicated that there was still some opposition against his plans. The Minsk speech was published in Pravda after Khrushchev's return to Moscow, on January 25.[41]

Although he had promised that the reform would be executed gradually, Khrushchev had a Central Committee Plenum convened for February 25-26 and proposed in his theses to proceed with the sale of the MTS machinary immediately without waiting for the setting of prices. In the public discussion that followed the Plenum and the Supreme Soviet session of March 1958, the implications of the new relations in the countryside were discussed; the issue of abolishing the MTS had clearly been decided. By the end of the year the number of MTS in the Soviet Union had dropped from nearly 8.000 to 345.

ISSUES IN SOCIAL POLICY

Family Law Reform, 1954-1968

In 1944, when it became apparent that the war would create serious population problems for the Soviet Union, family law was subjected to a quick reform in order to counteract the expected tendencies. It was felt that something had to be done if the scarcity of men and the consequent surplus of women was not to result in a severe decline of the economically active population. The banning of abortions in June 1936, the raising of barriers against easy divorce, and the introduction in November 1941 of a 6% birth-stimulation income tax on childless persons were not considered to be enough. At the time, according to computations made by Peter Juviler, for every six women between the ages of 20 and 39 there were only four men in the same age group.[42]

It was Nikita Khrushchev, then Party Secretary of the Ukraine and member of Stalin's Politburo, who proposed to put an end to paternity and support suits by unmarried mothers or their children.[43] The Family Decree of July 8, 1944, a decision (Ukaz) of the USSR Supreme Soviet's Presidium, in which his proposals were incorporated, precluded all legal relations between the natural father and his illegitimate child. In addition to the institution of medals, allowances and daycare facilities for the mothers of many children, and the extension of the birth stimulation tax to persons with less than three children, the legal recognition of unregistered marriages was brought to an end and divorce procedures were made costly and complicated.

In actual practice, Soviet family law now encouraged extra-marital sexual relations. The birth of children out of wedlock was apparently seen as a necessary supplement to the children born in 'normal', i.e. legal families. The state was in need of the maximum 'use' of femal reproductive capacities and encouraged men to procreate, either within or outside the family, preferably both. It protected them from unpleasant paternity suits and the payment of alimonies and supported unmarried mothers financially. But millions of illegitimate children became second rate citizens: instead of the name of their father, their identity papers showed a stroke, they had no right to support or inheritance from their father and even if the natural father was willing to recognize his paternity, the law did not allow him to do so. A situation against which Lenin had protested vehemently when it existed under Czarist conditions and which had been remedied in 1917, was now restored by the Soviet state.

Less than a year after the death of Stalin the Literary Gazette published a demand to reform the Family Decree. Journalist Elena Serebrovskaia demanded that the humiliating position of illegitimate children - of which at the time there were about four million[44] - be remedied. At the end of August of 1954, the paper reported a mainly positive mail response and expressed its support for a reform of the decree. Criticism of the more extreme reform proposals came from Grigorii Sverdlov of the USSR Academy of Sciences' Institute on Law, a respected specialist in family law. In his book on the 'Protection of the interests of children in Soviet family and civil law', signed for the press on December 18, 1955, he criticized the suggestion of the re-introduction of paternity and support suits, since these would endanger the peace in existing families. By way of compromise, however, he proposed to allow fathers to acknowledge their paternity, which was then to be entered in the child's birth certificate. A veritable reform movement developed in 1956, led by Alexandra Pergament, a lawyer at the All-Union Institute of Juridical Sciences, and several more female jurists. VIP's such as Dmitrii Shostakovich, Ilia Ėrenburg, Samuil Marshak and Georgii Speranskii, an eminent specialist on children's diseases, joined in.

Early in 1957 the issue reached a new and important stage. Alexei Rumiantsev, a member of the CPSU Central Committee who had in the fall of 1955 exchanged his position of head of the Secretariat's Department of Science for the chief editorship of Kommunist, supported the movement before a meeting of the Supreme Soviet, together with the delegate from Estonia, E.K. Pusep. Rumiantsev probably represented a liberal policy group in the Secretariat; what he did was to place the issue on the formal agenda. Just before this Supreme Soviet meeting Pergament had used a conference on codification organized by her institute to promote the drafting of a new family law. Several legislative proposals were designed, at juridical conferences, in professional journals and so on. By the end of 1961 a subcommission had completed a preliminary draft for Principles of legislation of the USSR and the union republics on marriage and the family, which was to overrule the 1944 Family Decree.

On December 3 of that year the legislative committees of the two Supreme Soviet chambers met jointly and heard reports of ministers, scholars and Central Committee Secretariat representatives. It was decided that the committees would prepare draft Principles for legislation, based on the existing preliminary draft. A special subcommittee on family law reform was created by the legislative committees and experts were invited to present their reports. During 1962 the subcommittee met with representatives of a great number of law faculties, institutes, central and republic government agencies, which were asked for comment. Members of the subcommittee visited institutes and government agencies in republic capitals to solicit reactions. The subcommittee's draft was completed by the end of 1962 and presented on a December 13-14 joint session of the legislative committees.[45]

Thus, early 1963 the draft was as good as completed and waited a final OK for publication. But this OK did not come. Olga Kolchina, chairwoman of the subcommittee, told a reporter of the _Trud_ newspaper in the middle of February, 1964, that the draft was 'apparently soon to be released for public discussion'. It simplified divorce procedures, allowed acknowledgement of paternity and, 'in certain cases', paternity suits. But it seems that these 'certain cases' were unacceptable to the conservative group in the central Party apparatus, for nothing was heard of the draft for a long time. It had apparently been shelved.

This deadlock in the decision-making process appeared at a time when the problem itself became more and more urgent. The number of illegitimate children had grown to about 7 million and the number of unmarried mothers to approximately 5 million.[46] Thus, if the existing law was to be changed, it might lead to the sudden accumulation of paternity and support suits by unmarried mothers. In the eyes of a conservative group in the Party Secretariat this would seriously threaten the stability of many legal families, and to them the family remained the cornerstone of a communist upbringing. Moreover, specialists such as Sverdlov had warned that 'a stable family is one of the most important prerequisites of a high birth rate'[47] and Academician Starovskii, director of the Central Statistical Administration had claimed that the 1944 decree had contributed to the raising of the birth rate 'during a highly unfavorable sexual balance in the population.'[48] Nikita Khrushchev himself was strongly committed to a high birth rate and large and stable families. It seems probable that the conservatives in the Party Secratriat appealed to him - who, after all, had suggested the 1944 measures to Stalin - to stop the new Principles of family legislation, and that he did in fact do so.

The dismissal of Khrushchev in October 1964 did not immediately lead to a revitalization of the draft Principles. At the end of 1965 a new divorce edict simplified divorce procedures somewhat, but only one year later, on December 20 1966, the Supreme Soviet Presidium decided to revitalize the work on a number of draft Principles, among them the draft Principles on marriage and the family.[49] In June 1967 the journal Soviet State and Law announced that in January 1967 an important conference had taken place at the Academy of Sciences' Institute of State and Law. Prominent 'scientific and practical workers' had discussed juridical questions of the family and child raising, and some other matters as well. Over fifty papers had been read and discussed. According to the conference report, quite a few of the participants recognized the need for revising family law;'more than once public men, scientific and practical juridical workers stressed the need for such changes.'[50] The report was quite frank in recognizing that the 1944 Family decree 'at the time was justified by the consequences of the war...'. It was outright cynical when it based its advice for a reversal on similar demographic arguments:

> ...at the moment the situation is different. According to demographic data, the disproportion between the total number of women and men in our country is basically still existing, but its influence on the normal conditions for the start of families has deminished sharply and its influence on the dynamics of the birth rate is almost zero now, for there are more men under forty years of age, than women.[51]

Such considerations, the report said, had prompted several participants to propose to speed up the adoption of Principles for legislation on family and marriage in the USSR and the republics. It listed the following guidelines for the contents of the draft Pinciples:

- Equal rights of children from married or unmarried couples; 'the children should not suffer for the conduct of their parents'.
- 'Both the mother and the father must be entered in the register of births. If any such entry is absent or a mistake has been made, or in case of discord between the parents on the parentage, the courts must get the right to apply the necessary corrections in the registration or to make a decision in any parentage conflict.'[52]
- The new family legislation must not be retroactive, but acknowledgement of paternity must also be made possible for illegitimate children born before acceptance of the new Principles.
- Unmarried mothers with extramarital children must receive more financial government support.

Finally, on divorce procedures the report said that 'the conference did not agree with the proposal to remove the majority of divorce cases from the jurisdiction of the courts to that of the registration bureaus (zags)'.[53] Alexandra Pergament, present at the conference, had already made such a proposal many years before; it was aimed at the many divorce cases where husband and wife agree to divorce and have no children. It was decided that a report containing the most essential proposals and recommendations would be sent to the scientific council of the Institute of State and Law and that those proposals approved by this council be sent to the proper state organs.

We may assume that this was done, especially since the Principles finally made into law by the Supreme Soviet in 1968 realized many of these proposals. On April 8, 1968 the USSR Supreme Soviet Presidium announced that draft Principles were ready and would be published soon. On the critical issue of the relation between the natural father and his illegitimate child the draft, published two days later, proposed in article 16 that:

> The parentage of a child whose parents are unmarried is established through the submission of a joint application by the child's father

> and mother to the state agencies for the registration of documents pertaining to civil status.
> If a child is born to parents who are unmarried and if no joint application has been made by the parents, paternity can be established by the court. In establishing paternity the court takes into account cohabitation and the maintenance of a common household by the child's mother and the respondent before the child's birth, or their joint rearing or support of the child.[54]

Illegitimate children (and their mothers) born before the new Principles would take effect, would be excluded from the new rights.

Soon after publication of the draft, over one hundred prominent family law specialists, lawyers, judges, Party and state functionaries again convened at the Academy of Sciences' Institute for State and Law for a thorough discussion of the proposal. In the weeks to follow over 7000 letters were sent to Supreme Soviet committees, 8000 to *Izvestia*, which published several of them, and many more to other papers. Many people took part in discussions of the draft at factories and kolkhozy. The period of public discussion lasted about six weeks. In his report on the Supreme Soviet M.S. Solomentsev, chairman of the Council of the Union's Legislative Committee, said that

> ...the discussion of this article (16-J.L.) aroused the greatest amount of commentary. The debate revolved around the question of the court's establishment of paternity and the circumstances the court must take into account. It was proposed, in particular, to expand the range of cases allowing for court establishment of the paternity of extra-marital children and also to take into account all other evidence that reliably establishes paternity, or to refrain entirely from specifying in the law the conditions in which the court may establish paternity. Other letters, conversely, proposed that the draft excluded the section on court procedures for establishing paternity, since court errors are possible. After discussing these proposals, the committees deemed it expedient to add to the published draft's list of circumstances to be taken into account by the court in establishing paternity. In the draft submitted to you (the Supreme Soviet,

J.L.), the fourth paragraph of article 16 has been changed as follows: "In establishing paternity, the court takes into account cahabitation and the maintenance of a common household by the child's mother and the respondent before the child's birth or their joint rearing or support of the child, or evidence that reliably establishes the respondent's own acknowledgement of paternity."[55]

This is how the final text, accepted by the Supreme Soviet on June 27, 1968 read. The reformers who had campaigned for over fourteen years, had won a partial victory. Acknowledgement of paternity was legalized once again and the rights of children born in de facto families were recognized, but paternity suits on behalf of children who were the result of occasional relations remained out of the question.

Introduction of Governmental Tort Liability, 1956-1961

State institutions are responsible for harm caused to citizens by improper official actions of their officers in the field of administration on general principles, unless other provision is made by a special statute. State institutions are responsible for harm done by their officials to organizations, by a procedure laid down by law.[56]

This explicit introduction of governmental tort liability in article 89 of the Principles of Civil Legislation of the USSR and the Union Republics (1961) was the result of repeated demands by law specialists in the period following the Twentieth Party Congress. Since the early 1920s governmental tort liability in the Soviet Union had been limited to cases specially prescribed by law (article 407 of the RSFSR Civil Code), and such cases had been rare. During the 1920s the extension of governmental tort liability had been a subject of discussion in Soviet law journals, but this discussion had stopped at the end of the decade and was not resumed until after the death of Stalin.

In the years preceding the Twentieth Congress many thousands of victims of Stalinist terror were rehabilitated, came home from camps and prisons. At the Congress itself Mikoian and Khrushchev shattered the taboo of Stalinist terror and re-instituted socialist legality as the guiding principle of Soviet law. An early sign of a revival of the tort liability discussion was a proposal made by Mikhail Strogovich in a 1956 issue of the journal Soviet State and Law, signed for the press on June 22. In an article on theoretical questions of Soviet legality Strogovich, a corresponding member of the Academy of Sciences and head of the criminal law and litigation section of the Institute of State and Law, made several proposals for improving socialist legality in the Soviet Union. He stressed that 'the protection of legality means the protection of the rights of the citizens and the violation of the citizens' rights is the violation of legality'[57] and explicitly referred to the violation of criminal procedure by 'Beria's gang'. 'The time has come', he wrote, 'to decide in legislative order the question of compensation of damage caused to a citizen by the illegal instituting of criminal proceedings, arrest or conviction in the event of his rehabilitation.'[58] Curiously enough, he tried to legitimize this extreme proposal by pointing to Czechoslovakia and Hungary, countries which had already realized such legislation.

The third section of article 89 of the Principles adopted in 1961 made the following restriction on the general liability of governmental institutions:

> Where harm is caused by the illegal official actions of officers of the agencies of police or preliminary investigation or the procuratura or of a court, the corresponding State organs are liable to make compensation in the cases and within the limits specially provided by law.[59]

This shows that the original demand expressed by Strogovich was not met, at least not in 1961 with the adoption of the Principles: the regulation of tort liability of these agencies was postponed. This is not to say that up to the last moment the inclusion of the police, procuratura and the courts in the general tort liability settlementwas in the picture. On the contrary, in the discussion that developed after 1956 the issue was soon reformulated and attention was shifted away from government liability for unjust arrest or imprisonment. Barry has written that 'the tendency among writers was to discuss the subject of liability without referring to the particular acts out of which liability might arise.'[60]

The February, 1957 session of the Supreme Soviet was an important milestone in the development of this issue. At the meeting at which Alexei Rumiantsev put the reorganization of family law on the formal agenda, S.V. Stefanik, a lawyer from Lvov, did the same for governmental tort liability. He declared that the existing situation 'contradicts the principle of socialist legality' and spoke of

> ...the necessity of broadening the property liability of governmental organs for damages caused by their workers. The broadening of property liability will promote the thorough protection of the rights of workers and the improvement of the work of the governmental apparatus.[61]

In the years to follow, lawyers from Lvov University were active on behalf of the widening of governmental tort liability. A draft for a new Ukrainian Civil Code contained the provision that there would be 'liability of the government in all cases except those specially prescribed by law.'[62] The RSFSR Civil Code draft, which had been worked out by the RSFSR Ministry of Justice and the All-Union Institute of Juridical Sciences was discussed in December 1959 at a conference in Moscow. In contrast to the Ukrainian draft, its article on tort liability was not different from article 407 of the Code that was at that time in force. At the conference this part of the draft Code met with strong opposition, and it was proposed to widen governmental liability.[63]

In the meantime, the legislative process for the Principles of Civil Legislation of the USSR and the Union Republics had started. According to the Kovalev report it lasted about five years, which lends credit to the assertion that since the February, 1957 meeting of the Supreme Soviet the government was working on new Principles of Civil Legislation. The first versions of the draft were prepared by a special government commission, which then presented its fifth version to the USSR Council of Ministers in September 1958, whereupon it was presented to the Councils of Ministers of the republics and to the republican and union ministries concerned.[64] A subcommittee was then created by the legislative committees of the Supreme Soviet for the specific purpose of hammering out one final draft of Principles of Civil Legislation, to be subjected to public discussion. The subcommittee met weekly and considered the draft article by article. It consulted scientists specialized in civil law, lawyers, attorneys and judges, procurators and many representatives of government departments and ministries. For a number of specially complicated problems sub-committees were created, consisting of members of the sub-committee and representatives of the government departments concerned. An editorial group of the subcommittee was responsible for handling proposals which came in from the outside world, presenting them at subcommittee meetings and formulating its decisions. For the formulation and editing of specific articles in the draft Principles scientists and government specialists were invited.

When the draft had been finished in the spring of 1960, it was published in a number of law journals, among them Soviet State and Law. The legislative committees wanted to have the draft discussed by the law community (obshchestvennost') and invited comments and proposals. A special section of Soviet State and Law was reserved for discussion of the draft, which lasted from the August 1960 through the March 1961 issue. Conferences for the specific purpose of discussing the draft were organized by the editors of Soviet State and Law jointly with the Moscow City Court and with the law community of Kaliningrad.[65] Many law faculties of universities and institutes organized conferences as well, whereas the draft Civil Codes of the republics were discussed at a number of republican conferences.

On governmental tort liability, just one out of a multitude of subjects in the civil legislation Principles, the draft was conspicuously evasive: it suggested to postpone a decision on the issue. In article 75 it said that:

> The conditions and limits of liability of governmental institutions for injury caused by improper official acts of their officials in the sphere of administration and judicial activity will be established by legislation of the USSR and of the union republics.[66]

What may be described as a storm of protest sprang up against this provision. Donald Barry has shown that during the discussion of the draft its section on governmental tort liability was severely criticized, almost exclusively by academic lawyers. The complete faculty of the civil law department of Leningrad University, for example, signed an article in which they proposed to rewrite the section thus:

> For injury caused by improper official acts of their officials in the sphere of administration and judicial activity, governmental institutions shall be liable according to general principles except in cases provided by legislation of the USSR.[67]

Many more prominent civil law authorities, such as B. Antimonov and E. Lifshits of the All-Union Institute of Juridical Sciences, insisted that the provision on governmental tort liability in the draft must be changed. The discussion in law journals stopped in the spring of 1961. Half a year later, on December 3, the legislative committees of the Supreme Soviet met in joint session to approve of the draft Principles as the subcommittee had revised them after the public discussion. The new draft was presented to the Supreme Soviet, which accepted it on December 8.

The legislative process on civil law was now completed, at least as far as the Union was concerned. At the same session at which the legislative committees approved of the revised draft, they decided to undertake the preparation of draft Principles of legislation on marriage and the family and to organize a special subcommittee for this purpose. The Civil Codes of the republics adopted after the Principles incorporated articles on governmental tort liability which were virtually identical to article 89 of the Principles. Since 1961 the urgency of accepting a special law persuant to section 3 of article 89 was repeatedly stressed by liberal jurists in the context of their comments on specific court decisions on damage caused by police or the procuracy. However, up to this moment nothing came of it, so that for the time being the police, the procuracy and the courts remain exempted from tort liability.

Anti-Parasite Legislation, 1956-1965

He who does not work, neither shall he eat: this principle of the Soviet attitude towards labor has been firmly rooted in the Soviet Constitution. In the times of Joseph Stalin labor relations were strictly regulated and the penalties for loafing, speculation or idling were severe. After he had died and his police chief Lavrentii Beriia had been deposed, his successors made a point of stressing their determination to terminate terror and to restore what they called 'socialist legality': a term loosely used for the observance of traditional rules of procedural law and the protection of basic citizens' rights, as well as the termination of arbitrariness in criminal and administrative proceedings. The Ministry of Internal Affairs' Special Board, which had practiced summary justice against 'socially dangerous' persons since 1934, was abolished in September 1953, scores of prisoners were rehabilitated by military and regular courts, and returned home.[68]

In the minds of the Soviet leaders the gradual restoration of due process of law did, however, create a problem. The fight against anti-social behavior - such as heavy drinking, hooliganism, prostitution, speculation, idling from work or, as frequently happened, any combination of such sins - became more difficult at a time when such behavior seemed to occur more and more often. Criminal law and criminal procedure did not always allow for the prosecution of socially harmful acts.

A new instrument for the fight against anti-social behavior was found in the promotion of popular justice. In the second half of the 1950s three forms of popular justice were introduced. Voluntary People's Guards (druzhinniki) were to aid the police in maintaining public order and picking up drunks, prostitutes, loafers and thieves. Social control in collectives was strengthened by the revival of Comrades' Courts in factories and apartment flats. Finally, anti-parasite decrees were adopted, allowing groups of citizens to exile people from among their midst to remote places for a period up to five years.

The campaign against parasites started in 1956 and was instigated by top Party leaders; Marianne Armstrong has identified Nikita Khrushchev as its pace-maker.[69] In the fall of 1956 a federal decree was published allowing People's Courts (the lowest regular courts, not to be confused with Comrades' Courts) to sentence wandering gypsies to banishment with corrective labor. The preparation of draft decrees against parasitism by the legislative committees of the Supreme Soviets of the republics was a matter of months. In the spring and summer of 1957 all republics except the Ukraine published draft laws or decrees 'On intensification of the fight against anti-social, parasitic elements', accompanied by a request for public discussion of the drafts in the press and at public meetings.[70] The differences in the contents of the drafts were only of minor importance. All of them were directed against

> ...adult, able-bodied citizens leading an anti-social, parasitic way of life, maliciously avoiding socially useful labor, and likewise living on unearned income; adult able-bodied citizens occupied in vagrancy or begging, and those beggars and vagrants unable to work or with limited ability to work who maliciously avoid placement in homes for invalids.[71]

Persons suspected of parasitism were to be tried by general meetings of the inhabitants of apartment flats, street committees or committees organized by village soviets. These general meetings could issue a warning or establish a trial period for the parasite during which he was to better his life; they could also by a simple majority of those present at the meeting decide to exile him for a period of two to five years. In his place of exile the parasite was obliged to perform socially useful work. After final approval of such a sentence by the executive committee of the city district or village soviet, the parasite was to be deported by the police. Appeal of the verdict at a regular court would not be possible.

The legal profession in the Soviet Union immediately responded to this challenge. In numerous articles in the local press academic jurists, *Prokuratura*-officials, legal consultants, judges, police officials and other jurists expressed their opinion. Many of them, in particular officials of the *Prokuratura* and academic jurists, advanced arguments against the procedural paragraphs of the decrees; they were concerned that the proposed procedure might lead to abuse and to violations of the rights of the defendant.[72] Many amendments were proposed. Nevertheless, in the five Central Asian republics, Latvia, Armenia and Azerbaidzhan the drafts were soon passed into law with only minor alterations in their texts. The demand of many jurists that the trying of suspected parasites be performed by regular courts instead of ad-hoc popular meetings, was not met.

The acceptance of the laws and decrees by the Supreme Soviets or their Presidia in eight republics took place between May 29, 1957 (Uzbekistan) and January 15, 1959 (Kirgizia). The majority of the Soviet population (RSFSR, Ukraine, Belorussia, Moldavia, Lithuania, Estonia, Georgia) was not submitted to anti-parasite legislation. In the meantime, and in 1959 and 1960 as well, the discussion on parasitism continued, more and more often with reference to concrete examples of the prosecution, sentencing and exile of parasites. It became obvious that the implementation of the decrees was no easy task and did in fact lead to all sorts of abuses and difficulties. This has led Marianne Armstrong to conclude that 'the regime' had decided in 1957 'to test the decrees in eight smaller republics.'[73] The continuing opposition by important segments of the legal profession was illustrated in 1959 when the chief draftsman of the All-Union Fundamental Principles of Criminal Procedure told a Western observer of anti-parasite legislation that 'in his opinion the antiparasite laws contradicted the Fundamental Principles and should be repealed in the republics which had passed them.'[74]

Fundamentally new provisions appeared for the first time in the Georgian decree, that was accepted on September 5, 1960. The Georgian draft had been published in August of 1957, a few days before those of the RSFSR, Moldavia and Belorussia. It did not differ significantly from the other drafts. The innovation of the Georgian decree of 1960 was that it dropped the idea of popular justice. The role of meetings of citizens was reduced from trying suspected parasites to requesting the executive committee of a soviet to take up anti-parasite proceedings. Only the executive committees of local soviets could pass sentence on parasites. This, it seems, was a compromise between popular justice and the demand of jurists for transferring anti-parasite cases to the regular courts. Furthermore, the Georgian decree reduced the maximum term of exile to two years, excluded village dwellers from possible prosecution for parasitism and mitigated several other provisions.

On May 4, 1961 the Presidium of the RSFSR Supreme Soviet enacted its own decree on parasites.[75] Thereby it closed the public discussion and spoke the ultimate word on anti-parasite legislation in the Soviet Union. In the weeks to follow all the remaining fourteen republics, Georgia included, quickly passed new or alterated anti-parasite decrees almost or fully identical to the RSFSR decree. Although the RSFSR decree was less liberal than the one adopted in Georgia shortly before, it did to a considerable extent meet the objections that had been expressed by jurists. To begin with, it specifically identified the sort of behavior that was to be considered parasitic: living off unearned income, for example from the exploitation of private cars, dachas or pieces of land, enriching oneself on account of the state, being engaged in forbidden business, speculation, begging and so on. Earlier decrees had not provided such a detailed definition of parasitic behavior. Furthermore, all suspected parasites who had no job were to be tried by People's Courts, those that had a job 'for the sake of appearances only' were to face either such a court or a meeting of their colleagues. The role of the public prosecuter (prokuror) in anti-parasite cases was increased: he became the person to decide whether such a case would be tried in a regular People's Court or in a general meeting at the defendant's place of work. As of now no more meetings of neighbours for the conviction of parasites were to be held. Under the RSFSR decree every defendant was to be granted the opportunity to better his life: the sentence of exile of two up to five years was to be preceeded by a trial period during which the parasite had to find an honest job. The decision of a People's Court or of the local soviet's executive committee - which as before had to confirm the sentence of a public meeting - was to be final; appeal to a higher court was not made possible.

The implementation of the decrees of May and June of 1961 has been a history of failure and abuse. Trial periods were often unrealistically short, innocent people were threatened or sentenced and convicted parasites often could or would not find employment in their place of exile.[76] The failing implementation of anti-parasite legislation was duly reported in the Soviet press and criticized by the USSR Supreme Court.[77] In the years 1961-1963 the Supreme Court directed the People's Courts to take specific measures to ensure due process of law in anti-parasite cases. By 1963, according to Marianne Armstrong, 'the professionals and the courts had clearly taken over from the public. General meeting at places of employment heard only 10 percent of all cases in 1961-1963 in Lithuania and only 2 percent in the Tatar Autonomous Republic.'[78]

The close tie between Khrushchev's populist approach of the regulation of social life and the fate of anti-parasite legislation became even more obvious when this legislation was almost completely thrown overboard after his ouster. A new RSFSR decree of September 20, 1965 reduced the number of categories of parasitic behavior and eliminated the general meetings at places of employment altogether. It also limited the penalty of exile to those parasites living in Moscow and Leningrad and ordered that prior to such a penalty the parasites should not only be given a trial period, but offered a job as well.

'In fact', Donald Barry and Harold Berman have concluded,

> ...almost nothing has been heard of the antiparasite laws since the 1965 amendments. Reports of antiparasite proceedings have been conspiciously absent from the Soviet press, and in August 1966 the President of the RSFSR Supreme Court told one of the authors that the antiparasite cases in the courts in 1966 could be counted on the fingers of one hand.[79]

ISSUES IN VARIOUS POLICY AREAS

Educational Reform, 1952-1959

Polytechnical education, i.e. the combination of academic and technical instruction in day-schools with work in factories or on farms, was introduced in the Soviet Union in 1959. A week before the beginning of the new year the USSR Supreme Soviet had accepted a law ordering a full-scale overhaul of secondary education.[80] This was followed in the spring of 1959 by laws in each of the fifteen republics, laws which were patterned after - and almost identical to - the law of the Russian republic.[81] With these new laws, an authoritative decision on the issue of educational reform had been taken. Here I want to investigate how the issue originated and how it developed. This issue is quite a complicated one, involving such sub-issues as curriculum content, access to higher education, polytechnization and the organization of new types of specialized secondary education. It will not be possible to deal with all sub-issues extensively.

To many observers the 1958 educational reform seemed to be Khrushchev's work. Even Joel Schwartz and William Keech, who are among the few who have seriously studied the issue, have argued that 'there can be no doubt whose initiative lay behind the proposed reform', namely the initiative of Nikita Khrushchev who in April 1958 at the Thirteenth Komsomol Congress had demanded fundamental changes in the educational system.[82] Though in general their stressing of the role of Khrushchev as a pace-maker in educational reform has been correct, they have not been justified in suggesting that the ideas for polytechnization of education were exclusively Khrushchev's. Six years earlier, at the Communist Party's Nineteenth Congress, polytechnization had been discussed and had been made a major goal for a reform of Soviet education. During the years between the Nineteenth and the Twentieth Party Congress innovations had gradually been introduced in the secondary schools of the Russian republic, and in December, 1955 and January, 1956 the RSFSR Academy of Pedagogical Sciences had organized two conferences at which educators and pedagogues had discusses and evaluated the results of these experiments.[83] In the main, however, the theoretical orientation of secondary education remained unchanged. Soviet primary-secondary schools were training youths for an academic career, i.e. for the continuation of their studies at an institution of general or specialized higher education.

At the Twentieth Party Congress Nikita Khrushchev criticized this situation and demanded that the schools not only introduce new subjects which would familiarize the pupils with technology and production,

> ...but also accustom them systematically to working in factories, on collective and state farms, on experimental allotments and in school workshops. The secondary school curriculum must be revised in the direction of greater specialization from the standpoint of production, so that young boys and girls leaving the ten-year school will have a good general education opening the way to higher education and at the same time be trained for practical activity, since the majority of school-leavers will immediately be absorbed into work in the various branches of the national economy.[84]

Other delegates supported his criticism and the Congress resolution noted the 'isolation of teaching from life' as being 'the most serious shortcoming in the work of schools', and it copied Khrushchev's demands.[85] Soon after the Congress, new curricula and syllabi were worked out by the RSFSR Academy of Pedagogical Sciences; they included quantitative changes only: the introduction of polytechnical lessons and practical work without a reduction in academic lessons. The total number of hours of instruction in the ten-year school would be increased by about one thousand, i.e. nearly 10%. This system of polytechnical education was to be tested in all secondary schools of the RSFSR.

During the school year 1956/7 585 schools adopted the new curriculum. Their number was enlarged to 2.500 - a quarter of all schools in the Russian republic - in 1957-1958 and 50% of all RSFSR schools in 1958-1959.[86] The experiment was directed and monitored by pedagogues of the RSFSR Academy of Pedagogical Sciences, especially of its Institute of Teaching Methods. In May 1957 the Academy organized another big conference on polytechnical education, in which over a thousand Siberian educators, pedagogues, managers, Party and state officials discussed the first results of the experiments.[87]

These experiments left the basic profile of the ten year school intact: the preparation of the pupil for higher education. They only added some polytechnical and vocational training, but did not turn Soviet schools into training centers for agriculture and industry. But not everybody was satisfied with the limited scope of these experiments. Late in 1956 the first protests against the direction that educational experimenting was taking, were heard. Literaturnaia Gazeta published two articles pleading for a better preparation of the school youth for their working life. Educators and writers from Leningrad proposed to shorten the period of compulsory general education from ten to seven years, after which most of the students would receive specialized training in some industry or trade. In the first months of 1957 the RSFSR Academy of Pedagogical Sciences developed a plan for a twelve-year system of education, including eight years of compulsory general education and four years of specialized training. In December it was announced that this new plan would be tested in 50 experimental schools in the RSFSR; they would require students in the upper grades to combine three days of school instruction with three days of work each week.[88]

It was at this point in the decision-making process that First Party Secretary Nikita Khrushchev actively interfered. In his speech at the Thirteenth Komsomol Congress, held in April 1958, he said that 'the Party Central Committee is presently considering the problems of improving the public education system and the training of specialists in the specialized secondary schools and higher educational institutions.'[89] The time had come for what Khrushchev called 'a decisive reorganization':

> The most important thing in this matter is to set forth a precept and to have this precept be sacred to all members of our society. All children entering school must prepare themselves for useful labor...[90]

In Khrushchev's conception, higher educational institutions were to admit 'a greater number of young people who have already had some experience and a record of practical work.' He was not explicitly saying that each and every high school student would have to take a job upon graduating, or that having or having had a job was a prerequisite for access to higher education. However, Soviet and Western scholars have drawn such conclusions from a later passage in Khrushchev's speech, a passage that had the style of one of his many improvised intermezzo's:

> Every young man and woman must realize that in studying they must prepare for work, for creating values useful to man and society. There should be only one road for everyone, regardless of parents' position - to go to school and, when studies are completed, to work. Those who would like to continue their schooling while working can enroll in night schools or correspondence courses for both specialized secondary and higher education... Let them study while they work for a year or two, and then later, when they get to the more advanced courses, they should be given some time off; two or three days a week, say, especially for school. For their last year or two (of study) it would perhaps be expedient to relieve such persons of work altogether in order to enable them to complete their studies...[91]

The publication of this speech triggered a large expansion in the discussion in the press and in educational institutions, in which, according to Donald Kelley, the RSFSR Academy of Pedagogical Sciences 'led the battle for the retention of the day secondary school.'[92] Kelley has performed content analysis of 876 articles that were published in the Soviet press between Khrushchev's speech of April and the adoption of the educational reform law in December. Although he has not distinguished the first phase of this public discussion from the second, and has not made explicit the way in which he has treated his raw data, his procedure provides for a less shaky basis for his conclusions than is the case with Schwartz & Keech. In order to illuminate the distinction in phases, I will run ahead of things and proceed with a description of the later stages of the decision-making process.

In the summer of 1958 Khrushchev presented his proposals on school reform - the so-called September Memorandum - to the Party Presidium, which, possibly after serious discussions and amendments, accepted them in September. The Memorandum was published on September 21.[93] A Central

Committee plenary meeting on November 12 approved of the draft-theses on educational reform which had been compiled by the Party Secretariat on the basis of Khrushchev's Memorandum. It ordered their publication for nationwide discussion and their submission to the Supreme Soviet.[94] The nationwide discussion which lasted one month after adoption of the November theses was of a different character than the public discussion that had taken place before. Up to November, the papers had been open to all kinds of proposals pro and con, but the adoption of the theses by the Central Committee in the name of the Central Committee and the USSR Council of Ministers signified that policy had been set. Consequently, the nationwide discussion acquired a much more orchestrated and propagandistic character, as is witnessed by the quantities that have been proudly presented by a Soviet source: more than seventy million participants in one million meetings at which about five million people had their say. In the course of one month over 650.000 letters were sent to papers, magazines, Party and state institutions.[95]

In the summer of 1958 the battle over educational policy raged in full intensity. Khrushchev had apparently not been able to forge a majority for his position in the Presidium. On August 13 he delivered a speech in Smolensk in which he demanded that work experience be an absolute prerequisite for study in higher educational institutions.[96] In _Komsomol'skaia Pravda_ of September 10 G.I. Zelenko, representing the USSR Council of Ministers' Labor Reserves Administration, made a plea for vocationalization (full-time training in a skill or trade) after the completion of a general eight-year polytechnical school. 'In this connection, it is necessary to develop an extensive network of specialized... technical vocational schools where young people, after the eight-year school, can acquire a trade while engaged on a job that is subordinate to educational purposes.'[97]
However, Zelenko did propose the retention of three-year general secondary schools for particularly gifted graduates from the eight-year school.

From his study of the Soviet press, Donald Kelley had concluded that secondary school educators and members of the educational bureaucracy almost unanimously opposed Khrushchev's plans and demanded the preservation of the full-time secondary school. So did teachers and administrators associated with existing vocational and part-time secondary schools, led by the Labor Reserves Administration, and from workers.

In September Pravda printed Khrushchev's Memorandum to the Party Presidium. From the fact that the law adopted three months later differed from this Memorandum 'not only in detail but in basic principle', Schwartz & Keech have concluded that Khrushchev had been rebuffed by other Party leaders in the Presidium, who had been activated and supported by protesting educators. This overlooks the fact that Pravda stated that the proposals in Khrushchev's Memorandum had been approved by the Party Presidium. What exactly were the most important proposals of September? Khrushchev wrote that in his opinion 'all students without exception should be drawn into socially useful work at enterprises, collective farms etc., after completing the seventh or eighth grades.'[98] Compulsory education, Khrushchev proposed, should be limited to seven or eight years of instruction in basic knowledge, polytechnical and labor training. He was less explicit on what exactly was to happen after the eight-year school had been completed and the student was to enter the labor force.

On the crucial issue of the length of compulsory education, the Party-government theses accepted by the Central Committee in November seemingly echoed Khrushchev's Memorandum: after completion of a compulsory eight-year school all young people had to take up work. Alternative ways were open to them to take up vocational training in correspondence, evening or factory schools, or in tekhnikumy. However, the theses also created the alternative of the student enrolling in a three-year 'secondary general-educational labor polytechnical school with production training', that would give access to higher education.[99] These provisions, which in fact accepted the formula of the polytechnical school proposed by the RSFSR Academy of Pedagogical Sciences after the Twentieth Party Congress, were eventually incorporated in the laws accepted by the supreme soviets of the USSR and the republics. From a comparison of the programs of the new eleven-year schools with those of the former ten-year schools Donald Kelley has concluded that 'general education was not being sacrificed to vocational training.'[100]

On the issue of access to higher education the November theses backed down somewhat and the final legislation compromised even more. Having worked after the completion of secondary school was not made a prerequisite for access to higher education; instead, it was ruled that priority would be given to applicants who had worked or were employed. During the discussion a considerable majority of teachers from institutions of higher education had protested Khrushchev's plans and had argued for direct entry from secondary to higher school. Three representatives of the USSR Ministry of Higher Education had supported these claims.[101]

The new educational system that evolved after 1958 was to be fully implemented by 1965. Its central element in the course of the early 1960s became the eleven-year polytechnical school with vocational training and part-time employment. Suddenly in August 1964 the reorganization of 1958 was undone and the old ten-year school was re-instituded; vocational training and employment were almost completely eliminated.[102] At this occasion the Minister of Education of the Russian republic declared that the 'prolongation of secondary schooling by one year, which was devoted largely to production training, has not justified itself in most cases' and added that production training was 'frequently a useless waste of time'.[103] In his study of this important policy change, Philip Stewart has convincingly shown that it came about as the result of the activities of a loose coalition of opposing forces - or 'groupings' - that existed in the RSFSR Academy of Pedagogical Sciences, the RSFSR *Sovnarkhoz*, the Commission of Education of the RSFSR Supreme Soviet, the Estonian Academy of Sciences, the editors of *Uchitel'skaia Gazeta* and some members of the Party Presidium.[104] Thus, a few month before it removed Nikita Khrushchev, the Presidium neutralized one of the policies that were most identified with his person.

Opposing Pollution of Lake Baikal, 1958-1978

Lake Baikal in Eastern Siberia is a unique lake; it is both the oldest and the deepest lake in the world. This fold in the earth's crust, over 600 kilometers long and 1620 meters deep, is filled with 23.000 cubic kilometers of exceptionally pure fresh water. In it hydrobiologists have found a very rich and varied flora and fauna, of which the Baikal seal, the omul and the transparent and viviparous golomianka are only the best known representatives. The tremendous intrinsic value of the lake is underlined by the fact that three quarters of the species that inhabit its waters is endemic to it: many of the worms, mollusc and fish of Lake Baikal will not be found anywhere else in the world.[105]

Long before the foundation of the Soviet state scientists and conservationists appreciated Baikal's priceless value. The Baikal Commission of the Imperial Academy of Sciences promoted research and organized several expeditions in which prominent scientists took part. When in 1924 Gleb Vereshchagin, a young enthusiast for the new science of limnology (the interdisciplinary study of lakes) was elected its Scientific Secretary, he immediately left for Irkutsk to develop a grand program for research of the lake. His efforts resulted in 1928 in the foundation of the Academy of Sciences' first research establishment in Siberia, the Baikal Limnological Research Station. In 1961 this Station was transformed into the Limnological Institute of the Academy of Sciences' Siberian Department. Grigorii Galazii, a geobotanist, was its director.

Until the middle of the twentieth century the lake has not been seriously threatened by human activities. By the late 1950s, however, fishing authorities and scientists began to perceive a decline in the quality of the waters of the lake's tributaries and of regions of the lake itself. At that time Selenga river, the major tributary, received waste from about fifty factories, including meat packing plants and lumber mills, and only nine of them treated their effluent in some way before discharge into the river.[106] Ulan Udė, a city of 175.000 in 1959, discharged its sewage untreated into the Selenga.

In April 1960 the USSR Council of Ministers admitted that many of the country's rivers and lakes had been seriously polluted by untreated effluent from factories and sewers and ordered the councils of ministers of the republics to take protective measures. To begin with, it prohibited that new factories be put into operation before adequate waste purification installations would be operative. Less than three weeks later the Council of Ministers of the Russian Republic took a decision specifically for the Lake Baikal basin.[107] Among other protective measures, the decision prohibited that the Selenginsk Cellulose Paper Factory and the Baikalsk Cellulose Carton Factory be put into operation before purification installations were operative.[108]

Plans for the construction of these factories had been developed in 1957 by Gosplan's State Committee for Wood, Cellulose-Paper, Woodworking Industry and Forestry, hereafter to be called the State Committee for Cellulose. The great scarcity of paper and high-quality cellulose for cord to be used in tires, and the simultaneous presence of enormous virgin forests and pure water in great quantities had made the Soviet planners decide to build the factories in East Siberia, one of them on the shores of Lake Baikal. As was revealed much later, the location decision had been prepared very poorly, for in many respects the site was unsuited for a factory of this profile and size. In addition, as synthetic fibers became available in the 1960s, the need for the production of high-quality cellulose cord declined.

Construction of the Baikalsk factory (named after the new town which housed its workers and their families, 13.000 in 1970[109]) was started in 1958. From the beginning, opposition was voiced by concerned scientists. Their initiator was Grigorii Galazii, director of the Limnological Station. In August of 1958 he availed himself of the fact that a great many scientists, planners, government and Party officials had come to Irkutsk for a large conference on the industrialization of East Siberia to launch his first public attack. In the Conference's section on Forestry and Wood industry he decried the managers and planners, none of whom had paid any attention to the need of purifying the waste of the Baikalsk factory. Several conference participants demanded that the lake with a surrounding area of ten to fifteen kilometers be made a state nature reserve.[110]

In February of 1959 the issue reached the national press. The Siberian writer Frants Taurin published an article in Literaturnaia Gazeta under the headline 'Baikal must become a nature reserve'; his demands were supported by the papers'editors. In October of the year before the same editors had printed a letter signed by thirteen concerned professors, writers and managers protesting against a plan to blow up the 'threshold' in the Angara river where it flows out of the lake; now they decided not to let the case rest. In March of 1959 more letters sent by concerned readers, among them academicians and other prominent scientists, were printed.

This shows that Marshall Goldman was wrong in suggesting that in July 1960 a 'poorly circulated pamphlet' written by 'a local writer, B. R. Buiantuev' was the first sign of protest and that 'the public at large was unaware until almost 1962 of the plans for the pulp and cellulose mills'.[111] Balzhan Buiantuev, moreover, was no local writer but a Buriat geographer affiliated with the East-Siberian Branch of the Academy of Sciences. He had been present at the industrialization conference of August 1958 and may very well have been one of the participants that asked for the lake to be turned into a nature reserve.

In 1961 Baikal got more attention. The Fourth All-Union Conference on Nature Conservation rejected the possible discharge of waste water from the Baikalsk factory into the lake. One professor Grushko warned in the _Vostochnosibirskaia Pravda_ of June 9 that the design of the purification installations was of bad quality and that such was also the opinion of a commission of experts of the Academy's East Siberian Branch. At the end of December Olga Serova and Sergei Sarkisian published a little book on Lake Baikal, which they concluded with an appeal to turn the lake into a nature reserve[112] and Grigorii Galazii succeeded in having a letter published in _Komsomol'skaia Pravda_. In his alarming letter, Galazii proposed three alternatives for saving the lake: the full recycling of the water used by the cellulose plants, transporting the effluents of the Baikalsk factory to Irkut river, i.e. out of the Lake Baikal basin, or not finishing the construction of the Baikalsk factory but expanding the cellulose factory at Bratsk instead. Obviously, in Galazii's conception the discharge of waste water into the lake, treated or untreated, was out of the question.

During the years 1962 - 1964 little was heard about the imminent pollution of Lake Baikal. The cellulose factory at Baikalsk was being built and in the meantime publications were apparently prohibited. A commission of the USSR Council of Ministers' Committee for the Coordination of Scientific Research had been installed in order to investigate Galazii's complaints; it concluded that pollution of Lake Baikal was inevitable, but kept its conclusion secret.[113] The scientists, however, did not rest. Galazii's Limnological Institute launched a research program aimed at demonstrating the range and details of the threat that the new factories presented to the lake.[114] A design for purification installations for the Baikalsk factory was published in 1964 after it had been approved by the State Committee for Cellulose. After purification the effluent would still contain 3,5 times as many mineral salts as pure Baikal water, and fifteen times as many suspended particles.[115]

The issue of Lake Baikal's fate came in the focus of public attention in 1965. Literaturnaia Gazeta published several articles in which the decision to locate cellulose factories at the lake was assailed and the threat to the lake was dramatized. Writers, scientists and institutions of the Academy of Sciences joined forces in their opposition to ministries and state committees. In this year, too, the scope of the research performed by the Limnological Institute was broadened considerably when five other institutes offered their help: the institutes of Hydrodynamics and Warmth Physics of the Academy's Siberian Department, its Computer Center, the Academy's Institute for Oceanology as well as the Marine Hydrophysics Institute of the Ukrainian Academy of Sciences. In 1966 the Chief Hydrometeorological Service of the USSR and Moscow State University sent expeditions to Lake Baikal.

On May 11, 1966, shortly before the Baikalsk factory was to start production, Komsomol'skaia Pravda printed a letter in which twenty academicians and many outstanding scientists and artists characterized the decision to industrialize the shores of Lake Baikal as a mistake and called for the dismantling of the factories. The first signatory of this letter was Academician Boris Konstantinov, who had only recently become one of the vice-presidents of the Academy of Sciences. Among the other academicians were Presidium members Artsimovich, Bykhovskii, Kapitsa and Trofimuk. This letter may have prompted the installation of the First Special Commission of the Academy of Sciences on Lake Baikal. That such a commission existed is known from Boris Komarov's book on The Destruction of Nature, published in Western Germany in 1978.[116] Komarov has written that there have been two such commissions, and that the first presented its report to the Academy's Vice-President Vinogradov after it had investigated the issue for about six months.[117] Alexander Vinogradov was elected Vice-President in May 1967,[118] so that the First Special Commission cannot have started its work much earlier than November 1966. Chairman of the Commission, according to Komarov, was Academician Innokentii Gerasimov, Director of the Institute of Geography. Gerasimov had been one of the signatories of the May 11 letter. In March 1966 USSR *Gosplan* had also created a special commission on Lake Baikal which was to give a 'final advice' on the situation.[119] This commission was headed by Academician Nikolai Zhavoronkov, also a member of the Academy's Presidium. In their comment on the May 11 letter, the editors of *Komsomol'skaia Pravda* attacked Zhavoronkov for refusing to comment on the letter before a final decision had been taken. According to Komarov, Vice-President Vinogradov refused to accept the report of the First Special Commission because it was too negative, whereupon the Presidium created 'its own' commission, headed by Zhavoronkov, a chemist 'who had never done work on the purification of effluent.'[120] At a session of the Presidium Zhavoronkov declared that the purification of the factory's effluent would be excellent and that the factories would present no harm to the lake. There were further discussions in the Presidium, and a total of four versions of the report of the First Special Commission. These developments show that the Academy of Sciences' Presidium was torn over the issue of Lake Baikal, with Communist Party members (Konstantinov, Bykhovskii, Trofimuk, Gerasimov and Zhavoronkov) and non-Party members (Artsimovich and Vinogradov) on both sides of the line.

The first section of the Baikalsk factory was opened in December 1966. Adequate purification installations had not yet been completed. At the last moment the State Inspection Service for Water Resources of the Ministry of Land Reclamation and Water Management tried to hold up the opening; its representative in the factory's Acceptance Commission refused to sign the acceptance document, so that the commission could not accept the completed section. Nevertheless, the USSR Minister of Cellulose and Paper Industry ordered the factory to open; later he sought and found a representative of the Ministry of Land Reclamation and Water Management who was willing to sign the acceptance document, appointed him to the Commission and had him sign the document. After the Ministry of Land Reclamation and Water Management had annulled this signature and had re-appointed the first representative, and after this representative had persevered in his refusal, the Minister of Cellulose and Paper Industry ratified the acceptance document nevertheless. Such an episode was repeated in 1969/1970 when the complete first production line of the factory was put into operation over the resistance of the Ministry of Land Reclamation and Water Management.

At the end of 1968 the Limnological Institute published the results of the research projects that had been undertaken since 1960. In a brochure of which 1.000 copies were printed it documented the serious consequences that the effluent of the cellulose factories would have for the lake. Among its ten conclusions were that the Baikalsk Cellulose Factory should be forbidden to drain its effluents into the lake and that these should be pipelined to Irkut river; that the Selenginsk Cellulose Carton Factory should undergo an overhaul and be turned into a factory not producing harmful waste water; and that factories producing harmful waste water should not be built in the Lake Baikal basin at all.[121]

In spite of their considerable efforts the scientists were not successfull in preventing pollution of the lake. The factories were opened whereas as late as 1971 their purification installations were not yet completed. There was recurrent evidence of pollution of the lake.[122] Nevertheless, the campaign of the 1960s did produce results in the form of improved purification installations and several high-level decisions aimed at driving back the threat to the lake. Early in 1969 the USSR Council of Ministers issued a decision 'On measures for the conservation and rational use of the nature of Lake Baikal basin', which said that the Baikal basin would have to become a 'water protection zone' with especially stringent rules. They were to be drafted by ministerial committees and Academy institutions.[123] Work on them was apparently frustrated repeatedly, for in June 1971 the USSR Council of Ministers took another decision, now jointly with the CPSU Central Committee. This decision contained additional measures and ordered several ministries and state committees to design and introduce protective measures during the first years of the 1970s. The USSR Committee for People's Control was ordered to create special posts for policing the implementation of these new measures.[124]

Of course these decisions did not immediately stop the threat to the lake; it was no easy thing to overcome the vested interests of the cellulose industry, to furnish the funds and expertise necessary for the construction of a great many purification installations, or to speed up the consultation process in the government bureaucracy. In the fall of 1974 the Ministry of Land Reclamation and Water Management issued temporary measures for nature conservation in the Lake Baikal area, whereas a Second Special Commission of the Academy of Sciences was still investigating man's impact on the lake.[125] It is not known when this commission, which was headed by the zoologist Academician Vladimir Sokolov, was organized. However, it is known that it reported its findings in 1976 or 1977.[126] According to Komarov, the Commission concluded that 'the threat of Lake Baikal's death had not diminished but had become more serious, and the whole lake is on the verge of irreversible changes.'[127] Its recommendation to the USSR Council of Ministers was to close the Baikalsk Cellulose Factory.[128]

In spite of Komarov's claim of a total ban since 1975 on the publication of information on the situation of Lake Baikal, alarming voices have appeared in print. In August 1978 Grigorii Galazii, who had been a member of both special commissions, wrote in the monthly _Priroda_ that the effluent of the Baikalsk factory still contained particles with toxic and mutationogenic (_mutagennyi_) properties. In 1976 experiments (of the Second Special Commission?, J.L.) had shown that of the test objects (amphipody, molluscs, etc.) which had been submerged in the polluted part of the lake, 90 to 100 percent had died after 64 days.[129] Galazii concluded that the discharge of effluent into the lake, whether directly from the Baikalsk factory or indirectly via Selenga river, should be stopped completely. In the _Kommunist_ issue of December 1977 the same conclusion had been reached by Academician Trofimuk in the name of the Presidium of the Academy of Sciences' Siberian Department.[130] Thus, the campaign by scientists, conservationists, writers and journalists has not prevented the pollution of Lake Baikal. The results of the campaign were two: First, without the campaign the pollution of the lake would probably have been much worse than it is now. Second, the campaign resulted in legislative measures that may in the very long run turn out to be useful instruments for curtailing and repelling the harm done to this unique body of water.

To pinpoint the taking of a decision in a closed political system such as that of the Soviet Union is no easy matter, especially when there has been no announcement of that decision in the press. Yet, both William Korey and Leonard Schroeter have felt confident to claim that in March 1971 Soviet authorities took a decision of unprecedented scope in the issue of the Jewish emigration movement.[131] Behind their confidence lay the unspoken assumption that the magnitude of the upswing in emigration numbers was unthinkable without a prior decision of the proper authorities. I agree with this assumption. Between the founding of the state of Israel in 1948 and March 1971 13.047 Soviet Jews had been allowed to emigrate, on an average of a little over 550 a year. To be sure, until the Six Day War of June 1967 the mean number of annual emigrés had been much lower, 315. In the years after the war it jumped to more than 1.400. Immediately preceding March 1971 they numbered about 90 a month. The total for 1971, however, was over 13.000 persons, and in the following year about 30.000 Jews left the Soviet Union for Israel. Between the periods January 1970 - February 1971 and November 1971 - December 1973 the mean number of Jewish emigrés jumped from 90 a month to 2.500 a month. Considering the radical implications and international consequences of large-scale Jewish emigration from the Soviet Union, such a change is quite inconceivable without a decision of some high decision-making body.

The question which were the 'proper authorities' - as I have called them - remains unanswered. It is not known which political body took the decision. Korey speaks of 'the Kremlin', Schroeter of 'the Soviet government'. It seems improbable that the office which grants exit visas (OVIR) was authorized to decide such an important matter on its own, and the Minister of Internal Affairs, to whom this office is subordinated, does not seem to qualify either. Because of the differing interests involved - internal security, foreign policy, ideology, religion, nationality affairs - it seems probable to me that the issue was on the Politburo agenda and that this body took the ultimate decision.

The Six Day War in the Middle East had a strong effect on Jewish national sentiment in the Soviet Union. Jointly with other developments,

Table 1
JEWISH EMIGRATION FROM THE SOVIET UNION, 1948 - 1979

year		number of persons
1948 - 1967 (June)		6.000
1967		1.412 (arrivals in Israel) '
1968		229 +
1969		2.979 +
1970		1.027 +
1971	1st. quarter	1.400 "
	1st. six months	5.000 " (3.750 visas)
	November-December	600 to 1.000 per week
	Total	13.022 + / 13.905 "
1972		31.681 + / 31.652 (arrivals) '
1973		34.733 + / 35.000 ++
1974		20.628 +
1975		13.221 +
1976		14.261 +
1977		16.736 +
1978	1st. five months	9.507 ++
	1st. six months	11.490 +
	Estimated total	22.000 ++
1979		51.320 +

SOURCES: Schroeter, p. 351-352; Jewish Agency ('); 'Fluctuations de la politique d'émigration envers des Juifs d'U.R.S.S. de 1968 à 1980', Les Juifs en Union Sovietique, Supplément au Bulletin Un mois avec les Juifs d'URSS, April 1980, p. III (+); Radio Liberty Research RL 137/78, June 21, 1978 (++); Soviet government (").

such as the Soviet anti-semitic campaign that followed the war, further restrictions on Jewish education and career opportunities, and Premier Kosygin's declaration of December 3, 1966, that 'the road was open' to those who wanted to leave,[132] the war led to an increase in demands for exit visas and to open defiance of the Soviet authorities. More and more Jews decided to renounce their Soviet nationality, and their documents and letters found their way into *samizdat*. In the West, both public opinion and governments were alerted to the Jewish emigration movement by groups of Jewish activists, and the support from the West strengthened the movement itself. Riga, Leningrad, Moscow, Kiev, Georgia and Lithuania became centers of Jewish activism.[133]

During these years more visas were granted than before, but the authorities also tried to intimidate the Jews with administrative and repressive measures. Then in June 1970 a group of Jews planning to steal a plane was arrested; they were tried in December. The death sentences for two of them created such an international uproar that only a few days later, in the defendants' appeal case, the Soviet prosecutor himself asked the Supreme Court of the RSFSR for their commutation; this was granted on the last day of the year.[134] In the meantime, more members of the Jewish emigration movement had been and were being arrested. But the Jews were not intimidated. On the contrary, the commutation of the death sentences under pressure from Western public opinion made them smell success. From now on, they showed a challenging khutzpah in their way of presenting their demands.

The occurrence of the Twenty-fourth Party Congress, to be held in Moscow, March 29 to April 7, 1971, was used to make the Jewish grievances heard and to voice demands. The Congress was good for an extra dose of attention of the world press for Moscow happenings; in the course of March many foreign delegations and journalists were expected to arrive in Moscow. On the morning of February 24, the day after a World Conference of Jewish Communities for Soviet Jews had opened in Brussels, Belgium, 24 Jews presented a statement on emigration procedures signed by 32 people to the reception office of the Presidium of the USSR Supreme Soviet and demanded an interview with one of the Presidium's officials.[135] They were told that there was no one there to receive them. When the office closed at 5 p.m. its administrator asked the Jews to leave, and after they had refused to comply he returned at 7:30 p.m. with the announcement that the Presidium would answer the questions in the statement by March 1. With this result the first sit-in, which had lasted for over eight hours, was quietly dissolved.

On March 1 over one hundred Jews returned and a delegation of forty -including the 32 signatories of the February 24 petition - had a conversation with government officials, including the chief of the Department of Jewish Affairs of the KGB and the chief of OVIR. They received a number of concrete promises. February 26, two days after the first Moscow sit-in, a group of over fifty Jews from Riga had gone to the Latvian Council of Ministers and its Ministry of Internal Affairs, demanding exit visas. After they had been refused, they decided to stage an even more sensational action, and left for Moscow on the evening of March 9.[136] They had contacted Jews in other parts of the country and coordinated upcoming events.

On the morning of March 10 the Riga group assembled in the reception office of the USSR Supreme Soviet Presidium and was joined there by Jews from Vilnius, Kaunas, Lvov, Berdichev, Tallin, Kislovodsk and Daugavpils. They were told that they would not be met by an official, whereupon the group of 156 persons declared a hunger strike then and there. The strike was to last until 4 p.m. the next day. Several members of the group were interviewed by Western correspondents, but the office was closed at 4 p.m. The demonstrators finally left the building at about 7:30 p.m., after they had been threatened with arrest. Instead of having themselves arrested, they re-assembled the next morning at the reception office and marched through the streets of Moscow to the Ministry of Internal Affairs. 'Spectators', says Korey, 'were stunned.'[137] After they had refused to be received at the Ministry on an individual basis, 'confusion seemed to reign as police officers went to and from various bureaus.'[138] The Jews were not satisfied by the guarded promises of several department heads, and refused to leave. Finally, colonel-general Nikolai Shchelokov, the USSR minister of internal affairs and member of the CPSU Central Committee, confronted the group. William Korey has described what happened:

> He jousted with the Jews, at first delicately: he had one and one-half hours before giving a scheduled lecture at the university. 'Perhaps there is someone among you who is the head?' There was no 'head', no organization. They wanted answers to the questions of principle on the right to leave: 'What categories of Jews will be given permits and what categories will be refused?'
>
> The minister, mixing humor and anger, spoke at length. Several considerations guiding policy-makers on emigration were elaborated.

> He answered inquiries; assured those present that 'Socialist laws' would be strictly observed; and, finally, promised to send, within a month, 'special representatives' with wide powers to various localities so that applications would be re-examined in the light of the 'principles' he outlined. It was 4:00 p.m. when the interview ended. The demonstrators had achieved their objective. The hunger strike was halted.[139]

The demonstrations of late February and the first weeks of March must have made a strong impression, both within the Jewish community of the Soviet Union and in government and Party circles. To the Jewish community they showed the road to success, for instead of arrest the protesters soon received the exit visas they had demanded. This indulgent approach of the authorities did not stop the movement; instead it triggered more sit-ins and demonstrations in Moscow and in republican capitals during the summer of 1971. To the powers that be the demonstrators showed that in the case of the Jewish emigration movement the tried tactics of intimidation and repression failed to reach the desired result: containment. Instead, the movement spread. They decided for a twofold response: to grant exit visas to a considerable percentage of those who risked the perils of an agonizing application procedure.[140] The decision to grant exit visas on a large scale has apparently been taken between March 10 and the beginning of the Party Congress. Against 180 emigrés in the first two months of the year, about 1.200 were allowed to leave for Israel in March, and 12.000 during the rest of the year. By the end of 1971 the number of emigrés had reached 600 to 1.000 a week.

The decision to grant exit visas on a large scale has been motivated by both internal considerations and foreign policy aims. Internally, Jewish activism was threatening security and stability and the Soviet economy was in urgent need of advanced technology such as only the Western countries could provide. But the Jewish emigration movement had attracted the attention of Western publics and politicians, especially that of the large and influential Jewish community in the United States. A dramatic highlight of Western concern was the World Conference of Jewish Communities for Soviet Jews which took place in Brussels, February 23 - 25, 1971. The concern of Soviet officials over the possible impact of this conference was shown by the fact that the Soviet Union sent its own delegation, led by general David Dragunskii who declared that the conference was the work of imperialist and zionist forces, supported by NATO.[141] The watchword of Soviet foreign policy of the early 1970s was the prevention of a rapprochement between Washington and Peking, and détente with the West. At the Twenty-fourth Party Congress Leonid Brezhnev launched his Peace Program which gave this policy its concrete form. Soviet leaders may have thought that a gesture such as the granting of exit visas would further the acceptance of their policy by Western publics and politicians.

Since 1971 there have been many attempts to frustrate Jewish emigration desires, most notably the 'diploma tax' instituted in August 1972, but revoked after strong pressure by the U.S.Congress. In addition, the number of visas granted is not as high as Soviet Jews would wish. Prospective emigrants remain the subject of harassment and in the case of refusal they are condemned to the life of pariahs. Nevertheless, the decision of 1971 stands: our people are going, be it slow.

3 Group Influence in Soviet Decision Making

The compilation of case studies in the foregoing chapter has shown a considerable variety of decision-making processes. A first impression is that they differ from one policy area to another and that the degree of influence of individuals and groups in the decision-making process was different. But what regularities can we establish on the basis of these data? What generalizations can be formulated on the role of individuals and groups, the relationships between policy coalitions and factions in the Party top, on the applicability of the three models of agenda building and on the relationship between issue initiation and the wielding of influence? Is it really possible to establish influence relationships in Soviet decision making? These questions will be dealt with in the present chapter.

The political entrepreneur

Individuals acting on their own behalf sometimes play an important role in the initiation of an issue. However, for this role to be effective they have to qualify for the issue at stake by being generally considered an authority in the policy area. Examples are Grigorii Galazii in the case of Lake Baikal, Alexandra Pergament in the case of family law reform, and Venzher and Sanina in the case of the MTS. These examples suggest that personal initiative - provided it is the initiative of the right person - may trigger real changes, on condition that the Party leaders are ready for change. One cannot imagine the director of the Baikal Limnological Institute seriously trying to initiate the abolition of the MTS or a lawyer like Pergament stirring up an issue such as pollution of Lake Baikal. Also, the Soviet political system being what it is, one can hardly expect agricultural organizations, by way of their official representatives, formally demanding the abolition of the MTS, or the Society for Nature Conservation to press the Party to stop pollution of Lake Baikal. It seems that _if_ initiative bubbles up, such occurs through individual actions, not through officially transmitted demands on behalf of organizations. This throws some light on the importance of the political entrepreneur in Soviet politics. A _political entrepreneur_ is someone who successfully initiates a political issue, i.e. who succeeds in getting the issue placed on the public agenda or directly on the formal agenda. Our data suggest that, in addition to members of the political leadership, such a role can be performed by specialists who qualify for the policy area concerned. With this term political entrepreneur I want to convey that it is a spirit of enterprise that is a necessary characteristic of individuals who initiate issues. Political entrepreneur is of course not a profession; is is a role which is played more or less often by different types of actors. Soviet political leaders are typical political entrepreneurs. It is they who are most often in a position to broach proposals for policy change. But specialists in specific policy areas may also attempt to play this role. They often occupy official positions, but in the early stages of issue initiation act on their own behalf, not as officials. The function of this is that if the issue is refused access to the agenda, it can be put aside as the pet subject of an individual, so that those who guard the gates of the agenda need not disprove the legitimacy of an official demand. If, on the other hand, the issue reaches the public agenda and is thereby accepted as a legitimate issue, the political entrepreneur may change his attitude and stress his official position as a spokesman for his institution.

Policy coalitions

In Chapter 1 I have distinguished three types of political groups: interest groups, opinion groups and policy coalitions. After reading the case studies in the preceding chapter it should now be clear that whatever we may find about interests and influence in Soviet politics, interest groups are not often found to be operating. None of the studies of decision making has provided clear-cut evidence on the three group criteria of Milton Lodge: group self-consciousness, ascribed group status and shared values and beliefs. However, we have found traces of the two additional critaria: interaction among group members and a conscious desire to influence decision makers. The desire to influence may be inferred from the expression of explicit demands. There can be no doubt that many participants in the decision-making processes that have been described, desired to influence the top decision makers, for they did express concrete demands. The nine case studies now lead me to the following conclusions:

Certain groups or institutions may perhaps be said to behave as interest groups and to qualify on the six criteria, but often the common interests of their members will be quite limited in number and will be overshadowed by their different and conflicting interests. With the exception, perhaps, of the RSFSR Academy of Pedagogical Sciences, I have found no evidence of a group or institution in Soviet politics qualifying and behaving as an interest group. Therefore, the concept of interest group seems to be of limited use in the study of Soviet decision making.

I have often found different opinion groups to exist within groups, institutions and the Communist Party. Whether or not these may in fact be termed 'groups' is difficult to establish, primarily because it is difficult for the Western observer to find out if they satisfy the first three group criteria. To get around this problem, Philip Stewart and others have used 'grouping' instead of 'group'. Stewart wants to use grouping 'when similar opinions on the same issue are expressed by more than one individual.'[1] This broad definition leaves the possibility open of two men, one in Kiev, the other in Vladivostok, expressing in front of their wives the same opinion on house-keeping, being called an opinion grouping. It seems to me that at the very least interaction among such persons and their common desire to influence decision makers must be present, if we want to call them a 'grouping'. This seems to be quite acceptable in view of the fact that in many cases it has proven to be possible to document such interaction and such desire.[2]

Policy coalitions emerge when and if the common interests of sections (opinion groupings) of different groups and institutions appear to be stronger than the interests which bind each section to its 'own' group or institution. Such policy coalitions coalesce around one policy position in an issue, and they will fall apart once the issue has died in a binding decision. Examples are the anti-production-education coalition organized by the RSFSR Academy of Pedagogical Sciences, the coalition against pollution of Lake Baikal, organized by the Limnological Institute, and varying coalitions of jurists from different juridical and other institutions for the liberalization of family law, the introduction of tort law and the repeal of anti-parasite legislation.

Communities and conferences

Policy coalitions are not being created in a vacuum. They come about on the basis of what the Russians call the '<u>obshchestvennost</u>'' (community), 'a stratum of society that takes active part in social life and represents public opinion'[3], such as the scientific or the literary community. A policy coalition on, say, an issue in literary policy, may - but will not often - involve the whole literary community, or only parts of it - the point being that it cannot exist <u>outside</u> the literary community. The essential activity of the community is communication.[4] Communication takes place through the press and through conferences.

The importance of conferences is not to be underestimated. Conferences are one of the main vehicles for interaction and coordination of action. I have found that in at least six out of nine decision-making processes several specialized conferences had been organized at which the specific community - or parts of it - gathered to discuss impending changes. In several cases these conferences were organized in an early stage of the decision-making process. For example, juridical institutions convened several conferences with the purpose of discussing legislative reforms in such fields as tort law and family law. In the case of educational reform sections of the educational community convened at the following occasions:

- Two conferences organized by the Academy of Pedagogical Sciences of the RSFSR in December 1955 and January 1956. Participants: school directors and teachers, teachers at teachers' training colleges, scientists of the Academy and other pedagogical research establishments, and representatives of the Chief Directorate of Labor Reserves, USSR Gosplan, several education ministries of republics and autonomous republics, factories, kolkhozy, sovkhozy and MTS.
- The Novosibirsk scientific conference on polytechnical education, organized by the Academy of Pedagogical Sciences of the RSFSR, 13-16 May 1957. Over one thousand participants from Siberia: teachers, pedagogues, education specialists, representatives of industrial, agricultural, Party, Komsomol and trade-union organizations.
- A conference for the purpose of 'determining the direction' of a discussion on secondary education, organized by the editors of *Izvestia* and published in its October 13, 1963 issue. Participants: scientists, pedagogues, education specialists.
- A conference in Tallin, organized by the Estonian Academy of Sciences and the Estonian *Sovnarkhoz*. Participants: directors of Academy institutes, academians, teachers, pedagogues, industrial representatives.[5]

What exactly happens at such conferences? Members of the '*obshchestvennost'*' get a chance to meet, to exchange information and opinions and to coordinate their actions. They make speeches in which they state their position on the issue at stake, and are being identified as representatives of their institutions. They thereby let it be known how different sections of the community think about the issue. Quite often the conference proceedings are biased in favor of one specific policy-position, such as the repeal of production education or the large-scale development of the Virgin Lands. Behind the transparent façade of 'businesslike discussions' such a conference is in fact meant to promote a specific policy. The publication of its proceedings in the press has the function of letting it be known that the policy position(s) expressed at the conference are backed up by enough institutional power to resist their being silenced by censorship. In addition, such publication may awaken dormant discontent in sections of the population, for it signals that an issue which has been taboo, may now be discussed again.

It is a mistake to think that such conferences are always organized and manipulated by the Communist Party or that their organization at least does not conflict with the interests of the Party. First, often 'the' Party does not exist. Factional disputes in the Politburo, departmental conflicts in the Secretariat and discord between Moscow and the provinces may be exploited by non-Party organizations. Second, in quite a few cases the theme and tendency of a conference has been in conflict with operative Party policy.

In cases where issues 'bubble up', the initiative for conferences is often taken by specialized institutions, such as academies or learned institutes. Conferences are therefore to be seen as one of the important instruments for organizing policy coalitions around issues, in a country where such organizing is supposed to be a monopoly of the Party. In case of decision-making processes which conform to the mobilization model the conferences are being organized primarily for the purpose of explaining new policy and for the mobilization of those who will have to implement policy.

We have seen that editorial boards of periodicals may, and sometimes do in fact, take part in policy coalitions. Since opinions are hardly effective if they are not distributed through the media, it follows that such editors occupy key positions in the policy coalitions. They may do a great deal towards the publication of demands and conference reports; they are the ones best qualified to judge when and how to get them through censorship.

Supreme Soviet committee hearings

Conferences obviously serve the function of demand articulation by the obshchestvennost', i.e. by the specialized public concerned. It turns out that in specific cases this function may also be performed by committees of the Supreme Soviet. We have seen that in two cases the legislative committees of the Supreme Soviet organized and stimulated a broad discussion of the issues. Such discussion took place inside the Kremlin walls, where specialists in the field were invited to give their opinion and present their case. Thus it seems that, provided the Party leadership has not yet made a final decision on a specific issue, hearings may be organized. This conclusion is supported by additional evidence from different periods of Soviet history.[6] Hearings are not public, but from the case studies one gets the impression that at least some of the pleas and arguments presented do find their way into print, in the form of contributions to the general press discussion on the issue. In the case of the introduction of governmental tort liability, such was more than obvious. (It should be remembered that this issue was not legislated on its own, but was part of the Principles of Civil Legislation.) First the subcommittee of the legislative committees invited representatives of the law community to comment on the proposed legislation before it drew up the draft of the Principles. That draft having been completed, it was put on the specialized agenda of the law community through its publication in law journals. The legislative committees stated that they wanted the law community publicly to discuss the draft. Thereby they turned the draft into an issue. It may be that governmental tort liability could be discussed as profoundly and extensively as it was, because it was only a small part of the Principles. Had it been legislated on its own, such an intensive and extensive discussion would perhaps not have been allowed. Members of the subcommittee on family law reform went even farther. In 1962 they not only invited specialists, but also travelled through the country themselves, visiting institutes and republican government agencies and polling the community on its ideas. In this case, however, the public discussion and the completion of the legislative process were arrested for four years (December 1962-

December 1966). Once the top leadership had given the go-ahead in December 1966, the Institute of State and Law immediately organized a conference for the law community, and, after six months, published a report on its proceedings. When the draft Principles on marriage and family legislation were finally published in April 1968 they were put on both the mass and the specialized-juridical agendas and were discussed throughout the country.

Policy coalitions and factionalism

My conclusion, as far as the group approach of Soviet politics is concerned, must be that if influence is wielded at all, the subjects are not tightly knit groups, but loose policy coalitions of different sections of a community. Policy coalitions do not always and ever get a chance to develop. It seems that the conditions under which they flourish are those when the top Party leadership announces change, but is not yet certain as to the exact content and direction of that change. On the other hand, if the Secretary-General is explicit in his pronouncement of what he wants, such as was the case in the *Sovnarkhozy*, Virgin Lands and MTS reforms, policy coalitions have few opportunities.

How does this conclusion compare to the findings of other researchers? Stewart has hypothesized that, at least in the policy area of education, interest groupings form primarily among individuals and 'on the basis of similarity of viewpoint on one or more issues. These groupings may be found either within a single bureaucratic structure or cutting across organizational lines.'[7] This hypothesis was validated by his research, and by ours as well.

I have said that the institution - the locale for authoritative decision making - is a third possible type of actor. On the basis of research done in the past I have assumed (Ch.1) that institutions are not necessarily monolithic and that their factions may, for tactical purposes, want to enlist the support of outside groups. This assumed relationship between factionalism at the top and group politics at lower levels has been a central theme both in Kelley's and in Schwartz & Keech's comparisons of two decision-making processes. On the basis of their findings Schwartz & Keech have formulated the following hypothesis:

> The more and greater the disputes on the top policy making level, the more likely it is that policy groups will be involved and listened to.[8]

To be 'involved and listened to' means: to be influential. This hypothesis thus makes explicit some of the conditions under which groups may influence top policy makers. It will be discussed later in this chapter.

Issue creation

In the traditional conception of Soviet politics, based in part on Soviet ideology, the prime and only mover is the Communist Party. Other organizations merely function as transmission belts for conveying the Party's decisions to the masses. Such organizations are seen as agents for the mobilization of the population. All initiative, in this conception, comes from within the Party. In this vein Alfred Meyer has written that

> All organizations function as transmission belts for the Party because their core is always the Party's primary organization or caucus, which often makes decisions before they are submitted to general discussion. Hence, if there is discussion, debate, or other grass-roots participation, it is rarely more than a prelude to the adoption of policies formulated by the leadership.[9]

I will use this statement as a hypothesis and, with the help of the case-studies presented in the foregoing chapter, try to disprove it.

A crucial stage in agenda building is the creation of an issue, and of crucial importance the question of who may succesfully create an issue. We have seen that, of course, the Party leader may do so, and may thereby act as a political entrepreneur: as in the cases of the Virgin Lands, the Sovnarkhozy reform and the anti-parasites campaign. We have also seen that initiatives of others may be nipped in the bud by denying them access to the public agenda. Such cases of non-decision making must be numerous, but are virtually impossible to trace. A rare instance of admitted non-decision making was when Stalin in his book on the Economic Problems of Socialism in the USSR announced that two economists had proposed to do away with the MTS. Whatever this may mean, it documents that even under Stalin two economists were not afraid to suggest such an almost heretical measure.

In contrast to what has been suggested by Meyer, we have seen several cases where issues have been succesfully created at a low level. The case of family law reform was initiated by editors of Literaturnaia Gazeta, who allowed a female journalist to demand the repeal of a decree that had been and still was strongly associated with the newly elected Party leader, Nikita Khrushchev. Since Khrushchev had proposed the 1944 decree and during the early 1960s arrested its repeal, it does not seem probable that in 1954 he would allow the creation of an issue out of this subject. Nevertheless, the paper published Serebrovskaia's letter and, given the sensitive character of the matter, initiated an issue.

Tort liability was an even more sensitive issue, for its possible introduction was of importance to the millions of citizens who had suffered under Stalinist terror. The creation of this issue, however, proceeded in somewhat easier circumstances than in the case of family law reform, for in this case official policy pointed in the direction of liberalizing measures. Before 1956 demands for the introduction of governmental tort liability had been suppressed or, in anticipation of such suppression, had not been formulated. Now that Khrushchev had committed himself to de-Stalinization and the re-institution of socialist legality, specialists felt safe to express their demand. This issue was created by jurists of the Academy of Sciences' Institute of State and Law, who were supposedly best qualified in these matters, and who used their own journal to formulate the issue and place it on a specialized agenda.

The Lake Baikal issue was also the product of efforts of a specialist, the director of the Limnological Institute. It was not easy for him to reach the public agenda, witness the fact that his first protests were printed in a note to the text of conference proceedings. It seems probable that in contacts with scientists and journalists he promoted the issue and mobilized support, as a result of which Literaturnaia Gazeta allowed a writer to express similar demands, early in 1959. The Jewish emigration issue was created by small Jewish groups, acting independently at first, but soon coordinating their activities. They were denied access to the public agenda, but nevertheless continued their protests. This resulted in a peculiar decision-making process which will be dealt with later in this chapter.

These cases disprove the hypothesis derived from Alfred Meyer's book. Initiatives which ultimately resulted in social change entered the political system not through the Party but from other organizations. For the time being there is no sign that central Party bodies activated these organizations through their local representatives. Thus I conclude that the Party is not the only motor for change in the Soviet Union and that under certain circumstances non-Party organizations may get a chance to create issues.

The crucial question, of course, is which circumstances promote issue creation. One of the most obvious of these is a sudden change in a social or political variable. Cobb and Elder have termed such sudden changes 'triggering devices'.[10] This concept is defined in terms of synonyms and examples: triggering devices are unanticipated events, 'circumstantial reactors'.[11] President Kennedy's assassination triggered the issue of gun control and the cave-in of a coal mine in West Virginia (1968) triggered the issue of miners safety. Of course none of these issues was created out of nothing. What Cobb and Elder mean is that trigger events serve as a catalyst. Demands which hitherto have been unable to penetrate the public agenda may profit from trigger events if an initiator puts the new situation to use. The interaction between trigger event, initiator and the public is one of the circumstances in which new public issues may arise. Cobb and Elder have neglected to present an explicit definition of trigger events. They have given many examples and nine possible types of 'trigger mechanisms' instead. As a result almost any change can be said to precipitate more change, which is a truism. Nevertheless, I believe that the term should not be thrown overboard, if only because it may sensitize us to significant differences between decision-making processes. I define trigger events as sudden changes which present an individual or group with the unexpected opportunity of becoming a political entrepreneur.

Issue redefinition

An issue has to be defined if we want to know what it is about. In every-day politics, however, issues are almost never being defined clearly, unambiguously and objectively. Instead, they are being formulated in polemics in which participants may consider it useful to remain vague about the exact issue content. Also, different groups may perceive the real issue differently and may in fact talk and argue about different things. It is no surprise, then, that <u>redefinition</u> often takes place during the life cycle of an issue, and that often the issue which is ultimately decided upon differs from the issue which had originally been raised.

One of the main causes of redefinition of issues in American politics is, according to Cobb & Elder, the need for the proponents to enlist support if they want the issue to make a chance for reaching the formal agenda. Such support from other social groups than the original group may be obtained 'by changing the cleavage lines or substituting one conflict for another.'[12] Thus, for example, a citizens group that opposes landings of supersonic airplanes at a nearby airport because of the noise and the value depreciation of their homes, will gain support by redefining the issue in more general terms and stressing the worldwide health hazards caused by supersonic transportation.

Redefinition may also result from the fact that at the outset the problem is not yet well defined. During the early phases of the decision-making process the task of policy analysis is then to define the problem. Charles Lindblom has shed light on this aspect when he wrote that

> ...policy makers are not faced with a <u>given</u> problem. Instead they have to identify and formulate their problem. Rioting breaks out in dozens of American cities. What is the problem? Maintaining law and order? Racial descrimination? Impatience of the negroes with the pace of reform now that reform has gone far enough to give them hope? Incipient revolution? Black power? Low income? Lawlessness at the fringe of an otherwise relatively peaceful reform movement? Urban disorganization? Alienation?[13]

Redefinition of an issue for the sake of winning the support of new sections of the mass public does not play a role in the Soviet Union. Soviet politics do not work that way, for the electorate cannot use its votes to change the make-up of decision-making bodies. However, redefinition may be necessary to win the support of the particular specialized publics, organizations or groups. Also, when policy coalitions are to be formed, redefinition of the original issue may be necessary by way of compromise between the demands of the participants in the coalition.

Some of the issues we discussed were rather unambiguous at the outset and underwent little redefinition. In February 1957 Khrushchev attacked the industrial branch ministries and a congress resolution advised that their administrative function be transferred to regional economic councils. In spite of a public discussion and an attempted coup, this was what finally happened. The sale of MTS machinery to the collective farms had been proposed as early as 1951 and was realized when in 1958 the MTS were abolished. Finally, the granting of an exit visa to any Jew applying for one, and halting the harassment of applicants was a clear enough demand. There was only limited redefinition in this case, aimed not at the Soviet establishment or the Soviet public opinion, but at foreign publics. For such publics the demand for emigration visa was reformulated in terms of the general right to leave one's country and the spread of anti-semitism and discrimination in Soviet Russia. Such reformulation contributed much to the mobilization of Western public opinion, which was able to put pressure on the Kremlin, partly through the White House and Capitol Hill.

The legislation cases emerged from quite unambiguous demands, but they underwent more redefinition than the first three issues. The demand for the institution of governmental tort liability had orininally been formulated in the context of de-Stalinization and had explicitly been tied to the fate of the surviving victims of Stalinist repression. Soon, however, the issue was redefined and reformulated in less drastic terms. When, after three years, the draft Principles of Civil Legislation emerged from a complex legislative process, they proposed to postpone a decision on the tort law issue. Thanks to large-scale protests tort liability was instituted, but not for actions of the police, the Procuracy and the courts. The case of family law reform showed a similar though somewhat less far-reaching redefinition.

During the early phases of the struggle against pollution of Lake Baikal its protectors demanded that it be turned into a nature preserve and that the discharge of waste water into the lake was to be prevented. Later both the location decision for the cellulose factories and their need were questioned, and their dismantling was demanded. The responsible ministry was criticized for its behavior. The conservation issue thereby turned into a broader economic issue and gained in support.

The most far-reaching redefinition, however, occurred when an issue was quite ambiguous when it was first raised. The development of the Virgin Lands was the result of a decision-making process that started with a demand for more extensive agricultural production, was specified as a demand for more agricultural production in the Volga region, Urals and Siberia, and then reformulated so as to include Northern Kazakhstan. Later the issue became how much land the Kazakhs were able and willing to develop, possibly with the help of other republics. This shows how an issue was reformulated from a qualitive into a quantitive one, as it often must be. Issue content was least stable in the case of educational reform. Here, too, the issue originated not from a particular grievance, but from general concerns about the proper function of secondary education, and was reformulated and redefined in an ever more detailed sense.

In several decision-making processes studied here - especially the ones which have 'bubbled up' towards the public agenda - we have seen representatives of the groupings involved fight against redefinition of their issue by the decision makers. It is in the interest of decision makers to redefine issues in such terms that they can be solved at minimal economic, social, political and ideological cost. It is the task of political entrepreneurs to counteract this tendency, at the same time trying to gain support for their position, which may necessitate redifinition of the issue by themselves. Decision makers may take a decision on a redefined issue and present it as their decision on the original issue, hoping that thereby the policy coalition which has demanded change, will fall apart. The truly capable political entrepreneur is to be recognized by the fact that he or she does not accept this partial solution, and restates the original demand, meanwhile struggling against the disintegration of the policy coalition which he has created. To sum up, redefinition efforts on any issue come from two directions. Initiators of the issue try to win support by broadening the issue content so that new groupings are lured to join the policy coalition. At the same time decision makers try to 'solve' or at least defuse the issue by proposing a solution that will cost them as little as possible. The actual redefinition that we observe during the life cycle of an issue is the result of these two opposite tendencies.

Testing models of agenda building

In Chapter 1 a description of the history of the issue of educational reform led me to the conclusion that its decision-making process conformed to the mobilization model: initiatives and decisions were taken by top leaders and society was mobilized for their successful implementation. As far as Schwartz & Keech are concerned the initiative was indeed Khrushchev's[14], and the history of educational reform started with his speech at the Thirteenth Komsomol Congress in April 1958. In the preceding chapter I have shown that it started much earlier, around 1952. I have hinted that one may discern three distinctive phases in the decision-making process, and I will now substantiate these.

The first phase started around 1952 and lasted until April 18, 1958. The second phase lasted from April 18, 1958, when Khrushchev spoke at the Komsomol Congress, until the middle of November. The third and final phase begins with the publication on November 16 of the joint Party-government theses on educational reform and ends in the spring of 1959 with the acceptance of new education laws by the supreme soviets of the republics. It turns out that only this third phase shows the typical characteristics of the mobilization model: the earlier phases do not, and neither does the decision-making process as a whole. Policy was set by the joint Central Committee-Council of Ministers theses of November 16, and the public discussion that followed was intended to mobilize the population for the implementation of the changes to come. It was of an altogether different character from the public discussions during the preceding phases.

In his study of the <u>repeal</u> of these changes, Philip Stewart has documented the active role of the RSFSR Academy of Pedagogical Sciences.[15]

From my case-study it is clear that this academy - or at least powerful opinion groups inside the Academy, led by its president Kairov - played an innovative role much earlier, starting with the birth of the issue of polytechnization. One gets the impression that during the early 1950s Party leaders, while stressing the need for polytechnization, still felt that the elaboration of their general ideas on polytechnization was to be left to specialists, of which many were organized in the Academy of Pedagogical Sciences. Such indeed happened, innovations were introduced and experiments were monitored and discussed by the specialists on education. The ideas of many educators and pedagogues differed from those of Khrushchev, who was prepared to sacrifice academic training for production training. During the school years 1956-1957 and 1957-1958 Khrushchev must have realized that the implementation of production education, which was being directed by the RSFSR Academy of Pedagogical Sciences, took a direction altogether different from his own ideas. The basic profile of the ten-year school was left intact, whereas he wanted it to change. At the same time some educators argued for a shortening of compulsory general education and the Academy started limited experiments with a more far-going form of production education. During this phase the actors involved were individual specialists and specialist institutions. The discussion was limited to national - but primarily Russian - educational institutions and publications, and the issue was on the specialized agenda of these publications. The general ideas of vocationalization expressed at Party congresses were elaborated and neutralized in such a way that they contained no threat to the position and the ideas of the educational community.

Khrushchev's speech of April 18, 1958 brought this phase to an end. His interference signalled that the pace and content of educational innovation had been insufficient. Through publication of the speech in the mass circulation newspapers, the issue was put on the general mass agenda. What Khrushchev was doing in his speech was <u>not</u> to initiate a new issue, but to interfere in the ongoing discussion by changing issue content, i.e. re-defining the issue. Khrushchev let it be known that he, and possibly some of his colleagues in the Party Presidium, wanted the introduction of production education and that he wanted to see the changes realized soon. As against the careful testing of new plans by educational authorities the Party boss now put his own crude ideas and added a sense of urgency to the issue. During the spring and summer the Soviet press - both the specialized educational and the mass press - was engaged in a discussion of Khrushchev's proposals. During this discussion two opposing policy coalitions crystallized. Supporters of production education rallied around the Labor Reserves Administration. The coalition of opponents centered around the Academy of Pedagogical Sciences; it embraced teachers and administrators at secondary schools and higher educational institutions, and the RSFSR Ministry of Education.

In the summer of 1958 Khrushchev was both Party leader and (since March 27) Prime Minister. He commanded the two most important bureaucracies in the country and could, if he really wanted so, prevent the publication of unwelcome criticism. He had beaten and removed most of his rivals in the Party Presidium and enjoyed a power position that had never before been so secure. And yet Khrushchev's April speech was followed by multiple attacks. Why should he allow this to happen? Why did Khrushchev not prevent the publication of opposing views? If we want an answer to these important questions, we have to remember that in his April speech Khrushchev had not yet elaborated a full scale plan for educational reform. He had indicated the direction to be taken, but details had not yet been filled in. A detailed plan was being drawn up during spring and was presented to the Party Presidium in summer. Once we accept that policy had not yet been authoritatively defined, that specialists were asked for their advice, the fact that a discussion in the press was not suppressed does not seem so unusual. Khrushchev's September Memorandum contained his proposals which had been approved by the Presidium. It is possible that a minority of the Presidium members was opposed to the reform or to parts of it, but could not prevent the Memo from being approved by the Presidium. What they could do was to make sure that the proposals were presented as proposals of Nikita Khrushchev, not of the Presidium. The Party-government theses which were finally accepted by the Central Committee in November compromised on several points and accepted the formula of the polytechnical school proposed by the Pedagogical Academy. The nationwide discussion which was ordered by these theses was more spectacular than the preceding discussions had been, but of little use as far as the content of the reform was concerned. Policy had been set.

This issue also provides an excellent illustration of the crucial importance of the implementation phase in decision making. As Stewart has shown, after the realization of the 1958 reform, opponents of polytechnical education found new allies for their coalition. In the end they scored a full victory over the Party Secretary, and Khrushchev's innovations were completely neutralized.

The history of anti-parasite legislation shows a similar picture. Here, too, Khrushchev's proposal was partially realized, but in the course of many years was completely neutralized thanks to the persistent efforts of a policy coalition. In contrast to educational reform this issue started as a case in the mobilization model. The ideas for handling parasites trickled down from the top in the form of the draft laws and decrees published in 1957; thereby they were automatically both on the formal and on the public agenda. People were to be mobilized, for it was the people themselves who would have to identify and judge parasites. In the press discussion that followed, a policy coalition soon emerged, which directed its criticism against the proposed legislation. It proved to be so strong that the leadership decided not to force the issue, but to put the matter to the test in eight outlying republics, in order to learn if the objections of legal specialists were justified. Whether or not the Party Presidium was split over the issue is hard to tell, but it seems quite obvious that enough members of the Presidium were sensitive to the arguments of the opponents for them to prevent Khrushchev from pushing through his plans. Between 1957 and 1961 the legal policy coalition kept the issue warm and had the additional advantage that it was provided with arguments as to the bad functioning of the new legislation in the eight republics. Several of their objections were met, so that the laws and decrees adopted in the spring of 1961 left less possibilities for misuse than those proposed and introduced in 1957. This shows that it is misleading to start the case of anti-parasite legislation in 1961, as is sometimes done. What really happened is that in 1961 the implementation phase began. The legal profession, which had had limited success in preventing the adoption of extreme anti-parasite laws, now frustrated their implementation and kept the discussion going in the legal press, in journals such as _Sovetskaia Iustitsiia_, _Sovetskaia Zakonnost'_ and _Sovetskoe Gosudarstvo_ *i Pravo*. By 1963 the legislation had been neutralized, and after Krushchev's ouster it was quickly discarded.

These two case studies direct our attention towards one of the limitations of autocratic decision making. In both cases the desire for change was formulated by the Party leader at a time when he was not fully backed on each issue by his collegues in the Presidium. Through his announcements the issues were placed on both the public and the formal agendas. As a consequence, opponents got opportunities for voicing their criticism and building a coalition around each of the issues. It was one of Khrushchevs's bad habits to confront the Presidium with *faits accompli* in the form of public pronouncements which the other leaders had not approved and which they often had not even been informed about. Khrushchev has experienced that one of the drawbacks of this enterprising political style was that it made his colleagues in the Presidium susceptible to the objections raised by groups, individuals and institutions against his plans. The result was that by 1965 both polytechnization and anti-parasite legislation had been discarded, together with Nikita Khrushchev himself.

We have found that during the second phase of the decision-making process in the educational issue, Khrushchev's Memo was approved by the Presidium, but published only on condition of a nationwide discussion of the issue. This discussion provided Khrushchev's collegues with the weapons and arguments for checking his enthusiasm. They could point at the fact that great sections of the educational and scientific communities opposed the reform plans and they could use this as a weapon in Presidium discussions. Something similar happened in the case of the *Sovnarkhozy* reform. Moreover, this issue had serious and direct ramifications for the positions and work conditions of many employees of the state bureaucracy. It is therefore to be expected that they did their utmost to plead their case with 'their' representatives in the Party Presidium.

Had the Presidium members unanimously, or almost unanimously supported Khrushchev's proposals of February 1957, there would have been no need for a nationwide discussion. After all, this was an issue of administrative reform, not requiring the mobilization of great sections of the population. The issue might easily have been decided *in camera*, in discussions and negotiations within and between the Presidium, the Central Committee and the Council of Ministers. In such case, the decision-making process would have conformed to the inside access model. In reality, closed decision making failed because of discord in the Party Presidium. In February the Central Committee had announced a reorganization of industrial administration, thus placing the matter on the formal agenda. At that moment it was not yet a public issue, and it may not have been meant to become one. The Presidium and the Council of Ministers were ordered to draft detailed proposals, but instead of a binding joint resolution, Nikita Khrushchev presented his theses. With these theses the First Secretary placed the issue on the public agenda, making sure to remain somewhat vague on the question of which ministries were to be abolished, and to woo provincial Party secretaries. His opponents in the Presidium, it seems, were powerful enough to demand a public discussion as a condition for the publication of the theses. After all, if there had been no official discussion they would have been able to mobilize enough public opposition in the papers they themselves controlled. Khrushchev may have felt that it was less risky to have an officially proclaimed public discussion instead of a spontaneous discussion, manipulated by his opponents. Although the decision-making process was completed with the Supreme Soviet law of May 10, Khrushchev's opponents almost succeeded in undoing the reorganization, at the same time deposing its initiator. Weeks before the law was to be implemented they organized a coup which probably would have succeeded had they been more steadfast and had Khrushchev not received the help of the army.

It is evident that in 1957 closed decision making failed because of dissent in the top decision-making body. Three years earlier, when the Virgin Lands were to be developed, it had failed as well. Originally Khrushchev had taken the initiative and had tried to expand the cultivated area through private negotiations with officials from Kazakhstan. When it became clear that this tactics would fail because of the obstruction of the Kazakh Party leadership, the conflict was brought into the open and the issue was put on the public agenda. Even more interesting is the MTS case. During the reign of Stalin the demand for abolishing the MTS had not succeeded in penetrating the public agenda and becoming a public issue. It had been rejected behind closed doors. The public learned that there had been such a demand only after the decision not to abolish the MTS had been taken. It seems that all through the 1950s the Soviet countryside was witnessing a rather strong movement for the abolition of the MTS. How else to explain Stalin publishing his answer to the unpublished letter of Venzher and Sanina, than to get the message across to that movement that abolishing the MTS was out of the question?[16] After Stalin's death people and institutions at different levels took steps which assumed the gradual demise of the MTS. The issue itself was still taboo, because of its serious ideological implications. Thus, one cannot say that Khrushchev created this issue out of nothing. On the contrary, he seized an opportunity and legitimized the issue for public discussion. The fact that the issue had been decided within a few months after its first publication in January 1958 has tempted quite a few observers to state that this was another instance where Khrushchev played a major innovative role. In view of the history of the issue, however, I am inclined to conclude that his role was less prominent. This conclusion is supported by the fact that in the first years after Stalin's death the MTS still played an important role in Khrushchev's thinking about agricultural policy, primarily as an instrument for political control over agricultural production. Only when his reorganization schemes were failing and pressure for the abolition of the MTS gained in strength, he changed his mind.

Stalin's death was the biggest trigger event in the post-war history of the Soviet Union. Both the general internal relaxation of tension and the springing up of discord in the Party top allowed for ample opportunity to raise new demands and create new issues. The frontiers of what was possible and what was not, were shifting. For the first time in almost three decades there were opportunities to move frontiers, opportunities that were waiting for enterprising men and women to take them. In a general sense this new atmosphere has probably contributed to the geneses of the family law issue in 1954, though it is not possible to identify one particular trigger event. In two other cases, however, such is indeed possible.

Isolated demands for the introduction of governmental tort liability were probably voiced in the 1953-1956 period, when many prisoners were released and rehabilitated. However, they could not be heard in public.

The de-Stalinization of February 1956 and the Party's explicit commitment to 'socialist legality' served as trigger devices which were put to use by a prominent jurist. For a specialized public he uncovered the implications of these developments and explicitly called for the government to accept financial responsibility for its misconduct in the past. Much later the struggle of Jews for their right to emigrate to Israel was characterized by a virtual escalation of trigger events. First, the Six-Day War and the internal Soviet developments that followed it contributed to open defiance and increased demands for exit visa. Then the commutation of the Leningrad death sentences raised the Jews' sense of efficacy. Finally, at the Twenty-fourth Party Congress Leonid Brezhnev was to present his Peace Program aimed at détente; this added a sense of urgency, for the Soviet leaders must have felt that street demonstrations by Jews demanding exit visa would not contribute to the much wanted relaxation of tension between East and West. Via the Western press the issue threatened to come to play a role in East-West détente politics, and the Politburo has probably taken its decision of March 1971 hoping to prevent this from happening.

Together with the issue of the pollution of Lake Baikal these three cases were more or less congruent to the outside initiative model of agenda building. Their analysis is hampered by the fact that almost nothing is known about the policy positions of individuals, factions or departments in the Presidium and Central Committee Secretariat. Was the Presidium split over the issue of protecting Lake Baikal, and if so, who was for drastic measures and who was against? Which persons or departments were against liberalizing family law? Only in a few instances tentative answers to these and similar questions can be inferred from the course of events.

The most exceptional pattern of agenda building and decision making is presented by the case of Jewish emigration. No doubt the initiative came from outside the Party and government aparatus. It came about as individual demands were aggregated in local activists' groups which, after a while, coordinated their actions. The issue differed from the other eight issues in that it implied a total rejection of the Soviet system; it was an example of unorthodox dissent.[17] This and the international political ramifications turned it into a highly sensitive issue indeed.

These qualities prevented the issue from being allowed access to the public agenda. Nevertheless, it did reach the formal agenda, and very soon at that. This shows that at least in Soviet politics in addition to the mobilization, inside-initiative and outside-initiative models a fourth model of agenda building is possible, i.e. a hybrid of the inside and outside access models. It is applicable to non-orthodox issues which can only be suppressed at great cost because they have come to play a role in international politics. Such issues are decided *in camera* with the purpose of relieving the immediate pressure on the system.

The opposition against the pollution of Lake Baikal, on the other hand, was a classical example of outside-initiative. The issue reached the national mass agenda in 1958 in the form of demands only tangentially related to what later became the main issue. They were voiced by professors, writers and managers who had signed a collective letter. Both Grigorii Galazii and the editors of *Literaturnaia Gazeta* then acted as pioneers in redefining the issue in such terms that the lake would have to be turned into a nature preserve. In February-March 1959 the paper explicitly put this issue on the public agenda. Apparently it did not last long before it was transferred to the formal agenda, for in the spring of 1960 the Council of Ministers of the RSFSR announced a decision in which it tried both to redefine the issue and to appease the protesters. It promised that the two cellulose factories which were then being built would not become operative before their purification installations would be ready. But neither of the two strategies succeeded. Opposition in the press continued during the early 1960s and the issue itself was soon redefined back in its original terms: protecting the lake from any pollution at all. During the last three years of Khrushchev's reign there was apparently a publication stop, enforced by central authorities while the matter was under investigation. This meant, first, that the issue was still on the formal agenda, and second that Galazii's Baikal Limnological Institute had the time and opportunity to launch a research program which was to supply the scientists with precise documentation as to the consequences of pollution, and thereby with more arguments. After the removal of Khrushchev the press discussion erupted again. The wisdom of locating the cellulose factories near the lake was now publicly questioned and the decisions were criticized in central newspapers. At the same time the nucleus of a policy coalition 'for a clean Baikal' came about through the cooperation of several research establishments in the investigations of the Limnological Institute. Thus, the issue was allowed access to the public agenda and was duly transferred to the formal agenda. But as I have shown in the preceding chapter, the outcomes of the decision-making process were not very satisfactory to the conservationists.

The decision-making patterns in the two legislative cases have much in common. In both cases the de-Stalinization triggered rather large-scale discussions in the papers and in the specialized press, though the issue of family relations had reached the public agenda as soon as August, 1954. Both issues were transferred to the formal agenda during the February 1957 session of the Supreme Soviet. However, by that time the governmental tort liability issue had already been redefined and defused so as not to include the government's responsibility for actions of the police, the Procuracy and the courts. This issue was embedded in the Principles of Civil Legislation in the same way that the issue of illegitimate children became part of the Principles of Legislation on Marriage and the Family. The patterns of legislation should therefore not be considered typical for the issues, but for the legislation of Principles. In both cases the legislative committees of the Supreme Soviet created a subcommittee which was to consult with specialists and produce a draft. The draft Principles of Civil Legislation was published fairly soon (spring 1960) and with its publication the issue of governmental tort liability was once more put on the public agenda. It turned out that Party authorities wanted to shelve this issue, for the draft proposed to settle it by separate legislation.

However, the protests of jurists and juridical institutions made them decide to strike a compromise, so that in the Principles adopted on December 8, 1961 at least the general responsibility of state institutions was recognized. It seems that in the case of family law the Party authorities were not at all satisfied with the draft which the Supreme Soviet subcommittee had completed by early 1963. They, i.e. probably Khrushchev and some conservatives in the Party apparatus, held up publication. This interpretation assumes that these conservatives were not in a position to influence the outcome of the subcommittee's activities. It also assumes, as Peter Juviler has done, that the Party top was not united on the issue of family law and that Alexei Rumiantsev spoke for a reformist faction in the Secretariat.[18] Only after Khrushchev had been removed the legislative process was started again; in April 1968 it resulted in the publication of the draft, which once more put the issue on the public agenda. Again the final outcome of the legislative process was a compromise between conservatives and reformists, but we can probably say that this compromise was somewhat less dissatisfying to the reformist jurists than the one struck in 1961.

Influence

It is a sad truism of political analysis that the use of its central terms of power and influence by any of its practitioners should be prefaced by excuses over the disarray in the definition and use of these terms. In view of the nature of political analysis it is not probable that this situation will soon change. The definitions of power and influence used explicitly or implicitly by various authors will continue to differ as long as political science continues to develop in a free society. The individual practitioner of political analysis may, however, set himself the task at least not to add to the existing confusion and disarray. He may do so by making his definitions explicit and, preferably, by adopting one of the existing modal definitional frameworks. By embarking on this course he may set a first step towards the cumulation of knowledge on power and influence relationships.

In this book I am concerned with influence exclusively. I have selected Robert Dahl's definition as the appropriate definition for my analysis and I will use elements from his discussion of influence in both the first and the third edition of his _Modern Political Analysis_.[19] Dahl has distinguished manifest from implicit influence. In the tradition of Carl Friedrich, who introduced the rule of anticipated reactions, he conceives of _implicit influence_ of actor A over actor B if A's desire for outcome x causes B to attempt to bring about x without A having acted with the intention of causing B to bring about x.[20] This is the type of influence that I have dwelt upon in Chapter 1 . It is a type of influence that may be illuminated by giving two examples in which the direction of influence is opposite. On the one hand, Soviet authorities are careful in their employment and consumer policy, for they fear that job insecurity and rising scarcity may trigger popular revolt: here the population excercizes implicit influence over the authorities. On the other hand, citizens normally refrain from expressing radical demands for they anticipate severe reactions, in the form of reprisals and repression, from the authorities. Implicit influence in this direction is of course very strong in the Soviet Union. Its political culture does not generally promote or encourage citizens to raise political issues or participate in decision making; both historical experience and the present power structure discourage them from doing so. In other words: the populace is subject to strong implicit influence on the part of the authorities.

This conclusion, however, should not lead us to believe that individuals and groups may never influence government policy. In this book I am in search of proofs of their participation in decision making and of their influence on the content of decisions. This requires me to look for <u>manifest influence</u> relationships, where an actor A wants outcome x, acts with the intention of causing actor B to bring about x, and as a result of A's actions B does indeed attempt to bring about x.[21] Thus, manifest influence is a causal relationship between the actions of at least two actors. If we want to establish a manifest influence relationship, we will have to show that the influenced actor acted in a way that agrees with the demands expressed by the influencing actors, and that he did so <u>as a result of</u> the actions of the influence wielder. Depending on the phase of the decision-making process, influence may take different forms: the creation of an issue out of a policy that has gone unchallenged for some time, its entry to the political agenda, the definition or redefinition of that issue or the content of the final decision.

The field of sovietology is no exception to general political science as far as the disorder of influence terminology is concerned. In general, sovietologists tend to shy away from a narrow, precise definition that would force them to prove the existence of a causal relationship before speaking of manifest or actual influence. Peter Solomon, for example, writes that 'the mark of an actor's influence is the fact that, whatever the actual outcome, he has managed to make his preference more likely than it previously was.'[22] In his view influence then is the activity through which the probability of a given outcome is changed. Solomon makes a sharp distinction between cooperative decisions and conflict decisions and believes that a narrow definition of influence is only suited for the measurement of influence in conflict decisions, whereas his own definition is applicable to both. This solution, I believe, is unsatisfactory. The 'mechanisms of influence' through which in Solomon's view an actor can change the probability of outcome - such as taking part in discussions, providing decision makers with data and argumentation - in themselves in no way guarantee that the decision makers consider data or listen to argumentation. The only criterion is the decision maker's actual behaviour. Moreover, it seems to me that decision situations cannot be divided into two sharply separated classes, conflict decisions and cooperative decisions. As we have seen in the case studies, most decision-making processes are characterized by elements of both conflict and cooperation. Often issues are defined in an ambiguous way; they have many aspects which are stressed differently by the different actors. During the agenda-building and decision-making process issues are repeatedly redefined. Actors may disagree on some aspects of an issue, but often they agree on other aspects. Agenda building and decision making is therefore a process of both cooperation and conflict with conflicting elements predominating in one issue and cooperative elements in another.

Philip Stewart has also paid serious attention to the conceptual problems of political analysis of Soviet decision-making processes. He applies a framework that is somewhat similar to that of Dahl. Influence, he writes, is

> ....the recognition given the actions - positions, proposals, etc. - of one political participant by another or by others. The act of political influence consists of the communication of a policy position, proposal or attitude, by one individual, institition or grouping

> and its receipt by another. Influence may range from strongly negative, where the recipient becomes openly hostile to the initial communicator, through neutral, where the effect of the message is neutralized by other messages, to positive, where the recipient is motivated by the communication to respond favorably to the message.[23]

In his terms one may speak of positive influence if the subject is motivated by the reception of a communication to respond favorably.

My concern with influence, and not with power, results from the fact that I am trying to find proofs of the influence of individuals and groups on Soviet decision making. Influence wielding is the central activity of (interest) groups, policy coalitions and individuals. Such actors are expected to attempt to influence political decision making without wanting to accept formal responsibility for decision making. They differ from political parties, for parties aim to become governing parties. They seek rule, i.e. institutionalized political power. Both Marxists-Leninist doctrine and the Constitution of the Soviet Union allow only one such ruling party, and no other party may seek to challenge its monopoly. Interest groups, policy coalitions and other groupings, however, do not seek rule; they want only influence. Therefore, they are not *a priori* excluded from the Soviet political scene. Supposedly, i.e. constitutionally, the leading nucleus of each and every social and political organization in the Soviet Union is the Communist Party committee. This would imply that no such organization can act independently from Party directives and instructions. Only empirical research can show whether this is indeed the case.

When I speak of actual influence relationships I mean concrete, individual cases of manifest influence that can be shown to exist. Actual or manifest influence should of course be distinguished from *potential* influence and it should be kept in mind that quite a few actors in Soviet politics have potential influence on the decision-making process. In other words, the resources for actual influence are dispersed over a multitude of individuals, groups and institutions. The official position of individuals provides them with the opportunity for access to decision makers and the expression of demands. Policy makers are in need of expertise, which is provided by a multitude of organizations and individuals, from ministerial departments to individual scientists, from Academy institutes to professional organizations. The press, even though it is controlled by censorship, is so diversified - both functionally and geographically - that strict hierarchical control over each and every press item is impossible.

The role of editors and censors in determining what is acceptable for entry to the public agenda, and what is not, is of crucial importance. Of course the censorship Index provides guidance, but not each and every potential demand can be on that Index. This provides editors and censors with a certain elbowroom which has to be filled by their political feeling of what is possible and what not, when to ask superiors for guidance, and when not. A Politburo member or department chief of the Party Secretariat may suggest the editor of a central newspaper to print a controversial article. But alternatively, the editors and censors of a local paper or specialized journal may decide to print a controversial item without asking Moscow for permission. Thus, editors and censors perform the important function of keeping the gates of the public agenda, so that they can be said to dispose of potential influence.[24]

Potential influence in the form of access to the decision-making arena or public agenda <u>may</u> lead to actual influence. The question is, when does it and when not. What we can say at this stage is that potential influence is not a sufficient condition for actual influence. These considerations lead me to an operational definition of potential influcence that is very broad indeed. Those actors in Soviet politics are expected to have the potency to influence decision making that occupy official positions of some sort, dispose of expertise or have discriminating 'power' over the pointsof entry to the public agenda. It seems probable that these three qualities rather often combine in one actor.[25]

Dahl's definition of manifest or actual influence given above implies that the investigator has to show that the influencing actor has induced the other actor to act in a way that he would not otherwise, in the absence of the influence effort, have acted. Thus, when talking about relations of influence, we have in mind situations in which one person, group or institution induces another actor to do something the influencing actor wants to be done, or to refrain from doing something that the influencing actor would rather see not to be done. Persuading decision makers is only one of the possible 'mechanisms of influence'.[26] Other mechanisms are positive and negative sanction: the reward or 'punishment' of the decision maker if he does or does not decide conforming to the demands expressed by the influence wielder. Punishment of decision maker may take many forms, from non-implementation of the decision, to his unseating. In the cases of educational reform and anti-parasite legislation the policy coalitions opposing Khrushchev had a real opportunity of frustrating his demands. Deciding on new policy might be the Party's business, implementing new policy would be the business of the groups and institutions from which the policy coalition was made up. To Khrushchev's opponents in the Presidium the opposition of these key groups provided additional ammunition against adopting his proposals, for what was the use of adopting new policy when one was quite certain that its implementation would fail because of sabotage by key social groups. An obstructive republican Party leadership - such as the Kazakh secretaries in the Virgin Lands issue - could be removed from office, but such a measure could not possibly be taken against thousands of educators and jurists. Alternatively, in the case of the MTS Khrushchev was sure of broad support for his plan among kolkhoz chairmen, agronomists and others. In the case of Jewish emigration, the sensitivity of the Soviet leadership to Western public opinion provided the Jewish activists with a potential negative sanction. They made skillfull use of the few resources they had (such as contacts with Western journalists), thereby exploiting this sensitivity.

Influence is seen here as a causal relation between consecutive events. One of the common pitfalls of social research is the fallacy known as 'post hoc, ergo propter hoc'. The fact that an event occurs later in time than another event does not necessarily mean that it was causally related to the prior event. Therefore, even in cases where decision makers have taken a decision in conformity with the demands of a particular group or policy coalition, one may not conclude to an influence relationship, but has to establish its existence. Western politicians will quite often admit that their decisions have been influenced by specific interests, However, Soviet leaders will hardly ever admit in public that they yielded to certain social groups, and it is therefore not easy to establish an influence relationship.

A necessary condition for establishing an influence relationship is to show that prior to the influence-seeking effort the decision makers did not plan to do what the influence-seeking actor wanted them to do. The problem with my concept of influence is that it is not easy to establish that actor B would not have done what A wanted him to do, in the absence of A's effort to exert influence. As Martha Dethrick has remarked, using the word power where I use influence,

> Although we can discover that A wanted B to take a certain action, and we can observe that A has certain resources of potential power and used the available means to bring them to bear on B, and we can observe that B took the action that A intended, we still cannot be sure that B would not have taken the action without A's efforts.[27]

Situations where we can be absolutely sure that decision makers would not have changed their policy in the absence of influence-efforts are, of course, rare. This is especially so in the field of sovietology where we have to go by quite limited information on the intentions and motivations of decision makers. But it would be too fatalistic - and too easy - to conclude that it would be senseless to look for such certainty. In contrast to Solomon I do not want to speak of an actual influence relationship unless it can be established beyond reasonable doubt that the influence-seeking actor caused the decision makers to change policy or to refrain from an intended policy change. My definition of influence is therefore quite a narrow one.

Both Kelley and Schwartz & Keech have developed operationalizations of the influence concept that are more or less in conformity with what I propose. For Kelley the 'measure' of influence is 'perceptible alteration of policy along lines suggested by interest groups as seen in a comparison of the original proposal and the final legislation.'[28] It should be added that with such operationalization it is imperative to demonstrate two things. First, it has to be reliably demonstrated that the decision makers were firmly attached either to prevailing policy or, if the original initiative for policy change came from them, to their reform proposal. Second, we have to show that only after considerable effort on part of the interest groups the decision makers agreed to go along. Joel Schwartz and William Keech have adressed this crucial question in their interpretation of the school reform of 1958.[29] They have found that since Khrushchev in the September Memo identified himself with the proposal for sweeping reform and 'placed his public prestige squarely upon the line', it was quite unlikely that he would have changed his mind in the absence of the pressure exerted by the educators. In other words, had the anti-reform coalition not made such a fuss, Khrushchev's plans would have been fully implemented. But since it did, and since the plans were executed in a severely modified form, we may conclude that the policy coalition influenced decision making in the Party Presidium.

Another case where influence of a policy coalition can be reliably demonstrated with the help of the definition of actual influence, is family law reform. Since Nikita Khrushchev had personally been the initiator of the 1944 family decree and there is no evidence at all that in the 1950s he changed his mind on family policy, I conclude that the policy coalition of jurists was influential first of all in that it succeeded in initiating the issue. This shows that social groups may exert influence by creating issues on subjects where the leadership would rather keep things as they are. In this case the policy coalition initiated the issue and made sure that it was not shelved; the legislative process was completed with members of the coalition presenting their expert advice. However, when the new draft Principles on marriage and the family had been completed by early 1963, the Party top intervened and blocked the completion of the legislative process. It is not known who took the initiative to re-vitalize the issue in December 1966, forces in the Party Secretariat or interested jurists. Whatever be the case, the jurists seized this opportunity and resumed their campaign. As I wrote at the end of the case study, their efforts were partially successfull. What emerged from the legislative process in June 1968 was a compromise solution which testified to the influence of expert opinion and advice in some cases of Soviet decision making.

Anti-parasite legislation was a pet project of Nikita Khrushchev. His determination to introduce such legislation may be inferred from the simultaneous publication in 1957 of almost identical draft laws and decrees in all republics. The publication of these drafts and the call for a discussion meant that they had been placed both on the formal and on the public agenda. This in itself, however, did not yet turn the proposed legislation into an issue. It may be that severe opposition was not expected; it may also be that Khrushchev was opposed in the Presidium and could only publish 'his' drafts on condition that he allowed a public discussion. In any case we may assume that he and his partisans would have wanted the quick acceptance of the drafts and thereby the introduction of anti-parasite legislation in the whole of the Soviet Union. Instead, the numerous protests voiced by interested and expert parties turned the matter into an issue; they were followed by the acceptance of the drafts in only eight minor republics. This lends credit to Marianne Armstrong's interpretation that because of the unexpected heavy criticism, the leadership was forced to forego the quick introduction of anti-parasite legislation, and chose for the compromise solution of first putting it to the test. This testing, however, presented the opponents with the undreamt-of opportunity of providing them with real-life cases of abuse, which they could use as illustrations of their arguments, as weapons in their policy analyses. In the end, this testing proved to be an important contribution to their victory over Nikita Khrushchev.

Compromise solutions seem to abound, especially in legislative cases. One of the most obvious examples of this is the legislative history of governmental tort liability. Its formulation in article 89 of the Principles of Civil Legislation was a compromise formula. It did not go as far as Mikhail Strogovich or the faculty of Leningrad University's Civil Law Department wanted, i.e. to provide for the compensation of damages caused by political repression. On the other hand, it went farther than the draft Principles, which had wanted to take a non-decision, i.e. to postpone change indefinitely. The law text accepted after the public discussion included general tort liability, but made an exception for the liability of the police, Prokuratura and the courts: such liability was to be legislated through a special law. That law has never been made. In this case the influence relationship may be inferred from the fact that Party authorities apparently did not want to include a binding judgement on governmental tort liability in the Principles of Civil Legislation.

The case of Jewish emigration leads to stronger conclusions as far as influence relationships are concerned. Before the dramatic policy reversal of March 1971 the Soviet leadership had been rather rigid in its emigration policy. To allow Jews to leave en masse would mean to acknowledge once more the failure of its nationalities policy and to lose many of the best qualified scientists and technicians in the country. Moreover, it would complicate the Soviet position in the Middle East. In 1967 Israel had acquired vast new territories, and it welcomed the influx of new citizens. The Soviet allies in the Middle East, of course, did not. On the basis of these circumstances I assume that in the absence of pressure the Soviet leadership would not have changed its emigration policy.

This case throws some curious light on the relation between potential and actual influence, for we may safely say that the Jewish activists in the Soviet Union did not dispose of any potential influence in the form of official positions, expertise or access to the public agenda. The unorthodox character of their demand barred its legitimization for public discussion. Nevertheless they have actually influenced policy making. From this we must conclude that the operationalization of the potential influence concept has to be broadened, at least for issues which have international ramifications. The additional sources of actual influence are the international public agenda and the activities of Western powers in relation to the Soviet Union. Jewish activists in the Soviet Union made skilfull use of the international situation in the late 1960s and early 1970s, in particular of the support they received from groups in the West. Whether they have realized the full potential of the power of the Jewish lobby in the American Congress is unknown, but it worked in their favor anyway. Using the commotion that the Western groups stirred up in Western public opinion as the power resource, they made the Soviet leadership do something that it would not otherwise have done, granting them visa.

Influence and issue creation

What do the case-studies of Chapter 2 tell us about Stewart's hypothesis that interest groups will have more influence in cases when the Party leadership enters an ongoing policy discussion, and less if the issue was initiated by that leadership itself?[30] Before answering this question, it seems wise to analyze it in the light of Stewart's definition of influence. I have quoted this definition as 'the recognition given the actions - positions, proposals, etc. - of one political participant by another or by others. The act of political influence consists of the communication of a policy position, proposal, or attitude, by one individual, institution, or grouping and its receipt by another'. This means that *if* the Party leadership enters an ongoing policy discussion, that act itself shows that interest groups have (had) influence. They have had the opportunity to raise demands, to initiate an issue. Therefore, Stewart's hypothesis seems to be a circular argument; at the very least it is in need of a new formulation. I propose the following hypothesis: Policy coalitions will not often influence decision making in cases where the issue has been put on the agenda by a member of the Party leadership (Politburo or Secretariat), and they will relatively often be influential if the issue was initiated at a lower level.

The case studies tend to confirm this hypothesis. In five of the nine cases an actual influence relationship between policy coalitions and decision makers could be demonstrated with the help of my operational definition. Out of these five, three issues (family law, tort law and Jewish emigration) had bubbled upwards from the specialized communities. Their representatives had demanded more or less sweeping changes of established policy and had in the end been presented with compromise decisions. In four of the nine cases actual influence relationships could not reliably be demonstrated. These were primarily issues in economic policy which had been raised by Nikita Khrushchev in the 1950s: the Virgin Lands, MTS and the *Sovnarkhozy* reform.

The three remaining cases do not fully correspond to this pattern. The one other case where I could not demonstrate an actual influence relationship is the Lake Baikal issue, which originated at a low, regional level. The final conclusion on the policy coalition's actual influence depends upon one's estimate of what conservation measures the authorities would have taken in the absence of the Baikal campaign. Two cases with rather strong influence relationships are the school reform and anti-parasite legislation. These were by far the most complicated decision-making processes. Anti-parasite legislation was initiated at the top; nevertheless the juridical community succeeded in turning the demand into an issue and has had quite some influence on its realization and implementation. This shows that 'top issues' need not necessarily preclude influence of specialized communities. Much depends on the policy area and the presentation of the matter. In this case the decentralization of legislation provided ample opportunity for influence. The first draft-laws were published between April 3 and May 10, 1957, in the Three Baltic republics, one Transcaucasian and four Central Asian republics.[31] The discussion was opened in republican papers by two rather positive articles published in _Sovetskaia Estonia_ of 18 April, and continued with more critical articles in several republican newspapers in the middle of May, i.e. shortly after Khrushchev's sweeping _Sovnarkhozy_ reform had passed the Supreme Soviet. It just seems possible that opposition against anti-parasite legislation was fanned by Khrushchev's opponents in the Party Presidium, who during these weeks were scheming against the Party leader and tried to have him removed from office. If this was so, the proposed legislation was turned into an issue by, or at least with the help of members of what later came to be called the Anti-Party Group. However, this remains speculation; there is no proof whatsoever. To me it seems somewhat more probable that the opportunity of independent acting jurists for initiating the issue on a republican level was created by the fact that the Party top in Moscow was engaged in a power struggle that consumed just about all its energy.

In the case of school reform it is not possible to identify one initiator of the issue. The least one can say is that Khrushchev was not _the_ initiator, but that there were various groups and institutions striving for various forms of educational reform. The _repeal_ of production education in the early 1960s which Stewart has used to test his hypothesis, indeed originated in low-level institutions such as the Academy of Pedagogical Sciences and the _Sovnarkhoz_ of the RSFSR. Production education as an issue, however, had a long history, and the Academy had been active in the issue since the 1950s and had played an important role in its rise.

Issues may turn up on the public agenda roughly from two directions. First, they may bubble up to the public agenda from lower-level groups and institutions, i.e. via their publication in local or specialized periodicals (quadrants 2, 3 and 4 in Figure 1, Ch. 1). Examples of such cases are the demands for a revision of family law - first published in Literaturnaia Gazeta - for the introduction of governmental tort liability - put on the agenda by the jurist Strogovich writing in Sovetskoe Gosudarstvo i Pravo of June 22, 1956 -, and the protests against the pollution of Lake Baikal, put on the national public agenda by Literaturnaia Gazeta in February 1959. Access to the public agenda was through the specialized or local periodicals. In all cases, the issues were in need of legitimation by the leadership. The fact that they had reached the public agenda did not imply that they would be placed on the formal agenda as well. In the two legislative cases official recognition came on the February 1957 session of the Supreme Soviet, where delegates put them on the docket.

Lake Baikal has been the subject of a Russian government decision adopted a year after the publication in Literaturnaia Gazeta. The tactics of the government in this case has been to make small, incremental concessions. However, as a consequence of the perseverance of Galazii and other conservationists, the issue did not die. In 1959 Literaturnaia Gazeta had printed demands that Baikal be turned into a nature reserve, in 1960 the Russian government decreed that the cellulose factories would not be opened before their purification installations would be operative, a minimal concession. In 1961 a local Irkutsk paper disclosed that experts of the Academy of Sciences had judged these installations to be of poor quality and Grigorii Galazii demanded in Komsomol'skaia Pravda that *any* discharge of waste waters of the Baikal'sk factory be prevented. By this time the Party leadership probably decided that the issue had become too dangerous, for it seems that during Khrushchev's last three years in power it was deliberately kept off the public agenda. After his demise, the discussion erupted again. An important task (and merit) of the principle figure, Galazii, has been to counteract the tendency among government and Party officials to redefine the issue in such a way that an easy and cheap solution would be possible. The importance of his role in the decision-making process should be stressed, for as director of the Baikal Limnological Institute he was one of the very few in a position to learn all, or almost all developments, and to act on the basis of new knowledge. The policy area allowed him to order an analysis of the possible outcomes of different policy alternatives under the guise of scientific research.

Anti-parasite legislation was also turned into an issue by lower-level organizations, but only _after_ it had been put on the formal agenda. Legitimation had been implicit in the almost simultaneous publication of nine almost identical draft laws in April and May 1957, and the call for their public discussion. Had there been no dissenting voices in the press, there would have been no issue. But instead jurists attacked different aspects of the proposed legislation in republican papers. Thereby the legislation turned into an issue on several republican agendas.

A second direction from which an issue may reach the public agenda is the Party leadership. In such case it is expected to enter the agenda through publication in one of the leading national papers or magazines (Quadrant 1 in Figure 1., Ch. 1). This was indeed the case with the Virgin Lands and _Sovnarkhozy_ issues: Khrushchev's first reform proposals were printed in _Pravda_ and _Izvestia_. With the ideologically much more sensitive issue of the abolition of the MTS, however, he decided to proceed in a more cautious way. The first trial balloon was launched by Ivan Vinnichenko in a literary monthly, almost certainly on instruction of Khrushchev. Opposition was soon printed in other specialized periodicals, but Khrushchev dit not hesitate to show where he stood. Once he had succeeded in forcing the issue within the Party top, his position was printed in the national mass circulation papers, only two months after the Vinnichenko article. Therefore, we cannot say that in this case Khrushchev interfered in an ongoing policy discussion. On the contrary, he initiated the policy change and nipped a nascent discussion in the bud.

The conditions of influence

Influence, I have said, is a relationship. The relationship in which I am interested here is between political groupings and the top decision-making bodies. A precondition for influence is that the members of such top institutions are sensitive to the policy advice of political groupings or need their support. If a country is ruled by a tyrant or monolythic leadership, political groupings will generally have little chance of influencing policy making, for the lieutenants surrounding the tyrant will not usually be very susceptible to lobbying. After all, if they were, this might provoke the charge that they undermine the party's monolythic unity. With a collective and internally divided leadership, however, social groupings are presented with opportunities for actually influencing decision making. First, the points of access to the decision-making arena multiply so that the transfer of demands and policy positions to that arena is eased. Second, the groupings may try to exploit internal conflicts within the leadership with the purpose of furthering their interests.

This relationship between influence of political groupings and the character of the top Party leadership has been observed by several sovietologists.[32] Thus Schwartz & Keech have hypothesized that 'the more and greater the disputes on the top policy-making level, the more likely it is that policy groups will be involved and listened to.'[33]

This general relationship seems obvious but is hard to prove. First, in order to be able to do so one is in need of a yardstick with which to measure leadership conflict. Were the disputes of 1953 more and greater than those of 1957 or 1963? Is there as much strife in the present Politburo as in Khrushchev's Presidium after 1957? Even if we were perfectly informed about the disputes in the Politburo and about the positions of the participants, it would be difficult to devise a yardstick. Barring this information, such is impossible.

Second, the general relationship says nothing about the way in which influence is realized in case of intensive conflicts at the Politburo level. Is it because participants in such conflicts need the support of political groups? Is it because the groups provide them with policies and analyses with which to fight opponents?

Donald Kelley has gone one step further than Schwartz & Keech and has proposed that the influence of 'technically-specialized, issue-relevant interest groups' is related to the political sensitivity of the issue concerned. He has defined this concept as consisting of two factors. The first factor is reminiscent of Schwartz & Keech's criterion, i.e. the political milieu when the decision was reached, especially the degree of conflict within the Presidium. The second factor of political sensitivity is 'the natural sensitivity of the issue-area itself, that is, its impact on important interest groups'.[34] With this factor Kelley means to say that an issue which threatens either the power base of certain decision makers or their own formal positions and work conditions, or both, will be more sensitive than one that does not. In order to test his hypothesis on the impact of political sensitivity on group influence, he has compared the Sovnarkhozy reform with the school reform. The first issue was, in his definition, characterized by a high political sensitivity since Khrushchev's proposal threatened the power base of the state representatives in the Party Presidium, whereas the second issue did not threaten either that power base or the formal positions of Presidium members. No doubt these two issues were selected by Kelly because of their additional advantage that the first was decided during the power struggle of the spring of 1957, whereas the second was decided after this struggle had resulted in a victory for Khrushchev and the atmosphere in the Presidium had calmed down.

Kelley's conclusion has been that in high-sensitivity issues it is not the technical competence of political groupings that counts, but the political resources they may or may not offer participants in the power struggle: 'Only when the technically relevant groups also possess politically relevant resources or when their arguments are likely to convince others to alter their views voluntarily, would competing leaders choose them as allies.'[35] The most valuable resources, of course, are voting members of the Politburo, the Central Committee and the Secretariat.

Kelley, in my view, has confused his argument by giving two defining criteria for political sensitivity without indicating their mutual relationship. The 'degree of conflict' within the Presidium surely is not to be seen as a variable entirely independent of the 'natural sensitivity of the issue area itself'. As Kelley suggests, there is a relation between the two factors, but since at any time there are many issues on the agenda the question is what that relation looks like. In any case, issues with a high 'natural sensitivity' are not necessary resolved only during periods of a high degree of conflict within the Politburo. Moreover, the decision-making processes in quite a few issues cover a long period of time, spanning both periods of high and low degree of leadership conflict.

I will not try to put the nine issues in ranking order als far as the actual impact of the activities of opinion groups and policy coalitions is concerned. Instead I will arrange them in two categories. The criterion for placing an issue in one or the other category is whether or not I have been able to demonstrate that societal groups influenced decision making. These categories are called actual influence (first) category and possible influence (second) category. In the actual influence category the difference between original demand and policy outcome has varied from small to great:

actual influence category	possible influence category
Jewish emigration	*Sovnarkhozy* reform
School reform	Abolition of MTS
Anti-parasite legislation	Virgin Lands campaign
Family law reform	Lake Baikal
Governmental Tort liability	

A striking feature of the first category is that whereas the original demands had been presented as nonincremental changes, they were ultimately realized as nonrepetitive incremental changes. This is not an explanatory feature, but a symptom of the decision-making process typical for these issues: compromise solutions resulted from the struggle between policy coalitions and institutions. In the last two cases as well as in the Lake Baikal case we have seen that the Party leadership tried to satisfy a nonincremental demand by proposing a minimally acceptable, marginal solution, hoping thereby to appease the activists. Quite far-reaching, nonincremental demands were apparently necessary to bring about marginal changes in policy. A typical feature of the decision-making process in such cases is that the decision makers try to reduce the scope of the issue and to satisfy nonincremental demands with marginal solutions. We might therefore call this marginal decision making. From the point of view of the Party leadership it is successful insofar as it succeeds in getting the decision accepted as the solution to the problem as it has originally been raised. Often, however, members of policy coalitions see through this tactics and refuse to be appeased: they reformulate the original demand.

There are two major distinguishing features between the issues in the two categories: the policy area and the issue's role in the succession struggle of the years immediately following Stalin's death. With the exception of the Lake Baikal issue, the issues of the second category were all in the area of economic policy. The first category contains not one economic issue, but issues in law, social and education policy. I would have arranged the Lake Baikal issue in this category if it were not so that with the help of my narrow definition of influence an influence relationship could not be demonstrated. Another similarity of the issues in the second category is that, again with the exception of the Lake Baikal issue, they were all among the major issues through which the succession struggle of the years immediately following Stalin's death was fought. Unlike the issues of the first category, these issues ranked high on the agenda of the Party Presidium.

On the basis of these similarities and differences, one may conclude that in the three issues in economic policy which were selected by Khrushchev in his struggle for supremacy, nonincremental outcomes were the result of a decision-making process in which policy coalitions were not particularly influential. On the other hand, the role of such coalitions was considerably more important in issues which did not come to play an important role in the power struggle.

A further conclusion can be that, as far as internal policies are concerned, since the late 1950s nonincremental decisions have vanished from the Soviet political scene. True, the school reform of 1958 and anti-parasite legislation of 1961 have often been presented as examples of large, nonincremental changes typical of a communist regime wanting to drastically change society, but I believe that the case studies have shown that they were not. As we have seen, individuals or social groups may initiate a discussion on an altogether nonincremental issue. But since the early 1960s the decision-making process quite often transforms such nonincremental issues into incremental decisions. Large-scale social engineering projects and revolutionary economic schemes have made way for careful policy making. Since terror has worn off more power centers have come to play a role in the decision-making process. The Party can no longer brush aside the interests of social and occupational groups, for such groups are badly needed for the implementation of its policies.

4 The Reorganization of the USSR Academy of Sciences, 1954-1961

1961 was an eventful year for Soviet politics and Soviet science. The first manned spaceflight in the history of mankind was made by a Soviet citizen, triggering unmatched feelings of confidence among politicians and scientists alike. No doubt Izvestia caught the spirit of the day when it jubilated that Iurii Gagarin's journey into space signified 'the biggest victory of our system, our science, our technology and our courage.'[1] At the Twenty-second Party Congress de-Stalinization was continued and a fresh Party program showed the way to a brilliant future. It promised that by 1980 the construction of the foundations of a communist society would be completed. In the intermediate two decades the Communist Party would do all it possibly could to enhance the role of science, for the construction of the foundations of communism necessitated the maximum acceleration of scientific and technological progress.

Of course to the world the space flight proved that the Soviet Union had developed into one of the leading powers in technology. But in the Soviet Union men of science realized that this development had been unbalanced and that if the country wanted to keep that place, it could not afford to sit back and relax. So as not to fall behind in some branches of science and to catch up in others, fundamental research needed strong encouragement. For this reason the country's most important and prestigeous research institution, the USSR Academy of Sciences, was thoroughly reorganized and a new, powerful State Committee for the Coordination of Scientific Research was established. One out of every three of the Academy's research institutes was transferred from its jurisdiction to that of ministries and state committees. The establishments that were locked out of the Academy employed 20,500 persons, among them about 6.000 of the country's leading scientists. Hardest hit was the Department of Technical Sciences. It lost nine of its twelve research institutes.[2] The reorganization signified a profound change in orientation in the Academy's activities. From now on it was to leave technical and narrowly applied research to the research establishments of state committees. The Academy was to concentrate its activities on fundamental research and a limited number of applied projects that were considered to be of prime economic importance.

Graham's analysis

The Academy of Sciences reorganization has in the past been studied by the American historian Loren Graham. He has published his case study in the Juviler and Morton volume on Soviet policy making.[3] Graham attributed the initiative for the reorganization to Party Secretary Nikita Khrushchev. On the basis of a section of Khrushchev's report to the Twentieth Party Congress he suggested that in 1956 Khrushchev made a general call for reform, not yet offering concrete suggestions for improvement of the Academy's activities. This call was followed by a number of articles in the Soviet press advocating reform, whereupon on June 29, 1959 'Khrushchev again took up the subject of the Academy and this time advanced definite suggestions...'[4], namely to remove technical institutes from the Academy. Prior to his speech, Graham writes, 'a public defense of pure research had been impossible'; and 'Khrushchev's proposal was immediately interpreted by the theoretical scientists as an invitation to submit plans for restoring the status of fundamental research in the Academy of Sciences...'[5]

In this interpretation the initiative for the reallocation of values that ensued in 1961 came from above. It was Party Secretary Khrushchev who acted as a political entrepreneur - at least in the early stages of the decision-making process. It was he who voiced discontent with the existing situation, defined the issue and placed it simultaneously on the public and the formal agenda.[6] Thus, in Graham's conception the scientific community was activated by the topmost political leader, more or less in the same way as in the Virgin Lands, Sovnarkhozy and anti-parasites issues where the specialized communities were also activated by Khrushchev's initiative. According to this interpretation the agenda-building process was congruent to the mobilization model.

A different interpretation of the origin of the Academy of Sciences reorganization has been given by Linda Lubrano Greenberg.[7] She has stressed that Khrushchev did not initiate the idea of reorganizing the Academy. She also emphasized the independent role of Academy President Alexander Nesmeianov who in 1956 'tried to initiate reforms' in the direction of a concentration of the Academy's activities on fundamental research. According to her interpretation Nesmeianov received public support of key scientists only after Khrushchev's announcement of June 29, 1959. In this view the issue emerged not from the Party top but from the top of the Academy itself. Once the Party leader had been convinced by the arguments of the Academy's President and had legitimized the issue, it was placed on the public and formal agenda and its pro and cons became subject of a bitter debate between fundamental and applied scientists.

In this chapter I will present a summary description of the decision-making process leading up to the 1961 reorganization, starting with the early stage of agenda building.[8] This description will show whether Graham or Greenberg was right on the subject of issue initiation and to what extent either of their interpretations is in need of elaboration. I will put to use the conceptual framework that has been developed in the preceding chapters. Testing the hypotheses that have been generated in Chapter 3 will be reserved for the next chapter, in which I will draw general conclusions on the study of political decision making in the Soviet Union. The description of the decision-making process will be prefaced by a short account of the internal organization of the Academy of Sciences.

Internal organization

Just as with many foreign academies, the USSR Academy of Sciences is a meeting place for the most learned men in the land. Its members are the leaders of the different branches of science and schools in scientific thought. These academicians, as they are called, enjoy almost unequalled social prestige and privileges because of their membership of the Academy.[9] One step lower are the corresponding members. Academicians and corresponding members total only a few hundred. Up to 1959 the Academy also had honorary members (such as Stalin and Molotov) but since the new Charter accepted in that year it has only foreign members in addition to the academicians and corresponding members. In contrast to many foreign academies, however, the Soviet Academy governs an extensive research network and is the most important research establishment in the country. Sometimes its members work in establishments outside the Academy, but very often they have a well-equipped research institute or laboratory of their own. The internal organization of the Academy is rather complicated and has been subject to many changes. In this section I will present a somewhat simplified account of the Academy structure in the 1950s.

The Academy is, at least formally, governed by a meritocracy. The thousands of rank and file scientists, even the corresponding members, have no vote in its supreme organ, the General Meeting. Decisions in the General Meeting, which used to convene once or twice a year, are taken by a simple majority of votes of the academicians. The General Meeting is supposed to establish the general line of research within the Academy, to decide on the main organizational matters and to confirm the appointment of institute directors. However, the General Meeting has not been able to realize these rights: policy-making powers have been concentrated in the Academy Presidium. The only effective power of the academicians as voting members in the General Meeting is over the cooptation of new members. For the election of a new member a two-third majority of their votes, cast in secret elections, is necessary, so that a minority of one-third may hold up the election of a person they do not want in their midst.

The Academy Presidium is a rather large body consisting of about twenty members: the President, several vice-presidents, a Chief Scientific Secretary, the scientific secretaries of the departments and some other academicians. With the exception of the Chief Scientific Secretary they are elected by the General Meeting for a five-year period that is often extended. The Chief Scientific Secretary is elected by the Presidium itself. He controls the Academy's research establishments in the name of the President and oversees the recruitment of personnel.[10] For this task the Chief Scientific Secretary had during the 1949 - 1959 period at his disposal a Scientific Secretariat of the Presidium.[11] According to Alexander Vucinich, writing in 1956, 'there is not the slightest doubt today that the power of the Chief Scientific Secretary exceeds that of any other Academy member, group or institution, and that in reality he is responsible only to the authorities outside the academic world.'[12] He has claimed that through the Chief Scientific Secretary, the Scientific Secretariat and the scientific secretaries at all lower levels in the Academy structure, the Communist Party realizes its control over the Academy. The scientific secretaries are usually Party members and, again in the words of Vucinich, 'run their respective institutions, and through them the Party runs the Academy's entire system.'[13] About the powers and modes of operation of the Presidium the 1935 Charter said little, except that it was the highest decision-making organ in the period between general meetings. The Charter of 1959 reserved a section for the Presidium which gave a detailed account of its powers and duties. It is quite obvious that whereas matters of research and organizational policy may be discussed in the General Meeting, the decisions are taken in the Presidium and its Scientific Secretariat.

Since 1938 and up to the early 1960s the Academy had eight departments for the scientific and organizational direction of activities of institutions in the respective branches of science. In 1957 a new and extraordinary department was created: the Siberian Department, subordinated both to the Academy and the Council of Ministers of the Russian Republic. In contrast to its sister departments, this department was based on the geographical location of its research establishments. In the general meetings of the regular departments both the academicians and - since 1959 - the corresponding members may vote. They choose a Bureau of the Department, headed by a Scientific Secretary, who is by office also a member of the Academy Presidium.

The most important research establishments of the Academy are its institutes, of which it had 143 in 1957.[14] Although the institutes were grouped in eight different departments according to their branch of

science, they were originally administratively subordinated to the Presidium. As an increasing number of institutes and other establishments were founded, this situation became untenable. The Academy, once a small learned society, was becoming an enormous scientific network. The broadening of the rights and duties of the departments was discussed in the early 1950s and formalized in the 1959 Charter.[15]
A novelty of this Charter was that it contained a section on the institutes of the Academy, which said that the institutes could be subordinated to either the Presidium, to one of the departments or one of the branches.

Institutes are headed by a director, who is assisted by a scientific council but is personally responsible for all of its activities. If the institute is subordinated to a Department, the director is elected by the Department's General Meeting. After this election the Presidium proposes (or does not propose!) the Academy's General Meeting to confirm this election. Finally, in several geographical regions the Academy has branches (filialy) with their own research establishments. Several of these were turned into academies of science of the union's republics.

Traditionally the Academy has had a number of prerogatives. These concern the exchange of scientific literature with foreign countries and the publishing and distribution of books and magazines in the USSR itself. Thus the 1935 Charter, as amended in 1937, said that 'publications and works that are printed by the Academy and have been signed by the President, are not subject to censorship.'[16] The President's control over the Academy's publications - i.e. the internal censorship - is excercized through the Editorial and Publishing Council. It is quite obvious that if the President is party to an issue which is debated in the Academy, this position provides him with an enormous headstart.

Issue creation

The USSR Academy of Sciences has a long tradition of fundamental research. Founded by Peter the Great in 1724, it was originally staffed by foreign, primarily German scientists. With them Russia imported an admiration for theoretical research and broad descriptive studies. Applied research was generally looked down upon, by foreigners and Russians alike. As late as 1905 the general attitude of the academicians was that science's first task was to gather knowledge, regardless of practical considerations.[17] When Russia came to be ruled by a mobilizing communist regime the survival of this attitude came into jeopardy.

Even during the period of forced draft industrialization the Academy might conceivably have continued to serve as a haven for pure science. After all, it was not the only scientific establishment in Soviet Russia. The applied and technical research that industry needed might have been performed in state research establishments outside the Academy. But a communist system does not allow ivory towers. Not only was the Academy brought under communist control, but one of its main tasks became to contribute to the construction of a socialist society. During the 1930s the Academy, which had had few research institutes of its own, was transformed into the central institution of Soviet science and greatly expanded in size.

This transformation started with the entrance of communist academicians and academicians who were specialized in applied science and technology. It continued with the change of the Academy Charter which was made to stress the Academy's tasks in the construction of socialism. Then in 1935 a Department of Technical Sciences was added to the two existing departments. Its task was to direct the selection of applied research programs, coordinate their execution and advise state institutions on technical problems. This meant that the learned Academy henceforth was obliged to respond to even the most fatuous demand for help by a ministry or state committee. The creation of institutes for applied and technological research ensued only at the end of the 1930s. Research institutes were created in such fields as mechanics; metallurgy;mining and machine science. During the 1940s and 1950s these institutes grew to enormous proportions, sometimes with a staff of 1,000 and with many chairs and laboratories.

By the late 1950s the Academy of Sciences had accumulated all the functions that Vladimir Lenin had originally planned for a commissariat for science and technology, and even more. It had become the topmost science institution in the country, it supervised and coordinated science and technology policy and controlled the country's best research establishments in both the fundamental and the applied sciences. The Academy had become the unrivaled director of science in the Soviet Union. The position of the Technical Sciences Department was very strong and growing. The Department was surpassed in number of institutes only by the Biology Department. It had over twenty percent of all academicians and devoured about a quarter of the Academy budget.[18]

Judging from the criticism that was voiced against the Technical Department, its institutes spent much energy - and Academy funds - on petty technological research and on advising ministries and industrial plants. Apparently the staffs of the institutes often neglected to acquit themselves of their basic task: to keep a sharp lookout for new discoveries and developments in the fundamental sciences and to ensure that new discoveries would lead to economic progress in the shortest possible time.

The first questions we must now ask are, Where did the demand for removing the technical institutes from the Academy of Sciences come from? How did the issue arise? Who brought it up and how was it originally defined?

The evidence on the origin of this issue is inconclusive. In the absence of detailed accounts of the persons involved it remains impossible to find out who mentioned the demand first, and on what occasion.[19] I have to rely on printed sources and can therefore only determine when the first sounds reached the press. These sources show that soon after the death of Joseph Stalin, when the stifling pressure of terror was falling away, people in the top of the Academy bureaucracy decided to launch a number of trial balloons to see whether change was possible. Before selected publics - the readers of the Academy Herald and the participants of a conference of industrial personnel - Academy President Alexander Nesmeianov and Chief Scientific Secretary Alexander Topchiev voiced the first, barely audible sounds of reform, cloaked in long accounts on the achievements of Soviet science. The nucleus of the issue as it later grew could be found in their words: Nesmeianov said that the Academy was to concentrate on long-term problems and Topchiev blamed institutes of the Department of Technical Sciences for not producing scientific work in the course of many years. To what degree Nesmeianov and Topchiev acted on their own behalf or as spokesmen for a group in the Academy Presidium, I do not know. However, since they remained the most active participants in the decision-making process right up to the late 1950s, they may be called the pioneers of Academy reorganization. Nesmeianov in particular must be seen as the political entrepreneur in this issue.

Alexander Nesmeianov had been elected in 1951 and was the first Academy President to be a communist when he was chosen by his peers. But he was also an authoritative organic chemist who enjoyed the respect of many of the old academicians, scientists whose prime loyalty was to the pursuit of knowledge instead of the pursuit of political goals. As President of the Academy and member of the Communist Party, Nesmeianov was subject to various cross-pressures and could not always speak and write in all sincerity. However, according to one Soviet scientist who knew him well, 'his devotion and his heart were with the scientists, not with the Party.'[20]

At several occasions during the period 1954 - 1957 the Academy President stressed that Soviet technology was more or less on par with that of the West. The Soviets had reached this position thanks to the strong financial support of the authorities for the applied sciences. In Nesmeianov's view, Soviet applied science and technology had developed on the basis of this support _and_ on the basis of the results of fundamental research performed in Western countries. In the process, the development of Soviet fundamental research had lagged. If the Soviet Union now wanted to overtake the West, this could not be done by relying on Western fundamental research. Soviet fundamental research was therefore in need of strong support, and the place where that research would have to be concentrated was the Academy of Sciences. In short, Nesmeianov wanted the Academy to return to the profile it had had before the late 1930s.

It seems that already in this early stage there was talk of removing the technical institutes from the Academy. This may be inferred from the blame that Topchiev had shed upon them, and from a speech of mining engineer Nikolai Chinakal, who in April 1956 referred to '*persistent* proposals' to have the big technical problems solved by industrial branch institutes.[21] These proposals, he said, were symptomatic of a strong tendency within the Academy to 'escape into "pure" science' and withdraw from work on important 'scientific-economic problems'.

Alexander Nesmeianov did not experience great difficulty in placing the issue on the political agenda. In February 1956 he used the occasions of the Academy's General Meeting and the Twentieth Party Congress to voice a clear demand that the Academy concentrate on fundamental research. At the same occasions the technical institutes were criticized, but the demand for their removal from the Academy was not yet made, at least not in public. At the General Meeting Nesmeianov said that the institutes of the Technical Sciences Department 'too often passed the line that should separate the activities of an Academy institute with its responsibilities of solving fundamental problems of general importance, and went into details of an industrial branch character.'[22] At the Party Congress, two weeks later, he clarified what he meant by such details: 'superfluous, trivial activities' such as the development of automatic doors for Moscow's Prague Restaurant and the development of a new type of durable steel for pens. The activities of the Academy of Sciences, Nesmeianov said,

> ...should not be marked by results which are of limited, applied significance. The Academy's basic task should consist in discovering and studying new phenomena of nature and society, in establishing and generalizing the laws of relationships among phenomena and putting these laws to work in the interests of socialist society and its production.[23]

Khrushchev, however, was much less outspoken at the Twentieth Party Congress than was Nesmeianov. He made a short complaint about science policy in general, but did not single out the shortcomings of the Academy of Sciences. His remarks were reminiscent of those that had been made in a *Pravda* editorial earlier that month, which had criticized abstractness in science and the tendency to work on themes that were not related to the direct needs of industrial development.[24]

Alexander Nesmeianov's argument for reorganizing the Academy was clear: If the Communist Party's goals were to be met, Soviet science and technology could no longer rely on Western fundamental science. Therefore, fundamental science in the Soviet Union was in need of a strong boost, and this could be realized best by concentrating the Academy of Science's resources on fundamental research. But was this the only argument? If not, was it the main argument? Was it perhaps no more than a propaganda-argument meant for political consumption, a smokescreen hiding other, more pedestrian considerations? According to Alexander Lerner, it was indeed only one of the arguments of Nesmeianov and his supporters, and not even their most important one.[25] The main reason why they wanted to remove the applied sciences from the Academy was to secure the little elbow-room that they still enjoyed. The scientists engaged in applied research were under full control of Party and state officials, according to Lerner primarily because they consumed enormous funds. The specific weight of the applied sciences in the Academy was high and growing. The natural scientists, often 'old' and highly respected academicians, had been able to preserve certain prerogatives; Party and state control over them was less than perfect. They cherished a limited independence. They saw the strong development of the applied science institutes as a threat to this independence and hoped that their removal to ministries and state committees would benefit their own degree of independence. In addition, their work was hampered by a lack of resources, whereas the applied science institutes received ample funds. Nesmeianov and his supporters may have hoped that a removal of these institutes would free funds for their own use. These, according to Lerner, were the two main considerations of the natural scientists. The arguments that Nesmeianov used in public were only secondary; they were of a cosmetic character.

As I have shown, by the spring of 1956 Nesmeianov did not yet enjoy the explicit support of the Communist Party. But neither did the Party suppress his demands. His real demands may have been much more outspoken than he was allowed to ventilate in the press - a possibility that is impossible to investigate barring an interview with Nesmeianov - but he was in fact allowed to make a number of rather explicit statements. What then was the position of Party officials? The Party was interested in maintaining full control, especially over the applied sciences that were, after all, of first-rate interest to Soviet economic development. According to Alexander Lerner Party officials felt that such control, strong as it already was inside the Academy, could be perfected by removing the technical institutes to state organizations. Another consideration may have been that the development and introduction of new technology in industry was thought to be lagging because of the poor contacts between the technical institutes of the Academy, industrial research establishments and plants. The Soviets call this the vnedrenie (innovation) problem. The technical institutes were spoiled with ample funds and high status and income for their employees, but their output in terms of new production processes and new products was perceived to be disappointing. This malfunctioning of innovation processes was thought to threaten further economic progress. Party officials engaged in science policy apparently thought that such processes could be better controlled and thereby improved by 'bringing science closer to industry'.[26]

Thus, the motives of reformers and Party officials were quite different, but these differences did not preclude the possibility that the concrete policies that they would advocate, would coïncide. On the contrary, one gets the impression that Nesmeianov made skillful use of the opportunities that were provided by the Party's growing concern for technological progress. But he had to reckon with the Academy's Department of Technical Sciences, a strong department which could be expected to oppose his plans.

Aktiv

The preceding chapters have shown that in the development of quite a few issues conferences of specialized publics have played an important role in defining and redefining issue content and in forging communities into policy coalitions. Such conferences also took place during the history of this issue. In April and May 1956 the Academy Presidium organized three informal meetings for the discussion of the outcomes of the Twentieth Party Congress. Many different subjects were discussed at these meetings - from the coordination of the research activities of branches and republican academies to the harm that the 'personality cult' had done to scientific research in general and to the social sciences in particular. The atmosphere after the de-Stalinization Congress was one of openness and confidence in businesslike discussion, and in this new atmosphere the future profile and structure of the Academy of Sciences was one of the important discussion themes. These meetings took place in Leningrad (April 16-17, 1956), Novosibirsk (April 24-25) and Moscow (May 7-8). Reports were published in the Academy Herald. They were not meetings of any specific formal body of the Academy, but of the '_aktiv_ of scientists of the USSR Academy of Sciences'. This included not only academicians, corresponding members, directors and Party secretaries of institutes and other senior scientists working in the Academy system, but also representatives of Party organizations, ministries, the trade unions, industrial enterprises, establishments of higher education, industrial branch research institutes and leading personnel of the Academy's branches. Over 600 scientists and science administrators took part in the Leningrad meeting alone.

Why were these meetings organized and what was their function in the decision-making process? In order to be able to answer such questions, one has to know what an _aktiv_ is, and what it is supposed to do. The sovietologist who consults Western works on Soviet politics will be surprised to learn that they do not know this institution. It is hardly ever mentioned and its political significance has never been systematically investigated.[27] And yet, the _aktiv_ has been included in the Communist Party Statutes since more than forty years. In 1939, at the Eighteenth Party Congress, a new article was inserted in the Statutes, which said that

> _Aktivy_ of municipal Party organizations will be convened in all republican, district and provincial centers and in all more or less important industrial centers. They are to discuss the most important decisions of the Party and the government. These _aktivy_ must be convened not for show purposes or for the formal and solemn approval of these decisions, but for actual (_deistvitel'nye_) discussions.[28]

However, not only Communist Party organizations may convene meetings of its leading and most active (progressive, enterprising and experienced', according to the latest edition of the Great Soviet Encyclopedia[29]) members, but the Komsomol, trade unions, the Academy of Sciences and other organizations as well.[30] Such meetings are to be sharply distinguished from the formal meetings of the committees and bureaus of these organizations. First of all, in contrast to such committees and bureaus, the *aktiv* is not a clear-cut group of people in specific functions. It is up to the convenor to decide which persons to invite to a meeting of the *aktiv*, and therefore the composition of the meeting varies according to the issue or decision that is being discussed. Thus, it seems improbable that G. I. Ermolaev, director of the Kuznetsk Metallurgy Combine, who spoke at the *aktiv* meeting in Novosibirsk, would be included in the *aktiv* if the subject of a later meeting were, say, the development of the social sciences in Siberia. An *aktiv* meeting is a gathering of leading personnel that is deeply involved with one specific issue.

Second, in contrast to the committees and bureaus, the *aktiv* is not a formal organization. Its meetings do not function as formal arena's of decision making. On the contrary, such gatherings can be used to test new ideas, solicit the reactions of diverse bureaucracies and organizations that are involved with the issue, to foster support and fathom opposition against new policy proposals. It was exactly this function that was performed by the meetings in Leningrad, Novosibirsk and Moscow: they allowed the Academy Presidium and the Party to discuss their plans in an informal setting. However, *aktiv* meetings may also be used for the more limited purpose of discussing the execution of decisions that have been taken by other, formal organizations. Behind this façade of the discussion of formal decisions one may find more or less open debates; in the case of the Leningrad, Novosibirsk and Moscow meetings the formal occasion was indeed a discussion of the decisions of the Twentieth Party Congress, but these decisions had been sufficiently vague and the alternatives for execution still had to be outlined precisely. It would therefore be wrong to generalize and say that all *aktiv* meetings in Soviet history have been more or less open discussions of issues. We can only investigate concrete cases and try to find out whether or not this was in fact the case.

Both in Novosibirsk and in Moscow, Academy President Nesmeianov did his utmost to 'sell' his policy to his peers and to win supporters. Academicians and rank and file scientists got a chance to learn what exactly Nesmeianov and his supporters wanted to accomplish. In Moscow the Academy President started out by quoting the Party directives on the development of science. Although these directives prescribed both a 'broadening of theoretical research in all fields of knowledge' and a 'concentration of the efforts of scientists and material resources of scientific research establishments primarily on scientific problems that are of major economic importance', Nesmeianov chose to stress the importance of theoretical research. Interpreting the apparently contradictive directives in his own way and for his own aims, he said that

> ...it is necessary to pay special attention to the fact that the directives correctly call on us to broaden theoretical research in all fields of knowledge.[31]

At both meetings, too, he experienced opposition from within his own Academy. The overture to this opposition had been voiced by Academician Ivan Bardin, Vice-President of the Academy and one of the foremost applied scientists, at the General Meeting of the Department of Technical Sciences in February. There he had said that it was impossible to make a clear distinction between theoretical and practical institutes and research, and that such a separation, if made, would lead to the death of science, especially of technical science. Now, in Novosibirsk, Nikolai Chinakal, a mining engineer who later became Director of the Siberian Department's Mining Institute, warned that the tendency 'to escape into "pure science"' and to withdraw from work on important 'scientific-economic problems' was strong in the Academy.[32] Symptomatic of this were, in his opinion, the persistent proposals to have the big technical problems solved by the industrial branch institutes. These proposals, Chinakal said, underestimated the technical sciences. He was supported by G. I. Ermolaev, Director of the Kuznetsk Metallurgy Combine.

More opposing views could be heard at the Moscow <u>aktiv</u> meeting, from scientists such as Pavel Oshchepkov, Director of the Electrophysics Laboratory of the Institute of Metallurgy, Leonid Sapozhnikov, head of a laboratory in the Institute of Mineral Fuels, and Tigran Khachaturov, Director of the Institute of Complex Transportation Problems. Anatolii Blagonravov, Director of the Institute of Machine Science, reminded Nesmeianov of the fact that the Congress directives not only stressed the importance of theoretical research, but also the need to raise the role of Academy institutions in the cause of technological progress, and the necessity to draw science closer to 'the concrete needs of the national economy.'[33] Given these demands, he claimed, the role of the Technical Sciences Department was of special importance. It would have to take part in solving a number of the most important tasks of the national economy. Blagonravov's support for the opposition carried a special weight. He was a general who had been President of the Artillery Academy and who presently was heavily involved in the Soviet space program. At a time when he was helping the authorities to put an artificial satellite into orbit around the earth, some people were working to remove his institute from the Academy. In February 1957 Blagonravov became Scientific Secretary of the Department of Technical Sciences and member of the Academy Presidium.

However, Nesmeianov also received support, and quite valuable support at that. The provocative speech of Academician Kapitsa 'On leadership in science', that was published only ten years later, was probably delivered at this meeting.[34] Kapitsa complained that although Soviet science was presently capable of investigating every possible problem in science, 'there are still very few branches of science in which we are in a leading position'. To make things worse, Kapitsa said,

> ...the number of branches in which we are not leading is presently increasing. Before we were leading in a number of fields, but we lost the leadership position. Life shows that we very often give birth to new scientific ideas, but usually we do not succeed in developing them. This shows that there are fundamental shortcomings in our science organization.

He continued that in the preceding three to four decades scientific research in the Academy had lagged, mainly because the Academy did not have the ample funds that the government institutions had disposed of. Kapitsa explained the lack of leadership of the Academy 'by the fact that we do not cope with strategy well enough...' He proposed that it be turned into science's headquarters (shtab), directing the rest of science and determining its strategy. Kapitsa criticized the election procedures in the Academy and the bureaucratization of Academic science. He suggested that the Presidium be turned into 'a real authoritative scientific organization that provides science in our country with spiritual leadership and of course advises our government on all questions requiring a scientific appraisal...'

The three aktiv meetings adopted resolutions in which they identified problems, appealed to the Presidium to solve them and evoked scientists to display more boldness in theoretical and advanced research. The Moscow resolution said in particular:

> The immediate concentration of scientists' efforts and material sources on ... important scientific problems and the concentration of their forces on leading trends, is an important matter. With this aim the scientific establishments of the Academy must absolutely be freed from the tasks which can with success be solved by industrial branch institutes.[35]

The Presidium responded to these resolutions with concrete measures.[36] It conceded that much of the criticism was justified and complained that although the Moscow meeting had stressed the extreme importance of strengthening theoretical research, a considerable amount of research in many institutions was still not up-to-date enough. Its instructions to stop work on industrial branch and trivial research were being ignored.

The aktiv meetings had allowed for free and open discussion, but this did not satisfy all academicians. Speaking at the Fall 1956 General Meeting and voicing the opinion not only of himself but of colleagues in the Physical-Mathematical Department as well, Academician Tamm said that the aktiv meetings were of course necessary, but pointed out that their decisions were not binding to the Presidium; these informal meetings could not make up for the loss of decision-making powers of the General Meeting. A number of academicians wanted to democratize the Academy and call a halt to the tendency of the General Meeting to lose the little power over policy making it still had. Igor Tamm complained that

> ...for the past few years in a vast majority of cases the general meetings of the Academy were dedicated to the celebration of jubilees and carried a pure gala character. If there were individual sessions on really important questions, then in each case they concerned only isolated questions. General questions were touched upon only in the annual speeches of the Chief Scientific Secretary, which however were never subject to discussion. In such circumstances the General Meeting could not carry out its leading role...[37]

In the preceding chapters I have shown that a prolonged probe of the origin of the issue of educational reform must lead one to the conclusion that it cannot be properly described in terms of the mobilization model of agenda building, as had been suggested by Schwartz and Keech. In this model decision makers place issues on the formal agenda and, soon after a decision, have them expanded to the public agenda in order to generate the support that is needed for the decision's implementation. The same can now be said about the issue of Academy reorganization. In contrast to Loren Graham's findings, it was not Khrushchev who mobilized the Academy community. The development of the issue can therefore not be properly analyzed in terms of the mobilization model. In the 1954 - 1956 period the issue of reorganizing the Academy was raised within the Academy by its President, Alexander Nesmeianov. It was placed on the country's specialized political agenda concerned with science policy and was accepted by Party officials as an important issue. The issue was discussed at informal meetings which allowed its initiator to test the strength of his support and opposition, but did not bind him in any way. As far as the definition of the issue was concerned, several options remained open: merely to remove technical research projects from the plans of the Academy's institutes, or to transfer the technical institutes themselves - possibly even to abolish the whole Technical Sciences Department? During this early phase the opposition against reform manifested itself more strongly that the support. The Department of Physical-Mathematical Sciences fought Nesmeianov on procedural matters. It seems probable that many of its members agreed with Nesmeianov and the Communist Party on the need of reorganization, but demanded a price for their support: a democratization of the Academy's internal procedures.

As I have shown in Chapter 1, Cobb, Ross and Ross have distinguished two other models of agenda building: the inside initiative model, where issues arise inside institutions and the decision makers seek to prevent expansion of the issue to the public agenda, and the outside initiative model. In the issue of Academy reorganization, the agenda-building process did apparently not proceed according to the inside initiative model. Instead, the outside initiative model - with issues arising outside the formal decision-making bodies and then being expanded to the public and the formal agenda - is best suited for the analysis of this decision-making process. The remaining part of this chapter will illustrate that such a model is merely a crude tool for the analysis of a concrete process. Political life is more complicated than a model would lead us to believe.

Entrance, 1957-1959

For an issue to be accepted on the formal agenda it needs to be legitimized by Party authorities. Nesmeianov received this 'go ahead' in May 1957, in the form of an article in Pravda.[38] The authors of this article flatly stated that the Academy should be left to handle fundamental research. It was 'to develop the basic branches of science and to assist in the general advance of the level of science in the USSR'. This article was the joint product of two science administrators directly involved in the issue, the Academy's Chief Scientific Secretary and the head of the CPSU Central Committee Department for Science, Higher Educational Institutions and Schools. It bore the signatures of Alexander Topchiev and Vladimir Kirillin, a thermophysicist who had headed the Central Committee Department since 1955. Thereby the Party endorsed the Nesmeianov line and allowed the issue access to the formal agenda.

The appointment of Vladimir Kirillin to the Central Committee's Department for Science in 1955 has probably contributed a great deal toward the realization of the Academy of Sciences' reorganization. Kirillin was a relatively young man (42 in 1955) who had not served in the Party apparatus before. He had been a lecturer at the Molotov Power Engineering Institute in Moscow and had been accepted as a Corresponding Member of the Academy in 1953. Kirillin made a fresh start with science policy; his active support was of great help to the proponents of reorganization.

In November 1957 the leading Central Committee journal on ideological questions _Kommunist_ gave additional proof of Party endorsement for the reformers when it printed an article written by Topchiev, in which he repeated Nesmeianov's argumentation. At this occasion Topchiev went into ideological matters and tentatively presented the ideological foundation for the reorganization. He quoted Marx on the role of science in the transition to communism and implied that science was in the process of moving from the superstructure to the base. This of course would mean that science would soon stop being a dependent variable, but would become part of the base which conditions the development of society. It would also mean that the promotion of fundamental research would become a matter of utmost importance.

Except for the legitimation of Nesmeianov's demand by the Central Committee Secretariat, nothing much happened during this phase in the decision-making process. The issue had entered the political agenda, but for the time being this had no visible consequences. Through publications in _Pravda_ and _Kommunist_ the Party had told the general public and Nesmeianov's opponents that it backed the demand for reorganization of the Academy. However, the _issue_ had not yet reached the general public agenda. The fact that a section of the Academy was vehemently opposed to the reform remained hidden from the general public. Thus, while the demand for reform had been publicly legitimized, the issue lingered on the public agenda of the specialized community. In the absence of press reports we have no way of knowing what exactly went on inside the Academy during 1957 and 1958. However, it seems unlikely that the engineers had been silenced. They had opposed Nesmeianov's plans in 1956 and did not hesitate to oppose them again even after Khrushchev had adopted the reorganization proposal at the June 1959 Central Committee Plenum. One possibility is that while detailed plans were being worked out by the Academy Presidium in collaboration with Kirillin's Department, the issue was temporarily kept off the public agenda. Another possibility, suggested by Alexander Lerner, is that the reorganization plans were temporarily postponed.

Khrushchev interferes, 1959-1960

In 1959 the period of seeming tranquility came to an end. From two directions, the Communist Party and President Nesmeianov, new life was blown into the issue. The adoption of directives for the Seven Year Plan (1959 - 1965) at the Party's Twenty-first Congress served as trigger event. The Congress resolution envisaged a broad program of scientific-technological progress that would concentrate manpower and financial resources on 'the most important trends that are of practical and theoretical significance.'[39] The main trends were the following:

- Controlling thermonuclear fusion in order to acquire a virtually unlimited source of energy;
- Securing a broad application of nuclear energy for energy and transport motors;
- Broadening of the economic utilization of synthetic materials, products of nuclear splitting and radio-active isotopes;
- Solving the tasks of integrated mechanization and automatization of production processes and the creation for this purpose of new technical means, on the basis of a broad application of the achievements of physics, radio-electronics and computer technology.

Such were the demands of the Party towards the scientific community in general. They were, of course, not outstanding examples of fundamental research. At the end of March 1959 the Academy of Sciences' General Meeting adopted its own list of priorities. A comparison of this list with the Party's list shows us how the Academy planned to combine its

Table 2
PRIORITIES IN ACADEMY RESEARCH AS OF 1959, AND IN OVERALL USSR RESEARCH

	Research subject	department	rank in Pravda
1	Nuclear physics: controlling thermo-nuclear fusion; nature of elementary particles	PhMS	1
2	Exploration of cosmic space by satellites	PhMS	
3	Solid-state physics	PhMS	
4	Investigation and creation of new semiconductor materials, principles of constructing semiconductor instruments	PhMS	
5	Power engineering problems	TS	2
6	Mathematics: development of programming methods, principles of computer technology, creation of ultra-highspeed computers, etc.	PhMS	
7	Chemistry of high-molecular compounds	ChS	3
8	Chemistry of natural and biologically important compounds	ChS	
9	Development of new metals and alloys	TS	
10	Radiochemistry		3
11	Radioelectronics	TS	
12	Automation and remote control	TS	4
13	Mechanics	TS	
14	Geophysical research	GGS	
15	Mineralogy	GGS	
16	Geographic and oceanographic research	GGS	
17	'Creation of new technological processes and the improvement of existing ones in leading branches of industry (mining, ore enrichment, metallurgy, the chemical and petroleum industries)'	TS	
18-23	Biology, genetics, physiology, photosynthesis, etc.	BS	
24-30	Social Sciences, Linguistics, Literature		

Sources: VAN 1959:4, pp. 64-72; translated in CDSP Vol. XI, No. 25, pp. 9-11; Pravda March 16, 1959.

own interests with those of the Communist Party. This list, as shown in Table 2, was ranked more or less conforming to the ranking of the eight Academy departments as used in other documents of and referring to the Academy.[40] It supposedly showed the most important areas of research in the eight different fields of knowledge for which the Academy had departments. At the same time, however, it provided some insight into the relative ranking of these fields by the discrepancies between the ranking used in this list and the conventional ranking.

The priorities list conforms to the conventional ranking in placing the Physical-Mathematical Sciences at the top and the Social Sciences, Literature and Language at the bottom. Mathematical research, however, even though part of it is of an applied character, is considered less important than technical research into energetics. Chemistry in both cases occupies a second place, but the priorities list considerably upgrades a number of technical sciences by ranking them before the Geographical-Geological and the Biological Sciences. An exception is made for one particular type of very narrow applied research (17), which is ranked after the Geographical-Geological Sciences, and for research into energetics (5), which is considered so important as to justify ranking before mathematics and chemistry. Both this list and the Party Congress resolution placed the problem of controlling nuclear fusion at the top, thus conforming to Khrushchev's repeated demands on this subject. Although the Academy, by conforming to Pravda, took responsibility for this task, the differences between the formulations of the resolution and the Academy suggest differences in stress:

Resolution: ' 1- Controlling thermonuclear fusion in order to acquire a virtually unlimited source of energy.' [41]

Academy: ' 1- The problem of controlled nuclear fusion and the nature of elementary particles.' [42]

The first formulation suggests an ultimate interest in application, the second in theoretical problems. The fact that Pravda had specifically mentioned power problems, and had ranked them second, apparently caused the Academy to move this subject even further up than the other major technical problems, 'overtaking' not only the biological, geological and geographical sciences, but chemistry and mathematics as well.

In the period between the Twenty-first Party Congress and the Academy's General Meeting (March 26 - 28), the Party Secretariat had indicated the character of the country's research program in two articles in Pravda, one of them signed by Vladimir Kirillin.[43] It all boiled down to the Communist Party's demand that the Academy Presidium take measures to ensure that each and every scientist would keep a watchful eye on how he could contribute to scientific-technological progress. There was no place for scientists and institutions that worked on out of date research projects or that passively awaited requests for petty development projects such as - the example was Nesmeianov's - automatic doors for Moscow's Prague restaurant. Though the Party did not become a champion of fundamental research, its attitude suited the proponents of reform well. They, too, were opposed to Academy institutes working on unimportant development projects or on low-priority technological research. The funds that those institutes swallowed could better be used elsewhere.

The General Meeting of March 1959 was the occasion of a great many basic decisions which, one may suppose, had been prepared and pre-cooked by the Presidium and the Central Committee Secretariat's Department of Science. These decisions concerned the adoption of a new Charter, a new top structure (the establishment of a Current Problems Bureau of the Presidium), and the main research priorities. As a logical consequence of the new priorities it was resolved that the network of scientific institutions would be revised during the next three years. The Presidium was authorized to 'take under advisement several proposals concerning the network of scientific institutions'. These proposals suggest how the demands from both sides were to be reconciled and translated into organizational measures. They included the following measures in particular:

1. Concerning the Physics and Mathematics Department: 'to reassign certain work on magnetism and acoustics to other organizations.'[44]

2. Concerning the Technical Sciences Department: 'to provide for the most precise delimitation of work subjects with the institutes of the USSR State Planning Committee. In this connection, to clarify the specific functions of the Mineral Fuels Institute, Institute of Machine Science, the A. A. Baikov Metallurgy Institute and the G. M. Krzhizhanovskii Power Engineering Institute. To consider the advisability of transferring certain laboratories to the institutes of the USSR State Planning Committee and to the branches of the USSR Academy of Sciences.'[45]

3. Concerning the Geological-Geographical Sciences Department: 'to revise the structure of the institutes from the standpoint of a considerable reduction in the volume of geological research on subjects of narrow local or industrial application, shifting such subjects and the persons working on them to the geological organizations of the branches of the USSR Academy of Sciences, the institutes of the union-republic

academies of sciences and the USSR Ministry of Geology and Conservation. ...To reduce substantially the volume of narrow regional work of the Geography, Geology and Mineralogy Institutes, the Institute of Geochemistry and Crystallochemistry of Rare Elements and the Institute of the Geology of Ore Deposits, Petrography, Mineralogy and Geochemistry. To authorize the Presidium of the USSR Academy of Sciences to consider the question of merging the Oceanography Institute with the Marine Hydrophysics Institute. To decide the question of locating the Oceanography Institute near the ocean.'[46]

The General Meeting furthermore authorized the Presidium to review the plan for capital investments 'with a view to concentrating personnel and funds on the most important scientific projects and to completing their construction in the shortest possible time'.

In this way the campaign for more theoretical research was reconciled with the Party's demands for more practical results. These two aims were reflected in the General Meeting's summary on the Academy priorities, which said that it was essential

> ...that the efforts of the scientific collectives of the USSR Academy of Sciences be concentrated on the accomplishment of long-range tasks and the solution of major theoretical problems. Vigorous investigations must be carried out to this end. It is also extremely important that the USSR Academy of Sciences participate jointly with industry in the development of new technological processes and in the creation of new apparatus, instruments and materials.[47]

After the March 1959 General Meeting the direction for change had been indicated, but concrete measures were not yet agreed upon. The technical institutes managed to keep a place - even though a low one - on the Academy's priorities list. Their removal from the Academy was not yet explicitly announced. In the light of later events - specifically the June 1959 Party Plenum - it seems probable that opposition in the Academy Presidium against Nesmeianov was still too strong for him to be able to press his demands. This deadlock situation was finally resolved by the highest authority in the country, First Party Secretary Nikita Khrushchev.

June Plenum, 1959

At the June Plenum of the Party's Central Committee Academician Nikolai Semenov, the Soviet Union's first Nobel Prize laureate, threw his prestigious support behind Nesmeianov's demand for reform. His position made it clear that the demand for reform was backed by the Academy's Chemistry Department, of which Semenov was Scientific Secretary. Later Semenov would take over the initiative from Nesmeianov, but this was only after Khrushchev had interfered on behalf of the reorganization movement. Now Semenov complained that 'work in the field of deepening already known branches of science end executing concrete tasks for industry' had in the past been the most widespread in the Academy. He indicated that the two trends that it would henceforth have to concentrate its activities on, were fundamental research and creative proposals for and design of new or fundamentally improved technology. In contrast to Semenov, Nesmeianov had always stressed only the crucial importance of fundamental research. The tasks mentioned by Semenov in the second place had been lacking from Nesmeianov's speeches and articles. Therefore it appears to have been Nikolai Semenov who took the initiative to redefine the issue in such a way that the demands of Nesmeianov and the Party were reconciled.

On what was to become of the narrow applied research that had come to usurp so much of the Academy's resources since the early 1930s, Semenov was clear enough. He demanded that it be removed, so that the Academy might once again be allowed to concentrate on theoretical and innovative-technological research:

> Work in the field of deepening already known branches of science and executing concrete tasks for industry may, of course, also be done in the Academy; but basically such work should be carried out by laboratories of higher schools and by industrial branch institutes.[48]

I have no knowledge of what exactly went on behind the published façade of the Plenum, but it seems likely that in the corridors of the Kremlin Nesmeianov, Topchiev, Semenov, Kirillin and Khrushchev reached an agreement. The few facts that we know are these: In his speech on June 27 Alexander Nesmeianov said that he fully agreed with the considerations of Khrushchev and other speakers on the expediency of transferring the technical institutes to industry. The puzzling thing is, however, that such details had not yet been publicly discussed when Nesmeianov read his speech, and certainly Khrushchev had said nothing of the sort. This seems to be the reason why Pravda left this section of Nesmeianov's speech out of its report. But why did Nesmeianov say this in the first place? Was it to force the issue? Perhaps he had not yet come to an agreement with Khrushchev and wanted to force him to show his colors? This seems unlikely. It is known that specialists were often consulted on important policy speeches and it therefore seems more likely that Nesmeianov had had a hand in the preparation of this section of Khrushchev's speech and therefore knew what was coming.[49] It may be that Nesmeianov referred to the agreement he had reached with the Party leader in order to forwarn the participants interested in the issue of things to come; it may also be that he simply made a mistake: one can only guess.

In his speech of June 29 in which Khrushchev spoke the words that Nesmeianov referred to on June 27, the Party leader made it clear that the Academy President had his full support. He went even a step further than Nesmeianov had ever dared to go, and explicitly criticized the policy of the 1930s, when research fields such as metallurgy and coal mining were included in the Academy. Khrushchev said that the technical institutes would have to be removed in order to bring them in closer contact with industry and to speed up innovation processes. He made it clear that these policy proposals had been criticized ('Some scientists may disagree with me...') but through his speech he told Nesmeianov's opponents that in the fight over the final policy proposals in the Academy Presidium, Nesmeianov was backed by the First Party Secretary.

Once more we run up against a piece of missing information, and a crucial piece at that. In Chapter 3 we have seen that in the issues which 'bubbled up' we know near to nothing about the policy positions of the individual members of the Communist Party Presidium. It is therefore impossible to make definite generalizations about the relationship between leadership conflict and the actual influence of policy coalitions. This issue is no exception. We know that Nesmeianov was supported by Kirillin, the head of the Party Secretariat's Department in charge of science policy, and by Nikita Khrushchev. From the fact that in 1961 Alexei Kosygin took active part in the implementation of the reorganization we might possibly infer that he also belonged to its proponents. But unfortunately we know nothing about the positions of the other Presidium members. Since in 1961 the issue was finally resolved through a joint Party-state resolution, it seems likely that it was at that time discussed in the Party Presidium. But it remains unknown whether or not the issue was on the Presidium's agenda at any time before 1961. What we do know is that immediately following the June Plenum of 1959 the Presidium of the Academy convened for the discussion of a draft plan of the reorganization, which had been prepared during spring; it is also known that it was unable to reach a consensus on this plan.

Izvestia discussion

The press discussion on the future profile of the Academy that followed upon these developments had nothing in common with a 'mobilization discussion' where the political leadership uses the press to mobilize the population for a policy change. True, the discussion followed upon Khrushchev's endorsement of Nesmeianov's demands and Nikolai Semenov, who opened the discussion, explicitly referred to Khrushchev's speech. He made sure to note, right at the beginning of his article, that his demands had been endorsed by Khrushchev. In fact, in the best of Soviet tradition, he gave the impression that the First Party Secretary had been the initiator of these demands, as if there had been no discussion on the Academy's future since 1954.

To leave not even a trace of doubt on where the Party stood, <u>Pravda</u> of the next day published an editorial which supported the Khrushchev-Semenov line and said in particular that 'the work of the Department of Technical Sciences still does not meet the tasks of technical progress.'[50] It is also true that the issue was transferred from the subagenda of the scientific community to the general national agenda, for the discussion took place on the pages of *Izvestia*. Still, this was not a mobilization discussion at all. Semenov's opening article was soon followed by articles in which members of the Technical Sciences Department, led by Academician Bardin, criticized his proposals. Semenov had to wait more than two months before he received strong support from a group of four leading academicians representing the Physics-Mathematics Department and the Chemistry Department.

In his opening article Nikolai Semenov proposed an all-out reform. He disclosed what was probably the 'maximum program' of the reformers in the Academy Presidium, including not only the transfer of technical institutes, but also such measures as a reduction of the number of departments from eight to three (and thereby the abolishment of the Department of Technical Sciences), a streamlining of the supply system and of the geographic distribution of Academy institutions. No doubt budgetary considerations played a role. From what Semenov wrote when he closed the discussion four months later we may deduce that one of the main grievances of the fundamental scientists was that the technical institutes swallowed much too great a share of the Academy budget.

In the discussion that followed, the individual authors tackled different combinations of sub-issues. Not all of them made clear where they stood on the core of the issue: the concentration of the Academy's activities on fundamental research and major technological projects, and the transfer of technical institutes to state committees. Those that did, however, could be grouped into two categories, proponents and opponents. Tables 3 and 4 list all those who publicly spoke out on the central issue, right from its origin in 1954. The listing is in chronological order, beginning with the person who first made clear where he stood.

From these tables we may conclude two things. First, it turns out that the opponents of reorganization cannot be considered a policy coalition at all. They were instead a quite homogeneous group, consisting of leading personnel of the Department of Technical Sciences and of those institutes that were threatened with transfer. This was typically a group which acted on behalf of its own immediate interests that were being threatened. Its make-up satisfied both the sociological and the political criteria for group status. Of course the members of this

Table 3
PROPONENTS OF ACADEMY REORGANIZATION

Alexander N. Nesmeianov, organic chemist, Academician, Academy President, Director Institute of Elemental-Organic Compounds

Alexander V. Topchiev, organic chemist, Academician, Chief Scientific Secretary and Vice-President of the Academy, Director Institute of Petrochemical Synthesis

Vladimir A. Kirillin, thermophysicist, Corresponding Member, Head Department for Science, Higher Educational Institutions and Schools, CPSU Central Committee Secretariat

Petr L. Kapitsa, physicist, Academician, Presidium Member, Director Institute of Problems in Physics

Nikolai N. Semenov, chemical physicist, Academician, Presidium Member, Scientific Secretary Department of Chemical Sciences, Director Institute of Chemical Physics

Alexander G. Kurosh, mathematician, Professor at Moscow State University, Vice-President Moscow Mathematics Society

Gleb M. Frank, biophysicist, Corresponding Member Academy of Medical Sciences, Director Institute of Biophysics

Armenak L. Mndzhoian, organic chemist, Academician of Armenian Academy of Sciences, Vice-President Armenian Academy and Director of its Institute of Fine Organic Chemistry

Abram I. Alikhanov, atomic physicist, Academician, Bureau member Department of Physical and Mathematical Sciences, Director Institute of Theoretical and Experimental Physics

Martin I. Kabachnik, organic chemist, Academician, Laboratory head at the Institute of Elemental-Organic Compounds

Igor E. Tamm, physicist, Academician, Research associate at the Physics Institute

Mikhail M. Shemiakin, organic chemist, Academician, Bureau member Department of Chemical Sciences, Director Institute for Chemistry of Natural Compounds

Todor D. Pavlov, authority on science philosophy, President of the Bulgarian Academy of Sciences, Director of its Institute of Philosophy

Konstantin V. Ostrovitianov, economist, Academician, Vice-President, Candidate Member CPSU Central Committee

---

group argued in terms of the general interest: to remove their institutes from the Academy would cause harm to scientific-technological progress, to economic development and so on and so forth. But it is quite obvious that behind the 'unselfish' argumentation were their 'selfish' demands that their endeavours not be downgraded from Academy-status to

Table 4
OPPONENTS OF ACADEMY REORGANIZATION

Ivan P. Bardin, metallurgical engineer, Academician, Vice-President, Director Institute of Metallurgy

Nikolai A. Chinakal, mining engineer, Corresponding Member, Director Mining Institute of the Siberian Department

G. I. Ermolaev, Director Kuznetsk Metallurgy Combine

Anatolii A. Blagonravov, military mechanics engineer, Academician, Presidium member, Scientific Secretary Department of Technical Sciences, Director Institute of Machine Science

Pavel K. Oshchepkov, engineer, Head of the Electrophysics Laboratory at the Institute of Metallurgy

Leonid M. Sapozhnikov, fuel technologist, Corresponding Member, Head of a laboratory at the Institute of Mineral Fuels

Tigran S. Khachaturov, economist, Corresponding Member, Director Institute of Complex Transportation Problems

Alexander A. Skochinskii, mining engineer, Academician, Director Mining Institute

Alexander L. Mints, radio engineer, Academician, Bureau member Department of Technical Sciences, Director Radio Engineering Institute

Ivan I. Artobolevskii, mechanics engineer, Academician, former Deputy Scientific Secretary Department of Technical Sciences, Head of Department of the Theory of Machines at the Institute of Machine Science

Boris S. Stechkin, thermotechnologist, Academician, Director Motors Laboratory

Boris N. Petrov, power engineer, Corresponding Member, former Director Institute of Automation and Remote Control

N. V. Lavrov, engineer, Research Associate at Institute of Mineral Fuels

Kanysh I. Satpaev, geologist, Academician, Presidium member, President of Kazakhstan Academy of Sciences

Nikolai V. Mel'nikov, mining engineer, Corresponding Member, Deputy Director Institute of Mining

Nikolai P. Sazhin, specialist in chemical technology, Corresponding Member, Research Associate at Institute of Metallurgy

that of industrial branch research and that they not be robbed of the privileges that their affiliation with the Academy yielded. I have found no evidence that this homogeneous group received support from outside groups.

The opponents of reform did not shrink from strong words and innuendo.

Thus, Academician Bardin, a man of tremendous prestige both in the technological and in the political community, characterized the reform proposals as reactionary:

> Just why must the USSR Academy of Sciences, which was awakened to the need for contact with life by V. I. Lenin, constrict the range of its work and retreat to the ill-remembered Imperial Academy of Sciences? On the whole, Academician N. N. Semenov's proposition that 'the kind of detailed problems and such type of institutes were not included in the Academy in the past' sounds very strange in our time.[51]

Since this 'proposition' had also been made by Khrushchev at the June Plenum, Bardin's attack on Semenov amounted to an attack on the Party leader himself. He stopped only a fraction short of characterizing Khrushchev's position as un-Leninist.

Ivan Bardin was a much respected technologist, but not a member of the Communist Party. Insiders of the academic scene were soon to learn that even some communists refused to accept the proposed reform, in spite of the Party leader's endorsement. A few days after Bardin's article, *Izvestia* printed a joint article signed by academicians Blagonravov, Artobolevskii, Mints, Stechkin and Corresponding Member Boris Petrov. Thus, Vice-President Bardin received the public support of the Head of the Technical Sciences Department (Blagonravov, who was also a Presidium member and the Director of an important institute), one of its Bureau members (Mints, also Director of an institute), a former Deputy Scientific Secretary (Artobolevskii) and the directors of another institute and laboratory. Blagonravov was the only Party member in the quintuplet and the first Party member to speak out publicly against Semenov's proposals. That he permitted himself to engage in what might turn out to be a dangerous rebellion against Party policy, was probably related to the awareness of his indispensability because of his involvement with the space program.

Semenov's wholly unjustified contempt for the technical sciences, the engineers wrote, should be traced to its historical roots; and these roots, they speculate, have their origin in the remote past, 'when it was believed that true science should study the creation of God's hands, and that the study of the works of human hands was something lowly and unworthy of "lofty science"'.[52]

This attempt to discredit Semenov was renewed and further developed a few days later by Professor N. V. Lavrov, writing in Literaturnaia Gazeta. There was something suspicious about the fact that this article was printed in the literary paper, instead of in Izvestia; it was the only article article during the period of the discussion (August 9 - December 16) not published in Izvestia, and it represented the one and only time during this period that Literaturnaia Gazeta gave attention to the subject. Moreover, the content of Lavrov's article was, with a few exceptions, similar to that of the quintuplet. Lavrov explicitly identified Semenov as one of those scientists who have only contempt for the technical sciences, he attacked Khrushchev much more directly and finally suggested that if 'they' really wanted to exile the technical sciences, then it would be a good idea to create an independent Academy of Technical Sciences, composed of the Academy's 'former' Department of Technical Sciences and the industrial branch institutes. Quoting Lenin's 'Outline of a plan for scientific-technological work' and stressing that both the 1929-reinforcement of the Academy with 'great scientists who worked in industry' and the subsequent creation of the Department of Technical Sciences were logical outcomes of Lenin's Outline, Lavrov made the accusation that Khrushchev's words at the June Plenum were un-Leninist: 'This stage in the development of the USSR Academy of Sciences (1929 - 1934, J.L.), the correctness of which is now doubted by some scientists, followed logically from the theses of Lenin's "Outline of a plan for scientific-technological work"'.[53] There is, in my opinion, no doubt that over the head of Semenov, Lavrov was addressing his criticism to Party First Secretary Khrushchev. In this respect, one of his remarks is most revealing:

> If the reason for the expulsion of the technical sciences from the Academy is only the difficulty of leading the great number of scientific-research establishments of the USSR Academy of Sciences, then this task must not be solved rashly (ne s plecha), but by some kind of reasonable, constructive proposal.[54]

'If... as they say... the Presidium of the Academy does not have the power to lead the whole complex process of the development of the technical sciences...', then why not create an independent Academy of Technical Sciences? These remarks clearly referred to Khrushchev, not to Semenov; for it was Khrushchev who had said at the June Plenum that Nesmeianov was not and could not be 'omnipotent', that it was impossible for him to coordinate the innumerable establishments of the Academy. It was Khrushchev who had used this as one of the main arguments for reorganizing the Academy.

Why was this angry article not published in Izvestia, assuming that it had been presented to the editorial board? The reason seems to be that Lavrov's position and his way of saying things was unacceptable to Izvestia and to the prominent representatives of the Technical Sciences Department. First of all, in June 1959 Nikita Khrushchev's son-in-law Adzhubei had been appointed as Izvestia's new chief editor. The discussion on the Academy was one of the first features in the new style that he introduced. A Central Committee resolution adopted at the June Plenum had criticized Izvestia's former editorial policy and had decided that the editorial board must take a new, bold approach. An open discussion on science policy befitted such a new policy, but Adzhubei could hardly be expected to permit a frontal attack on his father-in-law in the paper of which he had just become the chief editor. Secondly, a comparison of the Lavrov article with that of the quintuplet leads one to the conclusion that Lavrov may have been going to sign this letter, but that some disagreement prevented him from doing so, whereupon he wrote his own article for Literaturnaia Gazeta. The content of Lavrov's article was, with a few significant exceptions, similar to that of the quintuplet. The main stumbling block may have been Lavrov's demand for an Academy of Technical Sciences. The idea of creating such an Academy was not new. It had been discussed for some time - though not in public -, but it was uncomfortable to both the applied scientists and to the academicians who promoted the reorganization. The first were afraid that an Academy of Technical Sciences would become a second-order academy, whereas the last feared that it would develop into the most privileged and best subsidized organization![55]

A second conclusion to be drawn from tables 3 and 4 is that the proponents of reorganization can be seen as a coalition of two groups, as illustrated in Table 5. Obviously the original impetus for reform came from prominent members of the Chemistry Department. Nesmeianov and Topchiev were organic chemists and occupied important posts both in this

Table 5
CORE OF THE POLICY COALITION FOR REORGANIZATION OF THE USSR ACADEMY OF SCIENCES

chemists	physicists
Nesmeianov	
Topchiev	
	Kirillin
	Kapitsa
	Semenov
Mndzhoian	
	Alikhanov
Kabachnik	
	Tamm
Shemiakin	

Department and in the Academy Presidium. They received support from physicists such as Kapitsa, Semenov, Alikhanov and Tamm. It seems that Nikolai Semenov has acted as broker between the two groups and has played a creative role in welding the policy coalition. But he had to wait a long time - and undergo severe public criticism - before the physicists Alikhanov and Tamm co-signed a letter of strong support with two leading organic chemists. This letter was published on October 21, more than two months after Semenov had opened the discussion. On the other hand, the four signatories were not to be sneezed at. Abram Alikhanov, the nuclear physicist who had helped develop the first Soviet atom bomb and, in 1949, had built the Soviet Union's first reactor with heavy water inhibitor, was a Bureau member of the Academy's Physical and Mathematical Sciences Department. Igor Tamm, the authority on nuclear energy theory and quantum mechanics, had received the

Nobel prize in 1958. These two physicists were joined by two organic chemists who had much in common with each other. Kabachnik and Shemiakin were of the same age, had both been elected Corresponding Member in 1953 and full member in 1958. In contrast to Alikhanov and Tamm, both were members of the Communist Party: Shemiakin since 1951, Kabachnik since 1957. The latter was an associate of Alexander Nesmeianov because he worked at Nesmeianov's Institute of Elemental-Organic Compounds and had headed its laboratory of Phosphorous-Organic Compounds since 1954.

From the outset the four academicians took it for granted that technical institutes should be removed from the Academy. They reminded their audience that Khrushchev had said so at the June Plenum and had initiated the _Izvestia_ discussion. The only legitimate question, therefore, could be 'which institutes of a technical profile must remain in the Academy system and which must be placed among the industrial branch institutes.'[56] The four wisely conceded that persons working outside the Academy were no second-rate scientists, and re-interpreted Khrushchev's and Semenov's motivation for the expulsion of the technical institutes. When the Soviet Union was young and when there were virtually no other scientific establishments than the Academy of Sciences, it was only natural that it engaged in such tasks as finding natural resources, solving energy problems, designing mines and machines. But, 'times have changed'. Now that the scope of this kind of research was widened immensely, the academicians wrote, and the country possesses a network of first-class industrial branch institutes, it would be counterproductive to retain this kind of research in the Academy. They wrote that it was now 'beyond the strength' of the Academy to engage in technical research, suggesting that they, too, were motivated by a desire for a thorough re-allocation of resources. Institutes engaged in research on 'complex, but concrete and for industry vital scientific problems' should be transferred, whereas the Academy should retain institutes working on 'the most important scientific-technological problems that do not promise results for contemporary industry, but must lead to the emergence of completely new branches (of industry)', as well as on industry-related but open-ended problems.

Such is the natural way of things. Times have changed. At the moment the presence in the USSR Academy of Sciences of a number of technical institutes that cater to fully developed branches of industry and concern themselves principally with perfecting existing branches of industry has become an obvious anachronism.[57]

However, the four did not believe that the Department of Technical Sciences sould be abolished, as Semenov had suggested. They proposed that the department remain in the Academy and that its basic function would be to 'evaluate and plan the directions of development of new technology in our country and to evaluate the results of (research) work and the means for its practical application.' In this function, the department should have authority over all major research institutes, irrespective of their formal subordination. And indeed, when in 1961 nine of the twelve institutes of the Technical Sciences Department were removed from the Academy system, the department retained control over the scientific activities of several of them.[58]

In December 1959 the discussion in *Izvestia* was closed by Semenov. He did not yield one inch to the engineers who had protested the removal of their institutes, but made a concession by retracting his demand that the number of departments be reduced to three. Opposition against this demand had come not only from the Technical Sciences Department, but from biologists as well. Even the four academicians who had supported Semenov had rejected his proposal, thereby suggesting a possible compromise. In addition, the demand that a new Academy of Technical Sciences be created, similar to the academies for medical and pedagogical sciences, had been brought up in public. Semenov now stressed that the Department of Technical Sciences should stay in the Academy even though it would lose its institutional base. Thereby he probably tried to appease some of his most outspoken opponents, especially the academicians-engineers who had stood to lose many privileges. A transfer of their institutes would mean that their formal boss would change, but the preservation of their own department inside the Academy would somewhat sweeten the bitterness of this pill. It gave them a power base inside the Academy and a voice in its Presidium.

Continued opposition

In spite of Semenov's partial retreat the Department of Technical Sciences did not stop its opposition. Although it had lost its most eminent spokesman - Academician Bardin had died on January 7, 1960 - the engineers resumed their campaign against reorganization at the February 1960 General Meeting. At this meeting, the pending reform was a major subject of debate. The meeting of the Technical Sciences Department that had preceded the General Meeting, had adopted a document concerning the main tasks and the place of the department within the Academy system, as well as the improvement of its activities. It had promised that a number of 'organizational measures' would be taken to remove 'secondary themes' and subjects of an industrial branch character from the work-plans of the department's establishments.[59] At the General Meeting itself, President Nesmeianov did not refer to Semenov's and his own proposals, but complained that in a number of cases research was not, as it should be, concentrated on the most important problems listed by the General Meeting of March 1959. He also spoke of complaints 'transferred, in part, to me,' that a number of the Academy's institutes were of a pure industrial branch profile and could be of considerable more use if subjected to the control of industry. Nesmeianov disclosed that on the basis of the discussions and proposals made in the spring of 1959, a draft (*proekt*; he did not say of what) had been made. It had been subjected to a preliminary discussion in the Academy Presidium at the beginning of July 1959. The basic outline of this draft, according to Nesmeianov, was 'the concentration of the efforts of the Academy on relatively few major and topical scientific problems and on the leading branches of science.'[60]

'On the whole', he added, the proposals had been greeted with approval. The discussion on and elaboration of the draft was to continue. In the discussion that followed Nesmeianov's speech, 25 scientists took part. Assuming that the reports of their speeches in *Vestnik*, *Pravda* and *Izvestia* were correct, nine of them criticized the proposals and only one supported them. The engineers obviously used the forum of the General Meeting to launch their heaviest counterattack. Apparently they did not yet feel beaten. The issue was not put to the test in the form of a vote of the General Meeting. No doubt the outcome of such a vote would have been far from unanimous. Opposition against the reform must have been rather strong in the Academy Presidium as well, for it did not come to a decision. The issue was left unresolved and taken off the public agenda. After the heated discussion of 1959 the press was now silent. But behind the scenes the engineers fought back. Directors of institutes organized the lobbying of members of the Central Committee and the Party Presidium. They wrote letters, visited Party officials and tried to involve well-known scientists in their activities.[61] But their efforts were to no avail. They lost. Suddenly, in April 1961, a binding joint decision of the Party and the government brought the stalemate to an end.

Party-government decision, April 1961

The joint decision 'On measures for improving the coordination of scientific research in the country and the activity of the USSR Academy of Sciences' (hereafter: Decision) was adopted on April 3. It ruled that several institutes, Academy branches and other scientific establishments were to be transferred to state committees, ministries, departments and the RSFSR Council of Ministers. It took more than a week before the Decision was made public; the timing probably had to do with a desire to implement the Decision before making it public. It had also to do with a desire to conceal the fact that, in the eyes of the Soviet leaders, the Decision could be seen as an admission of the backwardness of Soviet science.

On April 11 Izvestia reproduced three Supreme Soviet Presidium decrees of April 8, abolishing the State Science and Technology Committee, establishing the USSR Council of Ministers' State Committee for the Coordination of Scientific Research and appointing Mikhail Khrunichev as its chairman. The importance of this new position was stressed by making Khrunichev Deputy Chairman of the Council of Ministers. The Pravda issue of that day disclosed that on April 10 an 'enlarged meeting' of the Academy of Sciences' Presidium had discussed the Party-government Decision. Present at the meeting had been, along with members of the Presidium itself, academicians and directors of the biggest institutes, the newly appointed Mikhail Khrunichev and Party Presidium member and First Deputy Premier Alexei Kosygin. According to the *Pravda* report many academicians had spoken and approved of the new Decision, and the Presidium had unanimously adopted a resolution characterizing the joint Decision as 'a new manifestation of the care and attention of Party and government for the development of science in our country.'[62] The Presidium resolution also gave directions for the implementation of the Decision: it decided which institutes were to be transferred and which were not.[63]

The next day the April 3 Decision was published in *Pravda* and *Izvestia*. April 12 was also the day of the Soviet Union's greatest technological achievement so far, the manned spaceflight of colonel Iurii Gagarin. It seems obvious that the two events were related. On April 13 the jubilant newspapers congratulated scientists and engineers on their enormous achievement. The headline of *Izvestia* of that day, over the picture of Iurii Gagarin, said that a Soviet man in space was 'the biggest victory of our system, our science, our technology and our courage.' The publicity on this tremendous victory for Soviet technology overshadowed the recognition of defeat as far as science and technology policy in the past two decades was concerned.

In its introduction the Decision said that Soviet science and technology must in the shortest possible time succeed in occupying leading positions in decisive fields of global science and technology. 'Of fundamental importance in the present situation', it said,

> is the further strengthening of theoretical research on the most important scientific problems that are of economic value, bringing together science and production and securing the fast introduction of the results of scientific research into the USSR economy.[64]

The document put on the record a 'big shortcoming' in the activities of the USSR Academy of Sciences, namely that it had expanded its network of industrial branch-type research establishments considerably. As a result of this, the network had become 'extremely cumbersome and difficult to manage'.

> The presence in the USSR Academy of Sciences of a considerable number of industrial branch-type research establishments diverts attention from the solution of the major (perspektivnye) problems of science and disperses its forces and sources over many technical questions of industrial branch character that may be solved in specialized research institutes. A number of scientific establishments of the USSR Academy of Sciences has for a great many years worked on subjects that are of no theoretical or practical value.[65]

The cause of these and other shortcomings had been, according to the Decision, the lack of a 'general state organ for the coordination of scientific research' in the country. In its seventeen paragraphs the Decision established such an organization, ordered the Academy to implement certain changes in its structure and fixed the mutual relationship between the two establishments. Paragraph eight was concerned with the Academy structure and said that

> In connection with the realization of measures for the reorganization of the management system over the scientific research establishments of the country and the creation of the USSR Council of Ministers' State Committee for the Coordination of Scientific Research, and with the purpose of improving the work of the USSR Academy of Sciences, (the CPSU Central Committee and the USSR Council of Ministers) consider it necessary that the USSR Academy of Sciences concentrate its activities on the major (naibolee perspektivnye) and fast developing trends in science, that contribute to the development of the country's economy and culture.[66]

The Academy was to concentrate its forces on 'the most important research in the natural sciences and humanities' and the Central Committee and Council of Ministers said in paragraph nine that they had decided to accept the proposal of the Academy Presidium to transfer institutes, Academy branches and other scientific establishments to state committees, ministries,departments and the RSFSR Council of Ministers, though the Academy was to retain 'scientific-methodological guidance' over the branches.

In this way the leaders of the country overruled the opposition that had stood its ground for several years. They accepted a proposal that was not unanimously backed either by the Academy Presidium or by the scientists of the Academy as a whole. Thereby they ordered the rebellious engineers of the Technical Sciences Department to lay down their arms and collaborate in the implementation of the Decision. The realization of this order took place in the crucial Academy Presidium meeting of April 10, where important Party and state officials made sure that their decision was correctly implemented. The decision of this meeting included the following measures: In the institutes and at general meetings of the departments, the state of affairs and perspectives for the development of research were to be subjected to a thorough discussion. The department bureaus were charged with the task of preparing concrete proposals for the improvement of research in the most important problems of natural science and the humanities. They were to make sure that projects which were of no real theoretical or practical value were terminated.[67] They were also told to review research plans, the profile and structure of research establishments, the organizational forms of research coordination and finally the network of scientific councils and commissions of the Academy. All this was to be done in April and May of 1961.

Resignation of Alexander Nesmeianov

To the student of the Academy's reorganization it comes as a great surprise that shortly after what seemed to be his great victory, Alexander Nesmeianov resigned as President of the Academy. On May 19 Nesmeianov announced that since his ten year term (two five year periods) had expired in February, he was retiring as President. He proposed Mstislav Keldysh as his successor. Keldysh received support from the Presidium, in which Nesmeianov was to remain as a member, and the Party group, and was elected by the academicians. In his short acceptance speech he stressed the importance of the April 3 Decision.

Two things militate against the expiration of the ten year term as the true reason for Nesmeianov's retirement. First, the Academy Charter said that the President was chosen 'for a five year period' and contained no provision against re-election at all.[68] Second, in his memoirs Nikita Khrushchev later suggested that a disagreement between Nesmeianov and the government had been the cause. According to him, Nesmeianov had been criticized at a session of the Council of Ministers, whereupon he had proposed: 'Well, maybe you'd better think about promoting comrade Keldysh to the post...'[69] 'We said that was an idea worth thinking about', reports Khrushchev:

> After the session, we looked into the matter for a few days and came to the conclusion that, yes, it would be better to have Keldysh as president.[70]

Khrushchev left no doubt that it was the government - the Party - that appointed the new President, even though formally the academicians elected him. It remains unknown when this meeting took place and what the disagreement between Nesmeianov and the government was about. One possibility is that Nesmeianov insisted on abolishing the Academy branches, whereas the Party and government just wanted to transfer them, as was eventually done.[71]

Nationwide Conference of Scientists

At the end of May the newspapers announced that the Central Committee and the Council of Ministers had decided to convene a Nationwide Conference of Scientists for June 12-14, at which Keldysh was to report on the implementation of the April 3 Decision. The organization of this conference was entrusted to the new State Committee, whose director Khrunichev, incidentally, died in the night of June 1-2. His successor was Konstantin N. Rudnev, the former chairman of the State Committee for Defence Technology.

The first Nationwide Conference of Scientists ever held in the Soviet Union was opened in Moscow on June 12. More than 2.500 participants were present and, to stress the importance of the gathering, eleven members of the CPSU Presidium, among them Nikita Khrushchev, Alexei Kosygin and President Leonid Brezhnev.[72] That the conference was considered to be of utmost importance was also to be seen from the front page of Pravda of that day, dedicated almost exclusively to the occasion. The next day both Pravda and Izvestia opened with a special message to the conference from the Central Committee and the Council of Ministers.

The meeting was opened by Konstantin Rudnev, who claimed that the Soviet Union had reached a leading position in world science thanks to its successes in matters of energy, machine construction, metallurgy, the peaceful use of atomic energy and in space research. The main speech of the day, however, was delivered by Academy President Keldysh. He, too, dwelt upon the contributions of Soviet science to the economy. Up until then, Keldysh said, the forces of an enormous number of research institutions and scientists had been dispersed among 170 ministries and agencies, whereas coordination among them had been lacking. As a result a lot of parallel research had been carried out. As an example he mentioned the problem of direct conversion of thermal into electrical energy, on which about one hundred institutions were currently doing research without a proper allocation of tasks among them, and without central coordination. Later, during the discussion on Keldysh' speech, a conference participant mentioned that 80 'scientific collectives' were working on the problem of the laws of development and distribution of oil and gas deposits, but that there was no central research plan coordinating their activities.[73] Parallelism in science was according to Keldysh the most important cause of the slow pace of introduction of new technology into industrial production.

Keldysh suggested that a State Plan of Scientific Research be drawn up, listing the chief problems on which to concentrate the efforts and resources of science. Such a plan was to consist of three sections:
1- Major problems in experimental and design stages, such as automation, gas turbines, new metals and alloys;
2- Long-term research aimed at the solution of clearly defined problems such as thermonuclear synthesis, direct conversion of thermal into electric power; and
3- Basic research aimed at disclosing laws of nature that may open up

new paths of progress.
Drawing up the plan would be one of the tasks of the new State Committee of Scientific Research, with the Academy of Sciences preparing recommendations on the third section. On the allocation of resources to be laid down in the state plan, Keldysh proposed that the natural sciences receive priority over technology:

> As is known, the harmonious development of the whole national economic organism requires that the growth of heavy industry ensure the development of all branches of the economy and of consumer goods production. At the new stage of history, in the decisive phase of economic competition with the capitalist system, it is necessary that our technology develop more repidly than heavy industry and that the natural sciences, which form the fundamental basis of technical progress and are the main source of the most far-reaching technical ideas, outstrip the rate of development of technology. This fact must be taken into account in drawing up the State Plan for Scientific Research. Just as in industry the Soviet state is raising its general level while concentrating efforts on decisive sectors, so in science it is necessary to ensure a general front of scientific research while concentrating efforts on leading problems where the possibilities for practical application have already been disclosed.[74]

As the prime task of the Academy of Sciences, Keldysh listed research on the major theoretical problems in the natural sciences and humanities, and methodological guidance and coordination of research in these branches, performed by the republican academies and institutions of higher education.

In his speech the new President of the Academy revived several old ideas on science planning, ideas that had been associated with Nikolai Bukharin. Soviet scientists had been ideologically committed to these ideas since the 1930s, but nothing much had come of them in concrete terms. Of course, there had been some planning <u>for</u> science insofar as such things as its share of the national cake, the geographical distribution of scientific establishments and the creation of scientific cadres had been determined from above in a more or less systematic way; but no serious attempt at the planning _of_ science (i.e. planning the direction that research should take) had been made until the late 1950s. Now Keldysh proposed the creation of a State Plan for Scientific Research.

As the major guideline in the planning _for_ science, Bukharin had postulated in 1931 that 'the scientific research framework must grow even faster than the leading branches of socialist heavy industry'.[75] This idea that scientific research should be of topmost priority, higher even than heavy industry, was now again openly promulgated by Keldysh.

In the 'discussion' that followed Keldysh' speech, 33 participants spoke from the rostrum on various subjects related to the implementation of the April 3 Decision. Concerning its impact on the Department of Technical Sciences, Scientific Secretary Blagonravov said that it had been very strong. The tasks of the Department were changing. Now that it had lost most of its institutes, the main task of the Department was to promote the development of technical sciences in the country. 'In these new circumstances', he said, 'the scientists of the department must feel responsible not only for their own scientific work but also for the path of technical progress as a whole.'[76] He disclosed that the Department was considering the subdivision of its membership into councils or groups which would advise the State Committee.

Alexei Kosygin delivered a long speech at the end of the conference. He dwelt on several subjects, among them the possibilities of an increase in the allocation of resources for scientific establishments. If additional allocations were not to result in a reduction of funds for industry, agriculture etc., the scientific establishments would have to demonstrate that their research would result in the setting up of new branches of industry. If they were able to do so, Kosygin said, it might be useful and justified for the state to transfer funds from branches of industry to scientific research:

> Therefore, an increase in the allocations for science is in the hands of the scientists and depends entirely on the effectiveness

> of investments in science as compared with the effectiveness of investments for the expansion of capacity in corresponding branches of industry at the present technical level.[77]

Kosygin recited the well-known grievances against the existing system of planning and organization of scientific research and criticized the Academy of Sciences for having included 'a great number' of institutes of industrial-branch character. As a result, it had been distracted from the solution of the major problems of science, had dispersed its powers and means over too many problems and had lowered its organizational influence on the development of science in the country.

Concluding its work, the conference adopted two documents.[78] The first was an appeal to all scientific personnel in the Soviet Union, saying that the conference unanimously endorsed the April 3 Decision 'which had been taken on the initiative of comrade Khrushchev' and calling on Soviet scientists to do their utmost for the solution of the larger scientific problems and for communist construction. The second document adopted by the conference was a letter to the Party Central Committee and the Council of Ministers. In it, the conference claimed to speak for all scientists in the country, thanked the Party and the government for the April 3 Decision and promised that the tasks mentioned in the appeal would be fulfilled.

Impact

The discussions during the decision-making process leading up to the April 3 Decision, and that Decision itself, leave no doubt that the reorganization was to have a profound impact on the profile of the Academy. It is, however, quite difficult to establish the exact outlines of this impact since only very few public pronouncements have been made on the specifics of the reorganization. The Decision gave only the general outline of the reorganization, whereas the more specific decisions that the Academy's Presidium took on April 10 were never made public. Among the few communications that are at our disposal is President Keldysh' report at the November 1961 General Meeting, in which he said that one third of the Academy's employees (sotrudniki) and half the number of scientific institutions had been removed from the Academy, among them the following institutes:[79]

A. A. Skochinskii Institute of Mining;
A. A. Baikov Institute of Metallurgy;
G. M. Krzhizhanovskii Power Engineering Institute;
Institute of Electromechanics;
Forest and Woodchemistry Institute;
V. V. Dokuchaev Soil Science Institute;
Institute of Automation and Remote Control;
Acoustics Institute;
Precision Mechanics and Computer Engineering Institute;
Institute for Mineralogy, Geochemistry and Crystallochemistry of Rare Elements.

Most of these institutes were from the Department of Technical Sciences. Keldysh also indicated that a few institutions had not been removed and/or were not to be removed from the Academy's Department of Technical Sciences:

Institute of Mechanics;
Institute of Radio Engineering and Electronics;
Institute of Automation and Remote Control;
Laboratory of Data Transmission Systems.

No explanation was offered on the apparent contradiction regarding the Institute of Automation and Remote Control. An article in Pravda of November 17 on the General Meeting carried Topchiev's disclosure that the Academy at that moment employed 17.225 scientists (nauchnye rabotniki). At the general meetings of the Academy departments which took place shortly before or after the Academy Meeting, no further announcements were made on the specifics of the reorganization. In fact, since the November General Meeting data on the impact of the reform have only been published in the book The USSR Academy of Sciences, Headquarters of Soviet Science, which appeared in Moscow, 1968.[80] In this book, the number of scientific institutions removed from the Academy was given as 92 (or 'half the total number of scientific institutions of the USSR Academy of Sciences') and the total number of employees of these institutions as 20.500. Among the 92 institutions were 51 institutes and seven Academy branches.

These figures indicate that for a measurement of the impact of the reorganization it is helpful to distinguish three categories: the total and relative number of scientific institutions removed; the total and relative number of scientific and auxiliary personnel removed; and the changes in the Academy budget, i.e. overall changes as well as relative changes between the different departments. The question here is specifically: did the other departments receive more money following the pruning of the Technical Sciences Department? On the basis of a detailed quantitative study of Soviet sources a number of conclusions can be drawn.

Institutions. In the five-year period preceding the reorganization the number of scientific institutions of the Academy grew by one hundred percent or more. This growth rate was much higher than the growth rate for all scientific institutions in the country: they increased by 37 percent from 2.797 early 1956 to 3.828 early 1961.[81] This exceptionally strong growth rate was undone in 1961, when the Academy lost one out of every three institutions. The scope of the impact suggested by the numbers in Table 6, however, is somewhat misleading because the category 'research establishments' or 'scientific institutions' includes several types of minor institutions , sometimes even commissions with no research staff of their own. A more accurate picture is provided by the category of 'independent' Academy institutes. This category is not open to much dispute as to its content: these are the major Academy institutions, the crème de la crème of Soviet science. If we take the number of 148 institutes prior to the 1961 reform, the Academy lost nearly 35 percent of its institutes. If we take the data from the 1961 Yearbook of the Great Soviet Encyclopedia (i.e. 138 institutes, botanical gardens, observatories, museums etc. on December 31, 1960), the percentage would be even higher![82] Table 6 shows that in the years to follow, this 'loss' - if one can speak of a loss - was not fully made up.

Table 6
RESEARCH ESTABLISHMENTS IN THE USSR ACADEMY OF SCIENCES, 1955 - 1965 (*nauchnye uchrezhdeniia*)

End of year unless otherwise indicated

year	total number	index (1960=100)	scientific research institutes	index (1960=100)
1955 '	125	50	64	43
1956	195	78		
1957	200	80	143 [a]	97
1958				
1959	238	95		
1960	250	100	148	100
1961 ''	162	65	101	68
1962	166	66		
1963	192	77		
1964	194	78		
1965 '''	193	77	121	82

SOURCES: Komkov/Karpenko, *Shtab...*, p. 200 (1955, 1961); *Osnovnye printsipy...*, p. 262 (1956); *SSSR v Tsifrakh*, Moscow 1958, p. 365 (1957); Korol, *Soviet Research and Development...*, p. 24 (1959, 1962); *Vestnik Statistiki* 1974:4, p. 86 (1960, 1965); *Science Policy in the USSR* (OECD), p. 216-217 (1963, 1964).

' Total number includes 18 institutes of Academy branches, as a rule not counted in over-all statistics.

'' *Nar. Khoz. v 1961 g.*, p. 706 indicates a total number of 167; Komkov/Karpenko write on p. 200 that during 1961 92 scientific establishments - including 51 institutes and 7 branches - were removed from the Academy whereas their over-all total of 162 includes 4 institutes of Academy branches, so that the data for 1960 would be 162 - 4 + 92 = 250, i.e. exactly similar to the data supplied by *Vestnik Statistiki*. The number of institutes would be 152 instead of 148. *Nar. Khoz. v 1960 g.* ('signed for the press' on 24 August 1961), p. 787, however, claims that there were 241 scientific establishments at the end of 1960. The *Vestnik Statistiki* data for 1960 are also to be found in *SSSR v Tsifrakh v 1973 g.*, Moscow 1974, p. 65.

''' The total number of 193 is also supplied by *Nar. Khoz. v 1965 g.*, p. 714. Komkov/Karpenko claim that there were 209 scientific establishments including 122 institutes and 21 institutes of branches. Substracting the latter, one would receive a total of 188. For 1967 the numbers compare as follows: 215 sc. est. in *Nar. Khoz. v 1967 g.*, p. 813; 229 - including 130 institutes and 32 institutes

These data show that the reorganization did not hit the Department of Technical Sciences exclusively. On the eve of the reorganization this department counted twelve institutes. Only three of these 'survived' and remained formally subjected to the department; the other nine were removed to state committees and ministries, although the Academy retained 'scientific-methodological leadership' over those that were 'most closely related to the natural sciences'. The remaining institutes were technically oriented institutes from the departments of physical-mathematical sciences, geological-geographical sciences, chemical sciences and biological sciences. Since Soviet sources do not provide the names of all institutes that were removed, one suspects that a considerable number among them were secret establishments.[83]

Scientific personnel. To many scientists, engineers and other Academy personnel the persistent talk during the late 1950s about transferring their institutions to the jurisdiction of state committees must have sounded alarming. Their bosses, the academicians, had not much to fear, for their titles, income and privileges could not be taken from them. But for those who were of lower academic standing the transfer would mean a setback in work-conditions, status and income.

How many people suffered this setback? According to Table 7, prior to the 1961 reform the Academy counted 23.771 scientists (*nauchnye rabotniki*), and one year later 19.068. These are academicians, corresponding members, senior and junior research associates, holders of advanced degrees and academic titles and other personnel engaged in scientific research, categories which are not mutually exclusive. They do not include lower personnel. According to computations made by Korol around 1960 - 1961, scientific personnel constitutes about 30 percent of all the people on the Academy payroll.[84] It is therefore quite clear that

---

of branches - in Komkov/Karpenko. Unlike the other sources they do not explicitly indicate that their stocktaking took place at the end of each year; the note to their 1961 data, however, warrants the conclusion that at least for this year the numbers are those of the end of the year.

a According to *Ustavy Akademii Nauk SSSR* (Moscow 1975), p. 19, there were 143 'scientific research institutes' in the Academy by 1957.

Table 7
SCIENTISTS IN THE USSR ACADEMY OF SCIENCES, 1955 - 1965
(*nauchnye rabotniki*)

October 1st. (1955-1960) or November 1st. (1962-1965)

year		total number	index (1960=100)
1955		13.009	55
1956		15.716	66
1957		17.644	74
1958		20.650	87
1959		23.150	97
1960		23.771	100
1961	October 1st.	19.068	80
	November ?	17.225	72
1962		20.029	84
1963		22.119	93
1964		23.563	99
1965		25.471	107

SOURCES: (NKh 19.. = *Narodnoe Khoziaistvo SSSR v 19.. godu*). Korol, *Soviet Research and Development...*, p. 24 (1956, 1962); *SSSR v Tsifrakh*, Moscow 1958, p. 365 (1957); NKh 1959, p. 759 (1959); NKh 1960, p. 787 (1960); Topchiev in *Pravda* November 17, 1961 (1961, November ?); NKh 1961, p. 706 (1961, October 1st.); Nkh 1962, p. 586 (1962); NKh 1963, p. 594 (1963); NKh 1964, p. 704 (1964); NKh 1965, p. 714 (1965).

' During 1959 the 'scientific cadres' of the Academy increased by 2500, according to President Nesmeianov at the February 24, 1960 General Meeting (*VAN* 1960:4, p. 66). This number has been substracted from 23.150.

the number mentioned in the 1968 book on the history of the Academy (20.500) concerned the total personnel of the 92 institutions that were removed in 1961. Moreover, this number is nearly fully confirmed by Table 7 if one makes use of Korol's rule of three scientists on every ten Academy employees. If among the 20.500 persons were about 6.150 (30 percent) scientists, this means that 26 percent of the scientists that the Academy employed at the end of 1960 were transferred. This confirms the data supplied by Topchiev in November 1961 (17.225 scientists as against 17.621 in my own computations).

During 1961 the Academy's scientific establishments hired 1537 new scientists.[85]

Academy budget. Table 8 shows that 1961 witnessed a strong cut in the Academy budget as against the steady increase of the few years before. The figures in this table concern current expenses exclusively: they do not include investment expenditures. Of course Table 8 shows us only the net effect of the transfer of 92 institutions. The component parts of this net effect can be found thanks to the Chief Scientific Secretary's report on the Academy in 1961.[86] In this report Academician Fedorov said that 'the general increase in appropriations for the Acade-

Table 8
EXPENDITURES ON SCIENCE, USSR ACADEMY OF SCIENCES, 1955 - 1965
In 1961 rubles, millions of rubles (not including Siberian Department and investments)

year	expenses	annual change absolute	annual change relative
1955	122,9 "		
1956	n.a.		
1957	n.a.		
1958	123,4 ' estimated		
1959	138,6 ' estimated	+ 15,2	+ 12,3 %
1960	159,4 '	+ 20,8	+ 15,0 %
1961	129,2 "	- 30,2	- 18,9 %
1962	n.a.		
1963	n.a.		
1964	n.a.		
1965	152,2 "		

SOURCES: E. Zaleski et al., Science Policy in the USSR, Paris (OECD) 1969, Part 1, Table 9, pp. 98-99 ('); G. D. Komkov et al., Akademiia Nauk SSSR - Shtab sovetskoi nauki, Moscow 1968, p. 195 (").

my's activities during 1961 was (in comparative terms) 9,8 percent'. If one neglects the funds that must have been used by the institutions-to-be-transferred during the first months of the year, this may be taken to mean that the funds of the institutions that remained in the Academy after April 1961 amounted to 117,6 million rubles in 1960.[87] Therefore, the institutions that left the Academy in 1961 consumed 41,8 million rubles in 1960, i.e. 26,2 percent of the Academy budget. If we assume that their funding would have grown by the same percentage as that of the others, they took with them from the Academy's budget about 46 million rubles in 1961, i.e. a half a million rubles per institution in the average. This would tend to confirm that the reorganization concerned relatively many small Academy institutions, for in 1960 the average funding per institution was twenty percent higher than half a million (159,4 / 250 = 0,6).

Another and final conclusion is even more relevant: the 1961 reform did not mean that the institutions that remained in the Academy were now able to expand considerably, using funds that formerly went to the 'doomed' institutions. The 'cost' of the 92 transfers did not result in direct financial 'benefits' for the students of pure science. On the contrary, their funds grew probably at a slower rate than had been the case in the preceding years.

New Party Program

In 1957, on the fortieth birthday of the Soviet state, Academician Topchiev had quoted Karl Marx in saying that 'science becomes more and more a "direct productive force"', suggesting that science was in the process of moving from the superstructure to the economic base.[88] The implication was that in the future, once this process had been completed, the rate of development of science would become an independent variable. As long as science resided in the superstructure, its rate of development and the growth of its budget would be a variable dependent upon the rate of economic development. If science would (ever) have become part of the base, its development would condition other economic and social factors.

In Soviet science philosophy, science is still not yet considered as part of the economic base of society. For over a century it has been in the process of moving from the superstructure to the base, the process of becoming a direct productive force. An authoritative book on the development of technology in the USSR, published in 1967 by the Institute for the History of Natural Science and Technology, proclaimed that 'science is turning into a direct productive force' and that this process had started in the nineteenth century.

> In the second half of the twentieth century the process of science turning into a direct productive force developed further, became more tangible and is presently one of the factors that characterize the peculiarities of science and production.[89]

What this might mean in concrete terms, i.e. in terms of financial appropriations, had been revealed by Academy President Keldysh in his opening speech at the scientists' conference of June 1961, and was stressed again by Academician Topchiev, writing in _Vestnik_'s August issue. Without alluding to the Bukharinist origin of this idea, Topchiev said that 'the instruction that for the all-round development of material production the rates of development of technology must surpass the growth rates of production, and science must develop faster than technology' was of utmost importance.[90] It is necessary, he wrote, to start from this thesis when planning not only science, but the whole economy as well. What remains unclear, however, is why Topchiev attributed this so-called instruction to Alexei Kosygin's speech at the conference, whereas according to the published transcripts it was not Kosygin who had said something of the sort, but Keldysh.

The emphasis on these processes in 1961 was probably related to the preparation of the new Party program, which was long overdue. The second program of the Communist Party dated from 1919 and had become antiquated by the early 1930s. Since the Eighteenth Party Congress of 1939 there had been plans to replace the 1919 program, but not before 1961 were any concrete results announced.[91] Then, on January 10, 1961, the Central Committee decided to convene the Twenty-second Party Congress for October 17, and _Pravda_ of the next day announced that the new Party program would be one of the main subjects on the agenda. In mid-June, a few days after the closing of the scientists' conference, Khrushchev presented the new draft program to the Central Committee and by the end of July it was published in the press.

Khrushchev's new Party program as adopted by the Twenty-second Party Congress on October 31, was a long and grandiloquent document pretending to show the way for the development of Soviet society and the world towards communism. It said that in the 1960s and 1970s the Soviet Union would create the material and technical basis of communism and that by 1970 it would surpass the USA in per capita production. By 1980, the program said, the basis of communism would be completed and the Soviet people could start constructing a communist society. Since the foundation of communism would have to be laid within a period of two decades, 'the maximum acceleration of scientific and engineering progress' was said to be a 'major national task'; the Communist Party would do 'everything to enhance the role of science in the building of communist society' and 'science will become, in the full sense of the word, a direct productive force'.[92]

A special section of the program was dedicated to the tasks of the Party in science policy. As the first priority it gave the development of theoretical investigations, as second the improvement of the ties between science and production. On the first priority of science the program said that

> The further perspectives of scientific and technical progress depend in the present period primarily on the achievement of the key branches of natural science. A high level of development in mathematics, physics, chemistry and biology is a necessary condition for the advancement and the effectiveness of the technical, medical, agricultural and other sciences.[93]

It had been said on several occasions in the previous years, in the introduction to the April 3 Decision and at the scientists' conference of June: that Soviet science must 'take a leading place in world science in all key fields'. Now the program of the Communist Party of the Soviet Union officially declared that Soviet scientists were to strain every nerve so that this goal would be reached as soon as possible.

5 Conclusions

The history of the Academy of Sciences reorganization leaves the impression that both the reformers and the opponents of reform were actually influential. But does this impression stand as a conclusion if we apply my narrow definition of influence that says that only if it has been established that an actor has decided other than he would have in the absence of the influence effort, may we speak of actual influence?
It does not as far as the reformers are concerned. We cannot prove that the Communist Party would not have reorganized the Academy in the absence of the activities of Nesmeianov, Semenov and other reform-oriented academicians. On the contrary, the success of the reformers is to be explained by the fact that what they wanted was to some extent also wanted by Party authorities. To be sure, their ultimate goals were quite different: the academicians wanted less Party supervision over their research and their institutes, more freedom and more money, whereas the Party wanted more supervision and better results. But their means for reaching these goals coincided: the transfer of applied research themes - and possibly of whole institutes - out of the Academy of Sciences.

Sovietologists engaged in the interest group approach are sometimes tempted to see the Communist Party as a mediator between parties involved in an issue. In this view the Party authorities, having heard the arguments of all parties to an issue, weigh them and then take a decision that is binding to all. Such a characterization of the Party's role does not befit this issue, for it was not at all impartial to it. The fact that the plans of the reformers were well received in the

Central Committee's Department of Science gave them a tremendous head-start over their opponents. Nevertheless, they encountered persistent opposition in the Presidium of the Academy, opposition that was powerful enough to prevent Nesmeianov and his supporters from railroading a decision through the Presidium and the General Meeting. Although we cannot prove that the reformers were influential, we should not underestimate the importance of the agenda-setting activities of Alexander Nesmeianov and a few other pioneers of the issue. They may not have set the Party in motion against its own will, but their continuous badgering certainly helped a lot.

The opponents of reform were influential to a limited extent. They succeeded in postponing the decision: it is safe to say that because of their opposition the decision-making process took much longer than it would have otherwise. But in spite of the massive campaign that they organized in an effort to prevent the reorganization, in the end their institutes were transferred to state committees. Their rewards were only a few minor concessions, such as the preservation of the Department of Technical Sciences, now almost completely stripped of its own research base.

The actors involved in this decision-making process were many, from all categories of actors that I distinguished at the beginning of this book: individuals, groups and institutions. Several individuals played an active and prominent role, such as Nesmeianov, Semenov, Kapitsa, Bardin and Blagonravov. The most important institutions involved were the Academy's Presidium and the Central Committee's Department of Science, but the bureaux of the Academy departments, the General Meeting and possibly the Party Presidium should not be forgotten. As far as groups are concerned we can first of all establish that the opponents of reorganization can be considered an interest group with quite specific, 'selfish' interests. The scientists of the Technical Sciences Department can be said to share a set of beliefs and values that distinguishes them from other scientists, and to show both group self-consciousness and ascribed group status. In addition, the results of the case study leave no doubt that they interacted with each other and desired to influence decision makers. In Chapter 1 I have said that if a group wants to influence Soviet decision makers it improves its chances of success if it communicates its demands in terms of the 'public interest', whether these demands are 'unselfish' or not. The opponents of reform did indeed do so, but there is no doubt that their primary concern was their own position and that of their institutes. Their demand that the technical institutes not be downgraded from first-class Academy institutes (with corresponding high pay and status) to second-class state committee institutes, was quite selfish. The proponents of reorganization were not a homogeneous group but a policy coalition consisting of two opinion groups, one from the Chemistry Department, the other from the Physics-Mathematics Department. Although the members of this coalition also formulated their demands in terms of the general interest, it is obvious that they, too, were to a great degree motivated by 'selfish' interests: to retain a certain degree of freedom of action for their own institutes and possibly to receive more money and other resources for fundamental research.

Of particular interest are the relations between the different types of actors. The scientists who took part in the press discussion on the Academy's future should be seen as the representatives of the groups, not as the groups themselves. But they did not explicitly speak for these groups. In most cases they occupied important positions in the organizations involved in this issue: they were institute and laboratory directors, members of department bureaux and of the Academy Presidium. Moreover, several of them, both among the proponents and the opponents, were among the most prominent scientists of the Soviet Union and enjoyed great prestige. As a result, their expression of a policy demand in an official position came to carry much weight. The relations between these actors were characterized by both conflict and co-operation. In addition, there was considerable 'overlap' among the actors, meaning that several prominent individuals spoke for a policy coalition or interest group and for an institution as well, whereas they voted in another institution: the Academy Presidium. Together with the fact that Party policy and the demands of the reformers ran parallel, these are the reasons why it has not been possible to establish unequivocally that, in terms of the narrow definition of influence, the policy coalition influenced decision making.

If the history of the decision-making process on this issue leaves little doubt that they did nevertheless have influence, our conclusion should perhaps be that the narrow definition of influence is not well suited for establishing influence relationships in situations such as these. On the other hand, Chapter 3 has shown that in five out of nine other issues it has indeed been possible to establish actual influence relationships with the help of the narrow definition. The conclusions reached in those five cases rest on more solid ground than they would have, had we availed ourselves of the wider definition. It would therefore not seem wise to drop the narrow definition in favor of the wider definition that says that influence is the activity through which the probability of a given outcome is changed. Much more than is the case with this rather vague definition, the narrow definition may guide our research toward the in-depth study of decision-making processes. Its criterion of influence is quite strict, so that the investigator is not soon satisfied, in contrast to when he will use the wide definition of influence. Even in cases such as that of Lake Baikal and the Academy of Sciences reorganization, where the narrow definition does not allow us a conclusive proof of influence relationships, it is better suited to track down probable influence relationships. The wide definition tends to spoil the investigator, for he may be tempted to conclude after only superficial research that the probability of a given outcome has been changed by the expression of a few demands in the press. The narrow definition forces him to continue his research until he is satisfied that all sources are exhausted.

Such is the challenge of the measurement of influence: using a wide definition it is easy to establish influence relationships but the quality of the conclusions based on such measurement may be limited, depending, of course, on the exertions of the investigator. If, however, the investigator is guided by the narrow definition, it is more difficult to prove an influence relationship, but if he can do so - and I hope that my research has shown that this is no impossibility - his conclusions rest on firm ground. Even if he does not succeed, he will be inclined to postpone his conclusions as long as he is not satisfied that he has unearthed all the facts that he may possibly find.

In the introduction to this book I have presented Peter Solomon's four 'images' of the decision-making process in the Soviet Union. Solomon has concluded that the fourth image, which says that outside specialists do influence decision making and that the constraints upon them are not fundamentally different from those facing actors in democratic decision making, typified the relationship between criminologists and criminal policy makers in the middle and late 1960s. If we 'substract' the comparative aspect - which is essentially irrelevant for the analysis of Soviet decision making - from this conclusion, Solomon can be located in the third image.

My own analysis confirms his conclusions only partially. What we have seen is that, as soon as we broaden our outlook from only one to several policy areas, not one but several images are applicable. It may be that specialists influenced criminal policy during the 1960s, educational policy during the late 1950s and social legislation in the period between 1955 and 1965, but in other issues influence of outside specialists could not be shown. In one case, the issue of Jewish emigration, the proof on influence was quite conclusive but the wielders of that influence were not specialists: they were action groups acting explicitly in their own, direct interest, as well as Western publics and politicians. If the international situation of the Soviet Union had not been so favorable to the demand of the Soviet Jews (the planned proclamation of Brezhnev's 'Peace Policy' and the Twenty-fourth Party Congress) they might not have succeeded at all. In three other cases, the economic issues of the 1950s which became vehicles for the power struggle between Stalin's heirs, specialists could not be shown to influence decision making. Consequently, Solomon's conclusion should be specified in the following way: during the late 1950s and the 1960s specialists do influence decision making in specific, particularly the 'soft' policy areas, such as science and education policy, social policy and legislation. How their influence efforts and the results thereof compare to those of specialists in democratic political systems is an altogether different affair.

Leadership changes (1953, 1964) and the shock of de-Stalinization (1956) have allowed specialists in the Soviet Union to come with fresh initiatives or to reanimate issues which had been shelved as a result of indecision at the top or a high-level veto. This brings us to the question of the relationship between specialists' influence and leadership conflict. Is it really so that 'it almost goes without saying that during a struggle for power Soviet policy-makers become more responsive to the demands or aspirations of groups', as Brzezinski and Huntington have claimed?[1] The fact is that the issues which permitted me to conclude to actual influence relationships, were not or only to a limited extent related to power struggles at the political top. On the other hand, the three economic issues in which I could not positively establish an influence relationship were vehicles of the power struggle of the immediate post-Stalin years. This shows that Brzezinski and Huntington's generalization is not borne out by empirical evidence. We have seen in this book that specialists' influence was wielded primarily during periods of relative stability at the top.

In the first chapter of this book I have claimed that the early phases of the decision-making process cannot be neglected on penalty of an incomplete and therefore incorrect picture. This concerns especially the question of which persons, groups or institutions may create issues. We have seen that several issues have been created at a low level, disproving Brzezinski and Huntington's statement that all policy initiatives come from above and Alfred Meyer's claim that all Soviet organizations function as transmission belts for Party policy. It transpires that reality is somewhat more complicated than such general statements suggest. We have also seen that Schwartz and Keech were wrong in attributing all initiative for educational reform to Khrushchev, because they had neglected the early agenda-building phase (1952-1958). In 1958 Khrushchev merely interfered in an ongoing discussion by redefining the issue. He changed the tone of the discussion, but his redefinition was not even binding to the participants. In addition to these findings, the results of my own research of the Academy of Sciences reorganization confirm my original impression that an investigation of the early phases of the decision-making process may result in completely different conclusions as far as the question of issue creation is concerned. Loren Graham's analysis of the history of this issue had resulted in the conclusion that the initiative had come from above, from Party Secretary Khrushchev, and that only after the supreme leader had decontrolled the question of the Academy's profile, scientists dared to present concrete proposals for reform. In this view the agenda-building process was congruent to the mobilization model. If, however, we compare the few lines on the Academy that Khrushchev spoke at the Twentieth Party Congress with the much more outspoken activities of Alexander Nesmeianov during the years before and after this Congress, it turns out that he was the real initiator. This is not to say that Nesmeianov acted squarely against the wishes of science specialists in the Communist Party. His alliance with Alexander Topchiev - the link between Academy and Party - and with the Party's Science Department Chief Vladimir Kirillin, his relations with Khrushchev and the common intermediate aims of the reformers in the Academy and in the Party, all these factors show that Nesmeianov was more a skillful politician who knew how to put a favorable situation to work for his own aims, than an activist who pressed his will against overpowering opposition. The weight of his role as a reformer and initiator of issues was rather less than, for example, that of the local action groups in the issue of Jewish emigration or the jurists who forced Khrushchev to retreat in the anti-parasite issue. One of his main tasks was to define the issue in a more precise way than was done by Party authorities and to fight those who tried to redefine it so that the outcome would do the least possible harm to their interests.

In broad outline, the agenda-building and decision-making process in the Academy of Sciences issue conformed to the outside initiative model. It is obvious, however, that this model is much too simple to be able to capture the complexities of decision making. What we have seen was an intricate interplay between different actors in different arenas, an interplay that lasted for almost seven years. Some actors were on the side of initiative; they made sure that the issue was put on the public agenda and tried to convert their policy proposals into policy proposals of other, weightier actors such as the Academy Presidium, its General Meeting and the Party's Central Committee. Other actors tried to obstruct these efforts. All of them fought for the support of key Party officials. The reason why I believe that the outside initiative model is too simple is not only that the actors often seem to overlap. Another and more serious reason is that in many issues the decision makers are manifold and not easily identifiable.

One of the most puzzling questions of sovietology remains the problem of locating the proper and real decision-making arenas in any issue. If Soviet administrative law can give no better than broad or tentative answers to the question of the proper decision-making arena in an issue, there is no other alternative but to rely on empirical research to find out in what arenas issues were decided. But the Academy of Sciences reorganization shows that even such research will not always take away all doubt as to the proper decision-making arena. It may very well be that this issue was originally to be decided by the Academy itself - of course after approval of the Party's Science Department - and that the Party-government decision of April 1961 was only taken to overcome discord in the Academy Presidium. Much more cumulative research will have to be done to be able to induce empirical generalizations on the proper decision-making arenas in all sorts of issues.

Having analyzed the role of individuals and groups, the question of decision-making arenas now focusses our attention on the institutions involved. For institutions are organizations which make decisions. The first thing that one notices in a review of the institutions involved is that they are easiest identifiable in the three economic issues of the 1950s. These issues were decided in the Party Presidium, but in a quite extraordinary atmosphere. It was Nikita Khrushchev's favorite technique to bring pressure to bear upon the other members of the Presidium through premature public speeches, memoranda and the building of support in the Central Committee. The case studies make it clear that the smooth picture of a Presidium quietly, and free from outside pressure, proposing and disposing over a policy proposal, is far from the truth. In these issues the Supreme Soviet and the Council of Ministers played only a secondary role: they formalized the decisions taken by the Party top.

The role of these state institutions was much more prominent in the social-legal issues. The relation between natural father and illegitimate child, and the introduction of governmental tort liability were of course typical legislative issues. They were decided as parts of general legislation of the USSR which was to serve as guide line for republican legislation in family law and civil law. The decision-making process in these issues was therefore to a great extent determined by the procedures for bringing about general principles of legislation. Consequently, these issues were decided primarily in the arenas of the USSR Supreme Soviet and the USSR Council of Ministers, i.e. in their presidia and commissions. One must, of course, assume that the Central Committee Secretariat and the Party Presidium played a secondary role, giving general directions and vetoing specific proposals. The case studies have shown that the legislative procedures involved in settling these issues present specialists with many opportunities for influence. In the anti-parasite issue, which was decided via the legislatures of the republics, the main decision-making arena is not easily identifiable. Behind the obviously coordinated actions of the republican supreme soviets and councils of ministers, one suspects a hidden hand, possibly that of the USSR Supreme Soviet Presidium with the Party Secretariat.

With the probable exception of Jewish emigration, the four remaining issues were not decided in one, easily identifiable institution. Decision making on education was an interplay between the supreme soviets of the USSR and the RSFSR, the Party Central Committee, its Secretariat and Presidium. The Lake Baikal issue was also on the agenda of many different institutions and the decision making arena jumped back and forth between the councils of ministers of the USSR and the RSFSR, ministries and state committees.

An especially important type of actor in the Soviet Union is the scientific institute or Academy. The main function of this actor is of course to do scientific research. However, in the Soviet Union all human endeavour is supposed to contribute to the building of communism, and scientific research, whether of an applied or pure character, is not exempted from this task. This book has shown that scientists in the Soviet Union, as elsewhere, are eager to execute their obligations by giving advice and seeking influence. We have seen that in at least six out of ten cases academies or scientific institutes were repeatedly asked for advice. These actors hold a special place in the Soviet decision-making structure. Formally they are part of the state apparatus, controlled by the Party and therefore far from independent. And yet in reports and through the organization of conferences they often promote policies that run counter to the status quo or to the wishes of Party and state organizations. It is often through such scientific establishments that groups and individuals make themselves heard and are deputized to weightier decision-making arenas. The academies and scientific institutes of the Soviet Union are more than only centers of learning. They are to be seen as one of the main vehicles for specialists' participation in decision making.

What is to be expected concerning specialists' influence on decision making in the near future? In order to be able to answer this question we have to take a look at the present situation at the political top. The Kremlin is presently inhabited by elderly citizens, and several of the topmost politicians are in poor health. Biological laws dictate that a leadership crisis is to be expected relatively soon. Due to the persistent postponement of a rejuvenation of the political top during the past years, we may expect this leadership crisis to be a serious one, a crisis that will last for quite some time.

If we would believe Brzezinski and Huntington, such a crisis would open many fresh opportunities for specialists' influence on decision making, for they stated that during a power struggle policy makers become especially responsive to the demands of specialists and societal groups. Schwartz and Keech have suggested that 'it may be... that the conditions of tranquility lend themselves more effectively to more or less permanent and far-reaching group influence than do power struggles', but their ultimate conclusion is somewhat disappointing:

> We are not prepared to predict that group influence over policy will be greater under power struggles or more during ordinary policy conflicts, but we are prepared to argue that under either of these conditions of leadership conflict group influence will be greater than when the leadership is relatively monolithic. Such an hypothesis is at the core of our whole argument.[2]

The study of a number of decision-making processes in different policy areas enables me to specify this hypothesis. The general tendency which emerges from my findings is that the better we are able to establish influence relationships, the less it is clear which institution took the ultimate decision, i.e. who were the decision makers that were influenced. In the three economic issues, resolved during the turbulent years following Stalin's death, there was little doubt about the decision-making arenas: it was the Party Presidium which was locked in a quite serious leadership battle. In these cases, however, I was not able to give proof of influence by outside specialists or societal groups. In the other cases I often found evidence of influence relationships, but there was not one, easily identifiable decision-making arena. In many of these cases several institutions were involved in taking partial, tentative, overruling and ultimate decisions. Such situations, where the issue is not considered to be so important that the highest political leaders are immediately involved, are apparently conducive to the wielding of influence by specialists and societal groups. The implication of this conclusion is that the opportunities for influencing decision making are greatest in periods when the political top is not involved in a struggle for power, i.e. when there is relative stability in the Politburo, the Secretariat and the Central Committee.

In the post-Brezhnev leadership struggle several crucial issues which have been left unresolved or which have been 'solved' half-heartedly, will again come to the fore and will probably be used by the country's politicians to fight their power battle. These are in particualar the questions of economic planning and organization, agricultural production, the Soviet economy's dependency on Western technology in relation to détente policy and the recent foreign adventures, and the lack of labor resources in relation to the nationalities problem. In the seventeen years since Brezhnev came to power, societal groups and specialists have had ample opportunity to present their different opinions on the proper policy measures in most of these issues. It remains to be seen, however, whether in the end they will have much influence on the decisions - if any decisions are taken at all. One would expect considerations of power politics to dominate the decision-making process.

An empirical study of decision making should never claim universal applicability for its generalizations. Generalizations and conclusions are of a tentative, temporary character, limited as they are by the empirical evidence upon which they are based, by time and space.

A study of Soviet decision making in the area of criminology, or education, or economic administration, should not tempt the analyst to draw universal conclusions, applicable to all policy areas. Struck by the ease with which some sovietologists give in to this temptation, I have compared decision-making processes in a number of different policy areas. Thereby I have tried to amend a number of conclusions and to disprove some hypotheses. But what I have said above is also applicable to this study. My generalizations should not be seen as the last word. On the contrary, they should be considered as hypotheses that will hopefully be used as instruments with which to tackle decision-making processes in other areas and periods. They are open to amendment and specification. Ideally, a process of continued testing will bring us closer to the truth.

The range of my generalizations is limited in particular by the time factor. They focus on the Khrushchev period and say little about decision-making processes in the 1970s. Peter Solomon's conclusion that in the 1960s specialists' participation has become firmly entrenched in Soviet decision making is certainly not disproved by my findings, but it is not confirmed either. There is still much work to do, comparing different policy areas and time periods. A conditio sine qua non for meaningful empirical theory building is <u>cumulative</u> research. As I have written in the introduction to this book, sovietologists have too often worked in isolation, each with his or her own theoretical framework. I hope that with this study I have brought a number of loose threads together, so that the picture of decision making in the Soviet Union may have become somewhat clearer. We should proceed from here and enrich our body of knowledge with new empirical studies of how the Soviets make their political decisions.

Notes

Introduction

1 See Lawrence C. Mayer, Comparative Political Inquiry. A Methodological Survey, Homewood Ill. 1972, pp. 48-66.
2 These studies only seldomly succeed in establishing actual influence relationships. They are Merle Fainsod, Smolensk under Soviet Rule, Cambridge Mass. 1958; Philip D. Stewart, Political Power in the Soviet Union. A study of decision-making in Stalingrad, Indianapolis & New York 1968; David T. Cattell, Leningrad: A Case Study of Soviet Urban Government, New York & London 1968; Jerry F. Hough, The Soviet Prefects. The Local Party Organs in Industrial Decision-making, Cambridge Mass. 1969; William Taubman, Governing Soviet Cities. Bureaucratic Politics and Urban Development in the USSR, New York & London 1973; and Ronald J. Hill, Soviet political elites. The case of Tiraspol, London 1977.
3 Duverger quoted by Mayer, p. 59.
4 Peter H. Solomon, Jr., Soviet Criminologists and Criminal Policy. Specialists in Policy-Making, New York 1978, pp. 1-4.
5 Robert Conquest, Power and Policy in the USSR. The Study of Soviet Dynastics, London 1961; Sidney I. Ploss, Conflict and decision-making in Soviet Russia. A case study of agricultural policy 1953 - 1963, Princeton N.J. 1965; Carl A. Linden, Khrushchev and the Soviet Leadership 1957 - 1964, Baltimore Md. 1966; Michel Tatu, Le pouvoir en U.R.S.S. Du déclin de Khrouchtchev à la direction collective, Paris 1967.
6 Zbigniew Brzezinski and Samuel P. Huntington, Political Power: USA / USSR, New York 1964; Frederick C. Barghoorn, Politics in the

USSR, Boston & Toronto 1966; Alfred Meyer, The Soviet Political System. An Interpretation, New York 1965.

7 Donald D. Barry, 'The Specialist in Soviet Policy-making: the adoption of a law', Soviet Studies Vol. XVI, No. 2 (October 1964), pp. 153-165; Peter H. Juviler, 'Family Reforms on the Road to Communism', in Soviet Policy-Making. Studies of communism in transition, edited by Peter H. Juviler and Henry W. Morton, London 1967, pp. 29-60; Loren R. Graham, 'Reorganization of the U.S.S.R. Academy of Sciences', in Juviler & Morton, pp. 133-161; Philip D. Stewart, 'Soviet Interest Groups and the Policy Process. The Repeal of Production Education', World Politics Vol. XXII (October 1969), pp. 29-50; Joel J. Schwartz and William R. Keech, 'Public Influence and Educational Policy in the Soviet Union', in Roger E. Kanet (Ed.), The Behavioral Revolution and Communist Studies, New York 1971, pp. 151-186.

8 Jerry F. Hough, The Soviet Union and Social Science Theory, Cambridge Mass. 1977.

9 Solomon, p. 160.

10 Solomon, p. 161.

11 See the first chapter of Hough's recent book (note 8), 'The Soviet System: Petrification or Pluralism?', pp. 19-48. This chapter originally appeared as an article in Problems of Communism, March-April 1972.

12 Solomon, p. 128.

13 The distinction between orthodox and unorthodox dissent is from Brzezinski & Huntington, pp. 104-121.

14 Interest Groups in Soviet Politics, edited by H. Gordon Skilling and Franklyn Griffiths, Princeton N.J. 1971; see also Gruppeninteressen und Entscheidungsprozess in der Sowjetunion, Herausgegeben von Boris Meissner und Georg Brunner, Cologne 1975.

15 Loren R. Graham, 'Reorganization...'; see also Linda Lubrano Greenberg, 'Policy-making in the USSR Academy of Sciences', Journal of Contemporary History Vol. 8, No. 4 (1973), pp. 67-80.

16 In addition to a central systematic book and pamphlet catalogue, the

Institute houses a systematic articles catalogue. This catalogue was set up in the early 1950's; entries from over 150 Soviet newspapers, magazines and journals, as well as from Western periodicals and Soviet and Western 'readers' are being coded daily and filed in this catalogue.

1 Conceptual Framework

1 Roger W. Cobb and Charles D. Elder, Participation in American Politics. The Dynamics of Agenda-Building, Baltimore & London 1972, p. 82.

2 David Braybrooke and Charles E. Lindblom, A Strategy of Decision. Policy Evaluation as a Social Process, London 1963, p. 62.

3 Braybrooke & Lindblom, p. 64.

4 Zbigniew Brzezinski and Samuel P. Huntington, Political Power USA / USSR, New York 1963, pp. 225-226.

5 Braybrooke & Lindblom, p. 77.

6 David Easton, A Systems Analysis of Political Life, New York etc. 1965, p. 21; I am using 'binding' instead of 'authoritative' allocation of values to prevent the suggestion of legitimacy of decision making. See U. Rosenthal, 'Eastons definitie van politiek: een herinterpretatie', Acta Politica Vol. IX, No. 4 (October 1974), pp. 379-397.

7 The concept of non-decisions was introduced by Peter Bachrach and Morton S. Baratz in 'Decision and Non-Decision: An Analytical Framework', American Political Science Review Vol. LVII (September 1963), pp. 632-642. See also Peter Bachrach and Morton S. Baratz, Power and Poverty. Theory and Practice, New York etc. 1970, and C. van der Eijk en W.J.P.Kok, 'Nondecisions reconsidered', Acta Politica Vol. X, No. 3 (July 1975), pp. 277-301.

8 Charles E. Lindblom, The Policy-Making Process, Englewood Cliffs N.J. 1968, p. 4.

9 Bachrach & Baratz, p. 44. The idea behind the concept, however, is

not new; Carl Friedrich has argued in his treatise on influence that 'influence predominantly works for the existing state of affairs' because such state is better known than the future. See Carl Joachim Friedrich, Man and His Government. An Empirical Theory of Politics, New York etc. 1963, pp. 202-203.

10 Brzezinski & Huntington, p. 104.

11 See Cobb & Elder, and Roger Cobb, Jennie-Keith Ross and Marc Howard Ross, 'Agenda Building as a Comparative Political Process', in American Political Science Review 1976, No. 1, pp. 126-138.

12 Cobb & Elder, p. 14.

13 Cobb & Elder, p. 14.

14 Cobb, Ross & Ross, p. 126.

15 See Gayle Durham Hollander, Soviet Political Indoctrination. Developments in Mass Media and Propaganda Since Stalin, New York etc. 1972, pp. 104-108, and B. Paulu, Radio and television broadcasting in Eastern Europe, Minneapolis 1974, pp. 94-180. Ms. Hollander refers to the 'pervasive dullness' of Soviet radio and TV (p. 106), and Paulu reports that 'in 1967 several Zhurnalist authors complained that television was not willing to be as controversial as the newspapers'. (p. 116).

16 Philip D. Stewart, 'Soviet interest groups and the policy process. The Repeal of Production Education", World Politics Vol. XXII (October 1969), pp. 29-50 (p. 32).

17 Ibid.

18 The main exponent of this approach is Gordon Skilling who, with Franklyn Griffiths, edited Interest Groups in Soviet Politics, Princeton N.J. 1971. For an illuminating survey of this approach, see A.H.Brown, Soviet politics and political science, London 1974, pp. 71-88.

19 Milton Lodge, 'Groupism in Soviet Politics', in Frederic J. Fleron Jr. (Ed.), Communist Studies and the Social Sciences. Essays on Methodology and Empirical Theory, Chicago 1969, pp. 254-278.

20 Lodge, p. 255.

21 Lodge, p. 276.

22 See Joseph LaPalombara, 'Parsimony and Empiricism in Comparative Politics', in Robert T. Holt and John E. Turner (Eds.), The Methodology of Comparative Research, New York 1970, pp. 123-149 (p. 145).

23 H. Gordon Skilling, 'Groups in Soviet Politics, Some Hypotheses', in Skilling & Griffiths, pp. 19-45 (pp. 25-26).

24 Harry Eckstein, Pressure Group Politics. The Case of the British Medical Association, Stanford 1960, p. 9.

25 Eckstein, p. 9.

26 Graham Wootton, Interest Groups, Englewood Cliffs N.J. 1970, p. 44.

27 Skilling, 'Groups in Soviet Politics...', p. 28.

28 Stewart, pp. 33-34 and 39-40 has found that in the case of the repeal of production education advocates of production education found their mouth-piece in the Ministry of Education's Uchitel'skaia Gazeta, and opponents in Literaturnaia Gazeta and Izvestia.

29 On the frequency of meetings of the Central Committee, the Secretariat and the Politburo, and other aspects of such meetings, see my book on the Politburo, Het Russische Politburo. Geschiedenis, profiel en werkwijze, Assen 1978, pp. 111-127; english edition, The Soviet Politburo, Edinburgh (Canongate Publishing), forthcoming.

30 Fortunately, the battle over the question whether Soviet political leadership is or is not monolithic has been fought. Since the 1960's almost all serious students of Soviet politics have recognized that Soviet leadership since 1953 - if not under Stalin as well - has been diversified. Some of the most outstanding books are Robert Conquest, Power and Policy in the USSR, New York 1961; Sidney Ploss, Conflict and Decision-Making in Soviet Russia. A Case Study of Agricultural Policy, 1953 - 1963, Princeton N.J. 1965; and Carl A. Linden, Khrushchev and the Soviet Leadership 1957 - 1964, Baltimore Md. 1966.

31 See Schwartz & Keech's hypothesis No. 4: 'The more and greater the disputes on the top policy-making level, the more likely it is that policy groups will be involved and listened to'. Joel J. Schwartz and William R. Keech, 'Public Influence and Educational Policy in the Soviet Union', in Roger E. Kanet (Ed.), The Behavioral Revolution

and Communist Studies, New York 1971, pp. 151-186 (p. 177).

32 In his memoirs Khrushchev has documented how his high regard for certain scientists brought about his being influenced by them. See Khrushchev Remembers. The Last Testament, translated and edited by Strobe Talbott, London 1974, pp. 58-71.

33 Pravda - Izvestia April 19, 1958; translation CDSP Vol. X, No. 17, p. 17.

34 See Jerry F. Hough, The Soviet Union and Social Science Theory, Cambridge Mass. 1977, pp. 49-70.

35 Brzezinski & Huntington, pp. 203-205.

36 See for example Henry W. Morton, 'The Structure of Decision-Making in the U.S.S.R. A comparative introduction', in Juviler & Morton, pp. 3-27 (p. 19) and T.H. Rigby and L.G. Churchward, Policy-making in the USSR 1953 - 1961: Two Views, Melbourne 1962, p. 4.

37 Cobb, Ross & Ross, p. 135.

38 Cobb, Ross & Ross, pp. 132-134.

39 Cobb, Ross & Ross, p. 135.

40 Leonid Finkelstein in Martin Dewhirst and Robert Farrell (Eds.), The Soviet Censorship, Metuchen N.J. 1973, pp. 50-75. See also my article 'Het sovjetcolofon - een sleutelgat voor de Kremlinoloog?' Internationale Spectator Vol. XXXI, No. 1 (January 1977), pp. 21-32.

41 Examples are the 'white' TASS reports, secret KGB reports on the public opinion and limited-circulation publications. See Dewhirst & Farrell, pp. 68, 75.

42 Schwartz & Keech, p. 173. Their two other basic patterns are roughly congruent to - but less explicitly formulated than - the mobilization and outside initiative models.

43 Cobb, Ross & Ross, p. 127.

44 Easton, A Systems Analysis..., pp. 37-149.

45 David Truman, The Governmental Process, New York 1951, p. 218, as cited by Cobb & Elder, p. 105.

46 Cobb & Elder, pp. 105-106.

47 According to Cobb, Ross & Ross (p. 130) the issue of public financing of medical insurance was on the public agenda for many years

before attempts to place it on the formal agenda had any success.

48 Brzezinski & Huntington, pp. 202-222.

49 Cobb, Ross & Ross, p. 137.

2 Cases in Soviet Decision Making

1 Ploss, Conflict and decision-making..., pp. 66-101.

2 Martin McCauley, Khrushchev and the development of Soviet Agriculture. The Virgin Land Programme 1953 - 1964, London 1976, pp. 44-73.

3 Richard M. Mills, 'The Formation of the Virgin Lands Policy', Slavic Review Vol. 29, No. 1 (March 1970), pp. 58-69.

4 Mills, pp. 68-69.

5 Khrushchev Remembers. The Last Testament, London 1974, p. 120.

6 L.I. Brezhnev, 'Tselina', Novyi Mir 1978: 11, pp. 3-55 (p. 20).

7 David Joravsky, The Lysenko Affair, Cambridge Mass. 1970, p. 327; Zhores A. Medvedev, The Rise and Fall of T.D. Lysenko, New York & London 1969, pp. 96-99; 'Nikolai Maksimovich Tulaikov (1875-1938)', in N. M. Tulaikov, Izbrannye Proizvedeniia. Kritika travopol'noi sistemy zemledeliia, Moscow 1963, pp. 7-28.

8 N. M. Tulaikov, p. 16; L. I. Brezhnev, 'Tselina', p. 20.

9 See XVI S"ezd VKP(b), Stenograficheskii Otchet, Moscow-Leningrad 1930, p. 584, and L. I. Brezhnev, 'Tselina', pp. 20-21. Although, according to Brezhnev, the USSR Peoples Commissariat of Agriculture soon began to found sovkhozy in Kazakhstan, nothing came of the project because of lack of tractive power and because of the war.

10 Mills, p. 59.

11 Ocherki istorii kommunisticheskoi partii Kazakhstana, Alma-Ata 1963, p. 497.

12 Mills, p. 59.

13 Mills, p. 61.

14 M. L. Bogdenko, review in Istoriia SSSR 1965:5, p. 142.

15 This decision was executed and formalized by a plenary meeting of the Kazakh Central Committee, held early February 1954; the person-

nel changes were first published in Pravda of February 12. According to Brezhnev, the decision to remove the Kazakh Party top was taken at a session of the CPSU CC Presidium on January 30. See L. I. Brezhnev, 'Tselina', p. 4.

16 The conferences were: 1) a meeting of scientists and production workers organized by the USSR Academy of Sciences; 2) a conference of MTS personnel (January 25-28); 3) a nationwide conference of state farm personnel (February 3-5); and 4) a conference of advanced agricultural personnel in the RSFSR (February 11-15).

17 Mills, p. 64.

18 Ploss, p. 82.

19 Mills, p. 65.

20 Ocherki istorii..., p. 499.

21 Conquest, Power and Policy..., p. 293.

22 Izvestia February 16, 1957.

23 Conquest, Power and Policy..., p. 298.

24 Izvestia March 30, 1957 (thesis III.2).

25 Ibid., thesis VI.5.

26 Donald R. Kelley, 'Interest Groups in the USSR: The Impact of Political Sensitivity on Group Influence', Journal of Politics August 1972, pp. 860-888. These numbers have been computed from table 3, p. 879. Kelley has analyzed 821 articles published between March 30 and May 7, 1957; unfortunately, he has presented his findings in a very superficial form. From the 821 articles he has identified 110 requests for separate economic councils for the areas in which the authors were residing. Twelve republic Party secretaries made such a request (being 86% of all republic Party secretaries responding in print), and 39 oblast Party secretaries (78 %). His data do not make clear whether those Party secretaries not demanding a sovnarkhoz 'of their own' responded positively or negatively to the general idea. In the 'managerial elite' group (republic ministers, middle-level economic officials, Gosplan officials and factory directors) only 8 % of those that responded in print demanded a sovnarkhoz for their own region. This would not necessarily imply that 92 %

of the managerial elite was against the institution of sovnarkhozy.

27 For examples, see Conquest, p. 302.

28 In his speech of May 7 Khrushchev had indicated that the original proposal was 68 sovnarkhozy for the RSFSR, 11 for the Ukraine and one for each remaining republic, making a total of 92. Eventually 105 sovnarkhozy were founded. Izvestia May 8, 1957.

29 Khrushchev's closing speech in Izvestia May 11, 1957.

30 This case study is based on Theodore H. Friedgut, 'Interests and Groups in Soviet Policy-Making: the MTS Reforms', Soviet Studies 1976:4, pp. 524-547; Linden, Khrushchev and..., pp. 58-71; Robert F. Miller, One Hundred Thousand Tractors. The MTS and the development of controls in Soviet agriculture, Cambridge Mass. 1970; Ploss, Conflict and Decision-Making..., Chapter III, pp. 113-153.

31 V. Venzher, 'Vysokoproizvoditel'noe ispol'zovanie novoi tekhniki - osnova dal'neishego pod"ema kolkhoznogo proizvodstva', Voprosy Ėkonomiki 1951:3, pp. 25-37.

32 Oral communication of Professor Venzher to Robert Miller, see Miller, p. 385, note 56.

33 Cited by J. Stalin, Economic Problems of Socialism in the U.S.S.R., Supplement to New Times No. 44, October 29, 1952, pp. 37-38.

34 Miller, p. 307.

35 Oral communication by 'a prominent Soviet agricultural economist' to Robert Miller, see Miller, p. 314.

36 E. Kolesnikov & L. Petrov, 'O nekotorykh voprosakh organizatsii kolkhoznogo proizvodstva', Kommunist 1956:3, pp. 123-128 (p. 125).

37 Miller, p. 318.

38 See Ploss, pp. 105-106. In his memoirs Khrushchev has written that the idea of abolishing the MTS was suggested to him by Ivan Vinnichenko during one of his tours of the Virgin Lands, and that Vinnichenko convinced him. See Khrushchev Remembers. The Last Testament, London 1974, pp. 125-126.

39 Ploss, pp. 106-110, and Linden, pp. 61-69.

40 See Linden, pp. 63-64.

41 A comparison of the pictures on the front pages of Pravda issues of

January 24 and 25 learns that Khrushchev left Minsk no earlier than the late afternoon of January 23, and was in Moscow on January 24 at the closing session of the Thirteenth Moscow City Party conference.

42 Peter H. Juviler, 'Family Reforms on the Road to Communism', in Juviler & Morton, pp. 29-60 (p. 33); other sources used for this case study: John N. Hazard, Communists and Their Law. A Search for the Common Core of the Legal Systems of the Marxian Socialist States, Chicago & London 1969, pp. 269-309; Rudolf Benninger, Die sowjetische Gesetzgebung zur rechtlichen Stellung des nichtehelichen Kindes unter besonderer Berücksichtigung ihres Einflusses auf die Geburtenzahl, Berlin 1977; Andreas Bilinsky, 'Zu den "Grundlagen der Gesetzgebung der UdSSR und der Unionsrepubliken über Ehe und Familie"', Jahrbuch für Ostrecht Band IX, 1. Halbjahresheft (September 1968), pp. 181-208; Report by M. S. Solomentsev to the USSR Supreme Soviet, Izvestia and Pravda June 27, 1968, english translation CDSP XX:27, pp. 15-19; 'Pravovye voprosy byta, sem'i i vospitaniia detei', Sovetskoe Gosudarstvo i Pravo 1967:6, pp. 137-140. The text of the Decree of July 8, 1944, is to be found in Sbornik Zakonov SSSR, t. 2 (1938 - 1967), Moscow 1968, pp. 409-417.

43 Juviler, pp. 50-51.

44 Juviler, p. 34.

45 Izvestia December 16, 1962.

46 Juviler, pp. 43-44.

47 G. M. Sverdlov, Sovetskoe semeinoe pravo, Moscow 1958, p. 33, as quoted by Juviler, p. 50.

48 Report to the USSR Academy of Sciences, VAN 1962:5, p. 45, as quoted by Juviler, p. 50.

49 Vedomosti Verkhovnogo Soveta SSSR, 28 December 1966, pp. 1047-1048.

50 Pravovye voprosy..., pp. 137-138.

51 Ibid., p. 138.

52 Ibid.

53 Ibid., p. 139.

54 Izvestia April 10, 1968; english translation CDSP XX:16, p. 4.

55 Izvestia June 27, 1968; translation CDSP XX:27, p. 17. Since he is

not very generous with notes, it is not clear how Bilinsky can let Solomentsev say that 'the commission proposes not to change this article' (italics mine, J.L.). See Bilinsky, pp. 205-206.

56 'Principles of Civil Legislation of the Soviet Union and the Union Republics', translated by A. R. Kiralfy in Z. Szirmai (Ed.), Law in Eastern Europe, No. 7, Leyden 1963, pp. 263-298 (p. 289). Other sources used in this case study are Donald D. Barry, 'The Specialist in Soviet Policy-making: the Adoption of a Law', Soviet Studies Vol. XVI, No. 2 (October 1964), pp. 152-165 (Barry 1964); Donald Barry, 'The Soviet Union', in Donald D. Barry (Ed.), Governmental Tort Liability in the Soviet Union, Bulgaria, Czechoslovakia, Hungary, Poland, Roumania and Yugoslavia (Law in Eastern Europe, No. 17), Leyden 1970, pp. 21-77 (Barry 1970); Whitmore Gray, 'Soviet Tort Law: The New Principles Annotated', in Wayne R. LaFave (Ed.), Law in the Soviet Society, Urbana Ill. 1965, pp. 180-211; 'K obsuzhdeniiu proektov Osnov', Sovetskoe Gosudarstvo i Pravo 1961:2, pp. 86-92; I. K. Kovalev, 'Shirokoe uchastie obshchestvennosti v obsuzhdenii proektov osnov grazhdanskogo zakonodatel'stva i grazhdansokogo sudoproizvodstva', Sovetskoe Gosudarstvo i Pravo 1962:2, pp. 16-23.

57 M. S. Strogovich, 'Teoreticheskie voprosy sovetskoi zakonnosti', SGIP 1956:4, p. 21.

58 Ibid., p. 25; translation Barry 1964, p. 154. Strogovich has acted as spokesman of liberal jurists in other (criminal law) issues as well. See John N. Hazard, 'Social Control Through Law', in A. Dallin and A. F. Westin (Eds.), Politics in the Soviet Union, 7 Cases, New York etc. 1966, pp. 207-242.

59 Kiralfy's translation in Law in Eastern Europe No. 7, Leyden 1963, p. 289.

60 Barry 1964, p. 155.

61 Translation Barry 1964, p. 155.

62 According to M. I. Braginskii in 1961; see Barry 1964, p. 156 nt 19.

63 Barry 1964, pp. 156-157.

64 From the Kovalev report in SGIP 1962:2, pp. 16-17.

65 Reported in SGIP 1960:10, pp. 59-65 and 1960:11, pp. 77-79.

66 'Osnovy grazhdanskogo zakonodatel'stva Soiuza SSR i soiuznykh respublik, Proekt', SGIP 1960:7, pp. 3-22 (p. 17).

67 O. S. Ioffe et al., 'O proekte Osnov grazhdanskogo zakonodatel'stva Soiuza SSR i soiuznykh respublik', SGIP 1961:2, pp. 93-102 (p. 101).

68 H. J. Berman, 'Law Reform in the Soviet Union', American Slavic and East European Review Vol. XV (1956), pp. 179-189 (p. 183); other sources on which this case study is based are Marianne Armstrong, 'The Campaign against Parasites', in Juviler & Morton, pp. 163-182; R. Beermann, 'A discussion on the draft law against parasites, tramps and beggars', Soviet Studies Vol. IX, No. 2 (October 1957), pp. 214-222; R. Beermann, 'The law against parasites, tramps and beggars', Soviet Studies Vol. XI, No. 4 (April 1960), pp. 453-455; R. Beermann, 'The Parasite Law', Soviet Studies Vol. XIII, No. 2 (October 1961), pp. 191-205; Glenn G. Morgan, 'People's Justice: the anti-parasite laws, people's volunteer militia, and comrades' courts', in Z. Szirmai (Ed.), Law in Eastern Europe No. 7, Leyden 1963, pp. 49-81; Donald D. Barry and Harold J. Berman, 'The Jurists', in H. Gordon Skilling and Franklyn Griffiths (Eds.), Interest Groups in Soviet Politics, Princeton N.J. 1971, pp. 291-333.

69 Armstrong, p. 165.

70 Beermann, 'A discussion...'; the Ukrainian draft was published on May 28, 1958 according to Beermann, 'The law against...'.

71 From the draft of the RSFSR decree as translated by Marianne Armstrong, p. 166.

72 For some of the arguments, see Morgan, p. 72 and Beermann, 'A discussion...', pp. 215-221.

73 Armstrong, p. 171.

74 The observer was either Barry or Berman; see Barry & Berman, p. 327.

75 'Ob usilenii bor'by s litsami, ukloniaiushchimisia ot obshchestvenno poleznogo truda i vedushchimi antiobshchestvennyi paraziticheskii obraz zhizni', Ukaz Prezidiuma Verkhovnogo Soveta RSFSR 4 maia 1961 g., Sovetskaia Rossiia May 5, 1961.

76 Proponents of anti-parasite legislation claimed that it was successfull in that it had a largely prophylactic effect: under the threat

of the decrees a great many parasites bettered their lives and were not sent into exile; others found a job after having been warned. See I. D. Petrov, Sud i obshchestvennost' v bor'be s tuneiadtsami, Moscow 1962, pp. 19-20. Anti-parasite decrees were also 'successfully' applied to the persecution of religious believers and a number of dissident writers.

77 See Armstrong, pp. 175-178.

78 Ibid., p. 179. For a description of anti-parasite proceedings, see Andrei Amalrik's book Involuntary Journey to Siberia, New York 1970. Amalrik was sentenced to 2½ years banishment with corrective labour by a Moscow court in May 1965.

79 Barry & Berman, p. 328. Since 1965 the RSFSR decree has once more been changed on February 25, 1970 (Vedomosti Verkhovnogo Soveta RSFSR 1970:14, pp. 176-177). Anti-parasite proceedings are now to be initiated by 'the organs of internal affairs' and parasites are to be placed at local places of employment upon decision of the local soviet's executive committee. The decree has repeatedly been used as as a means to threaten Jews after the application for an exit visa had made them jobless.

80 'Law on the strengthening of the ties of the school with life and on the future development of the public education system in the USSR', December 24, 1958; translated in S. G. Shapovalenko (Ed.), Polytechnical education in the U.S.S.R., Paris (UNESCO) 1963, pp. 375-389. Other sources on which this case study is based are Donald R. Kelley, 'Interest Groups in the USSR: The Impact of Political Sensitivity on Group Influence', The Journal of Politics Vol. 34 (August 1972), pp. 860-888; Joel J. Schwartz and William R. Keech, 'Public Influence and Educational Policy in the Soviet Union', in Roger E. Kanet (Ed.), The Behavioral Revolution and Communist Studies, New York 1971, pp. 151-186; Nicholas De Witt, Education and Professional Employment in the USSR, Washington D.C. (NSF/GPO) 1961, pp. 9-21; Gerlind Schmidt, Die polytechnische Bildung in der Sowjetunion und in der DDR. Didaktische Konzeptionen und Losungsversuche, Berlin 1973.

81 Jerry Hough has compared the laws of the USSR and fourteen republics

with that of the RSFSR in De Witt, pp. 556-574. All but three of the laws of the republics were passed in April, 1959.

82 Schwartz & Keech, p. 153.

83 The proceedings were published at the time of the Twentieth Party Congress in *Politekhnicheskoe obuchenie v srednei shkole, iz opyta raboty gorodskikh i sel'skikh shkol*, Moscow 1956 (signed for the press February 16, 1956).

84 Khrushchev in his report of the Central Committee to the Twentieth Party Congress, as translated by Shapovalenko, p. 50.

85 *Pravda-Izvestia* February 25, 1956, translated in Leo Gruliow (Ed.), *Current Soviet Policies II*, New York 1957, p. 193.

86 Schmidt, p. 88, note 3.

87 See *Materialy novosibirskoi nauchnoi konferentsii Akademii Pedagogicheskikh Nauk po voprosam politekhnicheskogo obucheniia, 13-16 maia 1957 goda*, Moscow 1958 (Signed for the press December 20, 1958).

88 De Witt, pp. 10, 12.

89 *Pravda-Izvestia* April 19; translation *CDSP* Vol. X, No. 17, p. 18.

90 Ibid., p. 17.

91 Ibid., p. 18.

92 Kelley, p. 867.

93 'Ob ukreplenii sviazi shkoly s zhizn'iu i o dal'neishem razvitii sistemy narodnogo obrazovaniia v strane (Predlozheniia, izlozhennye v publikuemoi zapiske tovarishcha N. S. Khrushcheva, odobreny Prezidiumom TsK KPSS)', *Pravda* September 21, 1958. The Memorandum was signed N. Khrushchev. At the end of it he proposed the scenario that was actually followed: Central Committee Plenary Meeting, nationwide discussion, Supreme Soviet session, and implementation through laws of the republics.

94 *Pravda-Izvestia* November 14 & 16, 1958.

95 1959 Yearbook of the *Bol'shaia Sovetskaia Ėntsiklopediia*, Moscow 1959, p. 9.

96 *Pravda-Izvestia* August 24, 1958; translation *CDSP* Vol. X, No. 34, p. 3.

97 *Komsomol'skaia Pravda* September 10, 1958; translation *CDSP* Vol. X,

No. 35, p. 3.

98 Pravda September 21, 1958; translation CDSP Vol. X, No. 38, p. 4.

99 Pravda-Izvestia November 16, 1958; translation CDSP Vol. X, No. 46, p. 6.

100 Kelley, p. 873.

101 Kelley, p. 875.

102 Joint resolution of the Party Central Committee and the USSR Council of Ministers, published in Pravda August 13, 1964. See Nicholas De Witt, 'Recent Changes in Soviet Educational Policy', in Denis Dirscherl, S. J. (Ed.), The New Russia. Communism in Evolution, Dayton Ohio 1968, pp. 73-85.

103 E. I. Afanasenko in Uchitel'skaia Gazeta, August 13, 1964, as translated by De Witt, 'Recent changes...', p. 78.

104 Stewart, 'Soviet Interest Groups...'.

105 The main sources used in this case study are John Löwenhardt, 'De vervuiling van het Bajkalmeer', Internationale Spectator Vol. XXVI, No. 2 (January 22, 1972), pp. 146-174; Baikal i problema chistoi vody v Sibiri, Irkutsk 1968; Boris Komarov, Unichtozhenie prirody. Obostrenie ėkologicheskogo krizisa v SSSR, Frankfurt a.M. 1978, pp. 5-30 (English edition The Destruction of Nature in the Soviet Union, White Plains N.Y. and London 1980); Marshall I. Goldman, The Spoils of Progress. Environmental Pollution in the Soviet Union, Cambridge Mass. 1972, pp. 178-209; Donald R. Kelley, 'Environmental Policy-Making in the USSR: the Role of Industrial and Environmental Interest Groups', Soviet Studies Vol. XXVIII, No. 4 (October 1976), pp. 570-589.

106 Goldman, p. 182.

107 'Ob okhrane i ispol'zovanii prirodnykh bogatstv v basseine ozera Baikal', May 9, 1960; see Okhrana Prirody. Sbornik Zakonodatel'nykh Aktov, Moscow 1961, pp. 124-126.

108 Ibid., article 7, p. 125.

109 A. A. Grigor'eva, Narodnoe khoziaistvo Irkutskoi oblasti, Irkutsk 1973, p. 99.

110 Razvitie proizvoditel'nykh sil Vostochnoi Sibiri. IX: Lesnoe khoz-

iaistvo i lesnaia promyshlennost', Moscow 1960, note 1 on pp. 141-2.

111 Goldman, p. 183.

112 O. Serova and S. Sarkisian, Zhemchuzhina Vostochnoi Sibiri, Ulan Udė 1961, p. 162.

113 Komsomol'skaia Pravda May 11, 1966.

114 Baikal i problema..., p. 3.

115 K. V. Mataruev, 'Ochistka promyshlennykh stochnykh vod Baikal'skogo Tselliuloznogo Zavoda', Khimicheskaia Pererabotka Drevesiny, Sbornik 31 (1964), pp. 3-6.

116 Boris Komarov is the pen-name of a 'prominent Soviet specialist on nature conservation' living in the USSR. Unfortunately for the Western researcher, Komarov is often more outraged than he is precise. His account is more of an indictment than an accurate history of the pollution of Lake Baikal. In particular, it is a pity that he has not indicated the exact names, dates of installation and dissolution and membership of the two special commissions. As a consequence, it is difficult to establish the interrelationships between these two commissions and the other commissions that have been known to exist, or to determine in what way the 1968 report of the Limnological Institute was related to the findings of the First Special Commission. Perhaps this report was in fact the first, second or third version of the report of the First Special Commission of the Academy of Sciences?

117 Komarov, p. 12.

118 VAN 1967:6, p. 3; see also the 1966 yearbook of the Bol'shaia Sovetskaia Ėntsiklopediia. In October 1966 Irkutsk hosted a great number of Siberian fishery managers, scientists and conservationists for a conference on the biological productivity of Siberian waters, organized by Galazii's institute. Among other problems, the results of the research projects on the influence of waste discharge on Lake Baikal were discussed here. See Soveshchanie po biologicheskoi produktivnosti vodoemov Sibiri. Kratkoe soderzhanie dokladov, Irkutsk 1966.

119 Komsomol'skaia Pravda May 11, 1966.

120 Komarov, pp. 12-13.

121 Baikal i problema..., pp. 51-52.

122 See especially Baikal i problema...; my study, pp. 159-160; and Kelley, p. 584.

123 'O merakh po sokhraneniiu i ratsional'nomu ispol'zovaniiu prirodnykh kompleksov basseina ozera Baikal', January 21, 1969; in Resheniia partii i pravitel'stva po khoziaistvennym voprosam Vol. 7, Moscow 1970, pp. 255-259.

124 'O dopolnitel'nykh merakh po obespecheniiu ratsional'nogo ispol'zovaniia i sokhraneniiu prirodnykh bogatstv basseina ozera Baikal', Spravochnik partiinogo rabotnika, Moscow 1972, pp. 76-78. The resolution dates from June 16, 1971; the fact that he has found the text in Sotsialisticheskaia Industriia of September 24, 1971, has led Marshall Goldman to the wrong conclusion that the decision dates from September 1971; Goldman, p. 208.

125 Pravda November 20, 1974 and Literaturnaia Gazeta December 4, 1974, p. 11. See also D. P. Nikitin, Iu. V. Novikov, G. P. Zarubin, Nauchno-tekhnicheskii progress. Priroda i chelovek, Moscow 1977, pp. 125-126.

126 Komarov gives as dates of the Second Special Commission's report alternatively 1975-1976 (p. 15) and 1977 (p. 9). In Literaturnaia Gazeta of December 4, 1974 the USSR deputy minister of Land Reclamation and Water Management I. Borodavchenko declared that this commission would complete its investigations 'in one to one and a half year', i.e. in the first half of 1976.

127 Komarov, p. 9.

128 Komarov, p. 15.

129 G. I. Galazii, 'Ėkosistema Baikala i problema ee okhrany', Priroda 1978:8, pp. 44-56. See also P. N. Shternov, 'Baikal segodnia', Priroda 1978:8, p. 57, and the interview of Grigorii Galazii in Sovetskaia Rossiia March 18, 1979.

130 A. A. Trofimuk, 'Strategiia nauchnogo nastupleniia', Kommunist 1977:18, pp. 41-44 (p. 44); In the article mentioned in note 129, Galazii by mistake attributes this statement to D. K. Beliaev, Chief

Scientific Secretary of the Siberian Department. Galazii refers to Beliaev's article which begins on p. 44 of Kommunist 1977:18.

131 William Korey, 'Soviet Decision-Making and the Problems of Jewish Emigration Policy', Survey Vol. 22, No. 1 (Winter 1976), pp. 112-131; Leonard Schroeter, The Last Exodus, New York 1974. Other sources used for this case study are William Korey, The Soviet Cage. Anti-Semitism in Russia, New York 1973; George Ginsburgs, 'Soviet Law and the Emigration of Soviet Jews', Soviet Jewish Affairs Vol. 3, No. 1 (1973), pp. 3-19.

132 Korey, The Soviet Cage, p. 172-173. Kosygin's declaration was made at a Paris press conference.

133 Schroeter, p. 141.

134 See Telford Taylor, Courts of Terror. Soviet Criminal Justice and Jewish Emigration, New York 1976, pp. 8-9.

135 Schroeter, p. 328. See also the testimony of Viktor Polskii in Christian Jelen et Léopold Unger, Le grand retour, Paris 1977, pp. 215-216.

136 Korey, The Soviet Cage, p. 180.

137 Ibid., p. 181.

138 Ibid.

139 Ibid., p. 182.

140 Data on the number of exit visa applications that have been filed with OVIR are not available. Brezhnev has claimed in 1973, during his visit to the United States, that 95 percent of the applications were granted, but his claim has been judged a gross exaggeration by experts such as Korey and Schroeter.

141 Rolf W. Schloss, Lass mein Volk ziehen. Die russischen Juden zwischen Sowjetstern und Davidstern. Eine Dokumentation, Munich and Vienna 1971, pp. 296-310.

3 Group Influence in Soviet Decision Making

1 Stewart, 'Soviet Interest Groups...', p. 42.

2 Stewart distinguishes (p. 42) 'opinion groupings' from 'political interest groupings'. The first direct their activities towards 'persons who are not authoritative decision-makers in the issue area concerned', the second 'exist when the information communicated by an opinion-grouping is received by the relevant official decision-makers.' This implies that some opinion groupings turn into political interest groupings, while others do not. I believe this distinction to be unnecessarily confusing. 'My' opinion groups communicate their demands both towards persons and groups who are not decision makers (in order to gain support), ánd towards decision makers; they remain opinion groups even after their demands have been heard, accepted or implemented.

3 Slovar' sovremennogo russkogo literaturnogo iazyka, t. 8, Moscow-Leningrad 1959, column 527-528.

4 Paraphrasing Karl Deutsch (The Nerves of Government, New York 1963), Stewart has written that 'communication of an opinion on a public issue through public media is the essential activity of opinion groupings. It is precisely this activity that constitutes the grouping...'. Stewart, 'Soviet Interest Groups...', pp. 44-45.

5 Published in Uchitel'skaia Gazeta November 28, 1963.

6 That the two cases studied here are not exceptions, may be learned from D. Richard Little, who has investigated the composition and operation of the Supreme Soviet's standing committees. He has found that 'Typically, a legislative proposal assigned to a given committee will activate a broad range of individuals who will be directly involved in studying and analyzing the proposal. Government and Party officials, academic consultants, practical workers in the particular field, other deputies, representatives of major organizations and individual specialists will play important roles, along with committee members, in considering the matter... The consequence of all this is both to provide broad participation in the discussion of important legislative proposals, and to diminish the importance

of committee members in the process. D. Richard Little, 'Soviet parliamentary committees after Khrushchev: obstacles and opportunities', Soviet Studies Vol. XXIV, No. 1 (July 1972), pp. 41-60 (p. 51). Memoirs of Party and state officials such as Nikita Khrushchev, Vasilii Emelianov and Arseni Zverev have documented that under Stalin such hearings (organized by other institutions than the Supreme Soviet) also took place. See G. P. van den Berg, De regering van Rusland en de Sowjet Unie, Leyden 1977, and my book on the Politburo (note 29 of Ch. 1), pp. 122-125.

7 Stewart, 'Soviet Interest Groups...', pp. 31-32.

8 Schwartz & Keech, p. 177.

9 Alfred G. Meyer, The Soviet Political System. An Interpretation, New York 1965, p. 384.

10 Cobb & Elder, pp. 82-85.

11 Cobb & Elder, p. 83.

12 Cobb & Elder, p. 44.

13 Lindblom, The Policy-Making Process, p. 13.

14 Schwartz & Keech, pp. 153, 155.

15 Stewart, 'Soviet Interest Groups...', p. 34.

16 The suggestion is from Robert Miller, One Hundred Thousand Tractors.

17 See p. 5 . The demand to be allowed to emigrate was unorthodox in the view of Soviet decision makers, not in the view of the Jews themselves: they merely wanted to leave, they did not want to change the system. The cleavage between the Jewish emigration movement and the dissident movement in the USSR can probably partly be explained by this fact. A deep involvement with criticism of the Soviet system would, in the perception of the Jews, have made it more difficult for them to obtain exit visa.

18 See Juviler, 'Family Reforms...', pp. 37-39. On the transfer of the issue to the formal agenda during the February 1957 session of the USSR Supreme Soviet, Juviler writes that 'the true origin of the legislative initiative' of Pusep and Rumiantsev 'lies... somewhere between Party fiat and the deputies' own discretion.' I have not been able to find corroborating evidence for his tentative conclu-

sion that the activities of Pusep and Rumiantsev were coordinated and related to a movement in the Party top. What I have found is a marked difference in the way Rumiantsev's words were reported. According to the official report, cited by Juviler but not available to me, he said:

> What is to be done about the legal status of children born out of registered marriage? By recognizing only registered marriage, the edict of the Presidium of the U.S.S.R. Supreme Soviet of July 8, 1944, puts the children born out of registered marriage in a different position from that of children born in registered marriage.

(Zasedaniia Verkhovnogo Soveta SSSR, chetvertogo sozyva, shestaia sessiia, 5-12 fevralia 1957 g.: Stenograficheskii otchet, Moscow 1957, pp. 471, 512-513, as cited by Juviler, p. 38.) This section has been left out of the text of Rumiantsev's speech as printed in Izvestia February 12, 1957, p. 7. Pravda, however, printed the following text in its February 11, 1957 issue: Rumiantsev indicated that

> recently the obshchestvennost' is persistently reverting to the idea of restoring family law as it has existed in the past, as it was expressed in the first decrees of 1918, signed by Lenin. This law allowed for the equality of all children, irrespective of their parents' relations.

In this version Rumiantsev implied that the decree of July 1944 was un-leninist. In retrospect it seems probable that the Pravda text of February 11 (which was not presented as a literal transcript but in the form of a report) corresponded with what Rumiantsev had said; when editors of Izvestia realized the radical implications of his words, they may have decided to omit the sensitive passage. Finally, in the official text published later during the year a neutral compromise text acceptable to both Rumiantsev and his opponents, was printed.

19 Robert A. Dahl, Modern Political Analysis, Englewood Cliffs N.J. 1963 (first edition) and 1976 (third edition).

20 Dahl 1976, p. 31.

21 Dahl 1976, p. 30.

22 Solomon, p. 128.

23 Stewart, 'Soviet Interest Groups...', pp. 47-49. The definition of influence is adapted from Robert E. Agger, Daniel Goldrich and Bert E. Swanson, The Rulers and the Ruled. Political Power and Impotence in American Communities, New York 1964, p. 51.

24 Details on the daily work of editors and censors and on the imperfectness of the censorship system can be found in Dewhirst & Farrell and in my article on the colophon. An example of the outcome of the 'elbowroom' of editors and censors is to be found in Dina Spechler, 'Elite Images and Soviet Foreign Policy', Soviet Union/Union Sovietique Vol. 5, Part 1 (1978), pp. 36-73. Ms. Spechler has documented marked differences in the treatment and appraisal of détente as a Soviet foreign policy objective during the October 1973 Middle East War between Pravda, Izvestia, Krasnaia Zvezda, Sovetskaia Rossiia, Komsomol'skaia Pravda and Trud.

25 One would of course assume that potential influence as defined here is a necessary precondition for actual influence. But concepts may be operationalized in different ways and empirical research will have to show whether or not a specific operationalization is correct. If we find instances of actual influence without potential influence, the operationalization of this concept would have to be changed.

26 Dahl distinguishes rational persuasion, where the persuading actor provides only truthful information, from manipulative persuasion where the persuading actor intentionally violates the truth in his communications (Dahl 1976, pp. 45-46). An important technique where these two types of persuasion are often intertwined, is policy analysis. Policy analysis is a technique according to which the influencing actor presents his arguments in such way that the policy he desires to be implemented is shown to contribute to the values and policy goals of the actor whom he tries to influence. It plays at least as important a role in Soviet decision making as it does in non-communist polities because in order to gain acceptability for orthodox decision making 'selfish' interests need to be translated into 'unselfish' interests, i.e. in terms of the general interest. The nine case studies of Chapter 2 have not shown the full richness

of policy analysis in Soviet policy debates because for the sake of brevity most arguments had to be left out. For policy analyses the sources used in that Chapter may be consulted, in addition to Chapter 4 of this book. On policy analysis, see Lindblom, The Policy-Making Process, pp. 32-33.

27 Martha Dethrick, The National Guard in Politics, Cambridge Mass. 1965, p. 7, as quoted by Graham Wootton, Interest Groups, Englewood Cliffs N.J. 1970, p. 74.

28 Kelley, 'Interest Groups in the USSR...', p. 864.

29 Schwartz & Keech, p. 160.

30 Stewart, 'Soviet Interest Groups...', p. 32.

31 The drafts were printed in the republican newspapers of April 3 (Estonia), 11 (Latvia), 17 (Azerbaidzhan), 18 (Lithuania), 23 (Kirgizia), 26 (Uzbekistan), May 5 (Kazakhstan) and 10 (Tadzhikistan). In this period the national press was engaged in a major economic discussion , viz. on the impending Sovnarkhozy reform. Khrushchev's theses on the reform had been published in Izvestia of March 30, and the discussion lasted from that day up to May 7. The Sovnarkhozy law was accepted by the Supreme Soviet on May 10 (see the section on the Sovnarkhozy reform in Chapter 2).

32 A.o. Linden, pp. 7-8; Brzezinski & Huntington, pp. 193, 198. In the conception of Brzezinski and Huntington the opportunities for influencing policy making are limited to a succession crisis or 'serious power struggle'.

33 Schwartz & Keech, p. 177.

34 Kelley, 'Interest Groups in the USSR...', p. 863.

35 Ibid., p. 886.

4 The Reorganization of the USSR Academy of Sciences, 1954-1961

1 Izvestia April 13, 1961.

2 For a description of the impact of the reorganization, see one of the last paragraphs of this chapter, pp. 173-180 and 224-226.

3 Loren R. Graham, 'Reorganization of the U.S.S.R. Academy of Sciences', in Juviler & Morton, pp. 133-161.

4 Graham, p. 138.

5 Graham, p. 139.

6 Khrushchev added that 'We shall ask the USSR Academy of Sciences, its Presidium, to draft proposals for further improving the activity of the Academy', cited by Graham, p. 139.

7 Linda Lubrano Greenberg, 'Policy-making in the USSR Academy of Sciences', Journal of Contemporary History Vol. 8, No. 4 (1973), pp. 67-80.

8 This summary description is based on the author's case study 'The reorganization of the USSR Academy of Sciences, 1954 - 1961', unpublished manuscript.

9 For details on the privileges of Academy members, see Alexander Vucinich, The Soviet Academy of Sciences, Stanford 1956, pp. 90-97, and Zhores A. Medvedev, Soviet Science, New York 1978. Other sources used in the writing of this section are Ustavy Akademii Nauk SSSR, Moscow 1974; Wolfgang Kasack, Die Akademie der Wissenschaften der UdSSR, Wiesbaden 1972^2, pp. 22-28; and Science Policy in the USSR, Paris (OECD) 1969, pp. 207-221.

10 Ustavy..., p. 197.

11 Ibid., p. 196.

12 Vucinich, p. 33.

13 Ibid., p. 34; according to dr. Alexander Lerner this overstates the issue since the Central Committee's Science Department has direct access to all institutions of the Academy and the secretaries usually enjoy only limited authority in the scientific community. Interview with dr. Alexander Iakovlevich Lerner (born in Vinnitsa, 1913). Dr. Lerner has worked at the Institute of Automation and Remote Control of the USSR Academy of Sciences since the early 1950s, first as a starshii nauchnyi sotrudnik, then as a laboratory head and later as head of the Department of Large Scale Systems Control. He has been member of a number of advisory committees and editorial boards of scientific journals. Dr. Lerner is a cyberneti-

cist and, since 1954, Doctor of Technical Sciences. Academicians Vadim Trapeznikov (Director of IAT), Vladimir Kirillin (Chief of Science Department of the CPSU Central Committee Secretariat) and Boris Petrov (presently chief of the space program) were among his best friends. In 1971 dr. Lerner was dismissed from his job and all other positions after he had applied for an exit visa to Israel. The interview took place on August 14, 1979, in dr. Lerner's apartment in Moscow.

14 For a distinction of the different research establishments in the Academy, see the paragraph on the Impact, pp. 175 - 177.

15 Ustavy..., note 121, p. 200.

16 Ustavy..., pp. 148, 197; a corresponding article was missing from the 1959 Charter.

17 See Alexander Vucinich, Science in Russian Culture 1861 - 1917, Stanford Calif. 1970, p. 220.

18 See my calculations in one of the last paragraphs of this chapter. Alexander Lerner claims that the greater part of the Academy's resources was granted to the applied sciences, whereas 'for the fundamental sciences the amount of resources... became smaller and smaller every year'.

19 In search for answers to these and similar questions, I have written to both Academician Nesmeianov and Academician Semenov in the summer of 1976. A reply was received only from Nesmeianov, who declined to answer my questions because of lack of time. In the summer of 1979 I tried to interview Nesmeianov, Semenov and Vladimir Kirillin, but in spite of the support which I received from the Royal Netherlands Academy of Sciences and Her Majesty's Embassy in Moscow, the USSR Academy of Sciences' Presidium said it could not arrange for such interviews. Academician B. M. Kedrov agreed to meet me, but declined to answer my questions since he 'was afraid that he might not remember well enough to give me the correct answers'. I then made an interview with the cyberneticist dr. Alexander Lerner, who has been head of a department of the Academy's Institute of Automation and Remote Control; see note 13 of this chapter.

20 Interview with Alexander Lerner, see note 13 of this chapter.

21 VAN 1956:6, p. 35, italics mine.

22 VAN 1956:3, p. 14.

23 Pravda February 19, 1956; translation CDSP Vol. VIII, No. 9, p. 23.

24 Pravda February 6, 1956. In his report to the Congress Khrushchev complained about 'the weak contact between many scientific establishments and practical work, production. Some scientific institutes are working on problems that are not of great practical significance and are not generalizing the advanced experience of our development... This incorrect state of affairs must be rectified; scientific research institutions and higher educational establishments must be brought closer to production'. The next paragraph from Khrushchev's long report has been quoted by Graham as an indication that, in his opinion, Khrushchev wanted reforms in the activity of the Academy:

> The lack of concert in the work of research institutes of the Academy of Sciences, industrial research institutes and higher educational establishments is utterly intolerable. This lack of contact and absence of coordination in work hinders the concentration of scientific forces on the solution of the most important scientific and technical problems, gives rise to harmful parallelism, leads to waste and hampers the application of scientific and technological discoveries in the national economy.

Pravda February 15, 1956, translation CDSP Vol. VIII, No. 5, p. 12. See also Loren Graham, 'Reorganization...', p. 138.

25 Interview with Alexander Lerner, see note 13 of this chapter.

26 This is also the view of Linda Lubrano Greenberg, in 'Soviet Science Specialists: professional roles and policy involvement', in Richard B. Remnek (Ed.), Social Scientists and Policy Making in the USSR, New York 1977, pp. 59-85 (pp. 71, 82).

27 See Abdurakhman Avtorkhanov, The Communist Party Apparatus, Chicago 1966, for some remarks on the history of aktivy.

28 Article 24 in 'Ustav VKP(b), priniat edinoglasno XVIII s"ezdom VKP(b)', in XVIII S"ezd Vsesoiuznoi Kommunisticheskoi Partii (b), 10-21 marta 1939 g., Stenograficheskii Otchet, Moscow 1939, p. 680. Article 29 of the present Rules is a revised form of this article.

29 Great Soviet Encyclopedia Vol. I, New York & London 1973, p. 86.

30 Only the Academy Charter which was in force between 1959 and 1963 mentioned aktiv meetings explicitly: 'The Presidium of the USSR Academy of Sciences convenes, jointly with social organizations, meetings of the aktivy of scientists of the Academy of Sciences' establishments.' Art. 41 i., Ustavy Akademii Nauk SSSR, p. 159.

31 VAN 1956:6, p. 4.

32 Ibid., p. 35.

33 Ibid., p. 42.

34 P. L. Kapitsa, 'O liderstve v nauke; Vystuplenie na sobranii aktiva Akademii Nauk SSSR, 1956', in P. L. Kapitsa, Eksperiment, teoriia, praktika. Stat'i, vystupleniia, Izd. vtoroe, Moscow 1977, pp. 132-139. The first edition was published in 1966. From the text of this speech it could be established that it was read not before February 20, 1956. I have written that it was probably delivered at the Moscow meeting since it was apparently read at a sobranie aktiva in 1956. It remains possible that the speech was read in Leningrad or Novosibirsk, though Kapitsa worked in Moscow.

35 VAN 1956:6, p. 48.

36 Published in VAN 1956:7, p. 68 (Leningrad), 1956:8, pp. 81-82 (Novosibirsk) and 1956:9, pp. 85-86 (Moscow).

37 VAN 1956:11, p. 9. Tamm and some of his colleagues of the Physics-Mathematics Department used the occasion of the re-election of Alexander Nesmeianov to raise this issue.

38 Pravda May 7, 1957; translation CDSP Vol. IX, No. 18, p. 19.

39 'Rezoliutsiia po dokladu tovarishcha N. S. Khrushcheva "O kontrol'nykh tsifrakh razvitiia Narodnogo Khoziaistva SSSR na 1959 - 1965 godu"', in Materialy Vneocherednogo XXI S"ezda KPSS, Moscow 1959, pp. 139-165 (p. 152).

40 The consistent pattern of ranking Academy departments was as follows:

1. Physical-Mathematical Sciences
2. Chemical Sciences
3. Geographical-Geological Sciences
4. Biological Sciences
5. Technical Sciences
6. Historical Sciences
7. Economics, Philosophy and Law
8. Literature and Language.

41 Pravda March 16, 1959.

42 VAN 1959:4, p. 64; translation CDSP Vol. XI, No. 25, p. 9.

43 Pravda March 13, 1959 and March 16, 1959.

44 VAN 1959:4, p. 64-72; translation CDSP Vol. XI, No. 25, pp. 9-11 (p. 11).

45 Ibid., italics mine. All four institutes were among the Technical Science Department institutes that were eventually removed from the Academy's jurisdiction in the 1961 reform.

46 Ibid., italics mine.

47 Ibid., p. 9.

48 'Rech tov. Semenova, N. N.', in Plenum TsK KPSS 24 - 29 Iiunia 1959 g. Stenograficheskii Otchet, Moscow 1959, pp. 627-635 (p. 629).

49 This explanation was supported by Alexander Lerner. The two sentences in question were left out of the Pravda and Izvestia reports although both the preceding and the following paragraphs were almost identical to those reported in the Verbatim Report.

50 Pravda August 10, 1959; translation Survey of the Soviet Press 1959:121, pp. 17-19.

51 Izvestia August 28, 1959. Contrary to what Loren Graham believes, I consider it improbable that Bardin 'evidently failed to note that Semenov's reference to the Academy's traditional concentration on pure science was almost a direct quotation from Khrushchev's speech of June 29, 1959...' (Graham, 'Reorganization...', p. 142). At the beginning of his article Bardin referred to this speech and claimed that Semenov's article of August 9 was 'a living response of a Soviet scientist to what comrade Nikita Sergeevich Khrushchev demanded of science in his speech on the CC CPSU June Plenum.' Moreover, Khrushchev had said very little on the subject of science; his words constitute only a few paragraphs in the verbatim report. It seems improbable that Bardin did not read these lines very carefully. Graham was wrong in writing that Bardin was the 'head of the Department of Technical Sciences' ('Reorganization...', p. 142). Bardin never held that position.

52 Izvestia September 6, 1959; translation CDSP Vol. XI, No. 36, p. 21.

53 Literaturnaia Gazeta September 10, 1959. At the June Plenum Khrushchev had said that 'After all, these areas were not within the Academy's domain before.'

54 Ibid.

55 Interview with Alexander Lerner, see note 13 of this chapter.

56 Izvestia October 21, 1959.

57 Ibid.

58 In November 1961 the new Academy President M. Keldysh said that 'the Academy of Sciences maintains scientific-methodological direction over those removed institutes whose... work is the most closely related to the natural sciences (the institutes of Automation and Remote Control, Acoustics, Precision Machanics and Computer Engineering, and the Institute of Mineralogy, Geochemistry and Crystallochemistry of Rare Elements.' VAN 1961:12, p. 14.

59 VAN 1960:5, pp. 32-61 (pp. 48-51 on the Technical Sciences Department's General Meeting.

60 VAN 1960:4, pp. 63-69 (p. 67).

61 Interview with Alexander Lerner, see note 13 of this chapter.

62 Pravda April 11, 1961.

63 Ustavy..., p. 202, note 128.

64 'O merakh po uluchsheniiu koordinatsii nauchno-issledovatel'skikh rabot v strane i deiatel'nosti Akademii Nauk SSSR', in Spravochnik partiinogo rabotnika 1963, Moscow 1963, pp. 397-403.

65 Ibid., p. 398.

66 Ibid., p. 401.

67 According to Ustavy..., p. 202, note 128.

68 Paragraph 38 in the 1935 Charter, Par. 39 in the 1959 Charter. See also Ustavy..., pp. 196-197, note 103.

69 Khrushchev Remembers. The Last Testament, p. 61.

70 Ibid.

71 At the July 1960 Central Committe Plenum Alexander Nesmeianov had said that the branches of the Academy could be abolished. See Plenum TsK KPSS 13-16 iiulia 1960 g., Moscow 1960, pp. 231-238.

72 Pravda June 13, 1961. Two were candidate members. One of the eleven,

O. V. Kuusinen, was not present in the picture of the conference Presidium and its honor-guests in VAN 1961:7, pp. 12-13, though the picture was almost identical to the one in Pravda of June 13.

73 S. N. Simakov; see VAN 1961:7, p. 45.

74 Pravda June 13, 1961; translation CDSP Vol. XIII, No. 24, pp. 10-11.

75 Bukharin at the first Nationwide Conference on the Planning of Science, April 6-11, 1931, in Moscow, as cited by Graham, The Soviet Academy..., p. 57.

76 VAN 1961:7, p. 78.

77 VAN 1961:7, pp. 90-106; translation CDSP Vol. XIII, No. 24, pp. 13-15 (p. 15).

78 Pravda-Izvestia June 15, 1961.

79 VAN 1961:12, pp. 13-14.

80 G. D. Komkov, O. M. Karpenko, B. V. Levshin, L. K. Semenov, Akademiia Nauk SSSR - shtab sovetskoi nauki, Moscow 1968, pp. 157-158 and 200. At pp. 157-158 the 'obshchaia chislennost' sotrudnikov' is given as 20.500 persons, at p. 200 the total number of 'rabotniki' as 'more than 20.000 persons'. Paul K. Urban and Andrew I. Lebed are wrong when, in Soviet Science 1917 - 1970, Part 1 (Metuchen N.J. 1971), p. 35, they claim on the basis of the Komkov/Karpenko book that 20.500 of the Academy's scientific personnel was transferred with the 92 institutions. At the end of 1960 the scientific personnel of the Academy (i.e. nauchnye rabotniki) numbered 23.771, according to Narodnoe Khoziaistvo v 1960 g., p. 787.

81 Alexander Korol, Soviet Research and Development: its Organization, Personnel and Funds, Cambridge Mass. 1965, p. 8.

82 During 1961 seven new Academy institutes were established, four of them in the Siberian Department. See VAN 1962:3, p. 9.

83 Investigation of a number of different sources has permitted me to establish the names of 20 of the 51 institutes that were transferred from the Academy. They are listed on the following page.

Acoustics Institute (DPhMS)
Institute of Automation and Remote Control (DTS);
Institute of Motors (DTS);
Institute of Electromechanics (DTS);
Institute of Electronic Control Machines (DTS);
G. M. Krzhizhanovskii Power Engineering Institute (DTS);
Institute of Geology and Processing of Mineral Fuels (DGGS);
Hydrochemical Institute (DChS);
A. A. Skochinskii Institute of Mining (DTS);
Institute of Mineral Fuels (DTS);
Institute of Art History (DHS);
Forest and Woodchemistry Institute (DBS);
Institute of Machine Science (DTS);
V. A. Obruchev Permafrost Institute (DGGS);
A. A. Baikov Institute of Metallurgy (DTS);
Institute of Mineralogy, Geochemistry and Crystallochemistry of Rare Elements (DGGS);
V. V. Dokuchaev Soil Science Institute (DBS);
Institute of Applied Geophysics (DPhMS);
V. G. Khlopin Radium Institute (DChS);
Institute of Precision Mechanics and Computer Engineering (DPhMS);

DPhMS - Department of Physical-Mathematical Sciences.
DTS - Department of Technical Sciences.
DGGS - Department of Geological-Geographical Sciences.
DChS - Department of Chemical Sciences.
DHS - Department of Historical Sciences.
DBS - Department of Biological Sciences.

Among the other institutions were:

Laboratory of Aeromethods (DGGS);
Central Research Laboratory for Electrical Processing of Metals (DTS);
F. P. Savarenskii Laboratory of Hydrogeological Problems (DGGS);
Laboratory of Sedimentary Minerals (DGGS);
Limnological Laboratory (DGGS);
High Temperatures Laboratory (?);
Museum for the History of Religion and Atheism (DHS);
The Ural, Kola, Karelian, Bashkir, Kazan', Komi and Dagestan Branches of the USSR Academy of Sciences with a total of 60 scientific establishments.

Uncertainty remains on the fate of the following institutions:

Radio Engineering Institute (?);
Alpine Geophysics Institute (DPhMS);
Laboratory of Electric Welding Machines (DTS?);
Magnetics Laboratory (?);
I. V. Kurchatov Atomic Energy Institute (?);
Institute for Theoretical and Experimental Physics (?).

The government organizations to which these institutes and laboratories were removed in 1961 and 1962 include the following:

USSR State Committee on Automation and Machine Building; USSR State Committee on Fuel Industry; USSR State Production Committee on Energy and Electrification; USSR State Committee on Ferrous and Non-Ferrous Metallurgy; USSR State Committee on the Use of Atomic Energy; USSR State Geological Committee; USSR Main Hydrometeorological Administration; USSR Ministry of Instrument Building, Means of Automatisation and Management Systems; RSFSR State Committee for the Coordination of Scientific Research.

84 Korol, pp. 167-168.

85 VAN 1962:3, p. 9.

86 VAN 1962:3, p. 9.

87 E. Zaleski et al., Science Policy in the USSR, Paris (OECD) 1969, Part 1, Table 9, note 24 comes to the same conclusion, though the author does not make this assumption.

88 Kommunist 1957:13, pp. 70-84; translation CDSP Vol. IX, No. 41, pp. 3-8, 34 (p. 3).

89 Sovetskaia nauka i tekhnika za 50 let. VIII: Puti razvitiia tekhniki v SSSR, Moscow 1967, p. 258.

90 VAN 1961:8, pp. 17-21 (p. 18).

91 For the history of the Party program, see Wolfgang Leonhard, 'Adoption of the New Party Programme', in Leonard Schapiro (Ed.), The USSR and the Future. An Analysis of the New Program of the CPSU, New York & London 1963, pp. 3-22.

92 'Programma Kommunisticheskoi Partii Sovetskogo Soiuza', Pravda November 2, 1961.

93 Ibid., translation Leonard Schapiro (Ed.), op. cit., Appendix p. 306 (New Times translation of November 29, 1961).

5 Conclusions

1 Brzezinski & Huntington, p. 198.

2 Schwartz & Keech, p. 177.

Bibliography

General

Almond, Gabriel A. and G. Bingham Powell, Jr., Comparative Politics: A Developmental Approach, Boston 1966.

Bachrach, Peter, and Morton S. Baratz, 'Decisions and Non-Decision: An Analytical Framework', American Political Science Review Vol. LVII (September 1963), pp. 632-642.

Bachrach, Peter, and Morton S. Baratz, Power and Poverty. Theory and Practice, New York etc. 1970.

Barghoorn, Frederick C., Politics in the USSR, Boston & Toronto 1966.

Braybrooke, David, and Charles E. Lindblom, A Strategy of Decision. Policy Evaluation as a Social Process, London 1963.

Brown, A. H., Soviet Politics and Political Science, London 1974.

Brzezinski, Zbigniew, and Samuel P. Huntington, Political Power USA / USSR, New York 1964.

Cattell, David T., Leningrad: A Case Study of Soviet Urban Government, New York & London 1968.

Cobb, Roger W., and Charles D. Elder, Participation in American Politics. The Dynamics of Agenda-Building, Baltimore & London 1972.

Cobb, Roger, Jennie-Keith Ross and Marc Howard Ross, 'Agenda Building as a Comparative Political Process', American Political Science Review 1976, No. 1, pp. 126-138.

Dahl, Robert A., Modern Political Analysis, Englewood Cliffs N.J. 1963 (1st. edition) and 1976 (3rd. edition).

Dewhirst, Martin, and Robert Farrell (Eds.), The Soviet Censorship, Metuchen N.J. 1973.

Eckstein, Harry, 'Group Theory and the Comparative Study of Pressure Groups', in Eckstein and Apter (Eds.), Comparative Politics, New York 1963.

Eijk, C. van der, and W. J. P. Kok, 'Nondecisions reconsidered', Acta Politica Vol. X, No. 3 (July 1975), pp. 277-301.

Fainsod, Merle, Smolensk under Soviet Rule, Cambridge Mass. 1958.

Fischer, George (Ed.), Science and Ideology in Soviet Society, New York 1967.

Fleron Jr., Frederic J. (Ed.), Communist Studies and the Social Sciences. Essays on Methodology and Empirical Theory, Chicago 1969.

Friedrich, Carl Joachim, Man and His Government. An Empirical Theory of Politics, New York etc. 1963.

Greenberg, Daniel S., 'The Myth of the Scientific Elite', The Public Interest No. 1 (Fall 1965), pp. 51-62.

Helmers, H. M., R. J. Mokken, R. C. Plijter, F. N. Stokman, Graven naar Macht. Op zoek naar de kern van de Nederlandse economie, m.m.v. Jac. M. Antonisse, Amsterdam 1975.

Hill, Ronald J., Soviet Political Elites. The Case of Tiraspol, London 1977.

Hirsch-Weber, Wolfgang, Politik als Interessenkonflikt, Stuttgart 1969.

Holt, Robert T., and John E. Turner (Eds.), The Methodology of Comparative Research, New York 1970.

Hough, Jerry F., The Soviet Prefects: The Local Party Organs in Industrial Decision-making, Cambridge Mass. 1969.

Hough, Jerry F., The Soviet Union and Social Science Theory, Cambridge Mass. 1977.

Kanet, Roger E., and Donna L. Bahry, 'Mitwirkung, Einfluss und Anpassung in der KPdSU. Eine Literaturübersicht', Osteuropa 1976:1, pp. 34-43.

Khrushchev Remembers. With an Introduction, Commentary and Notes by Edward Crankshaw. Translated and Edited by Strobe Talbott. Boston & Toronto 1970.

Khrushchev Remembers. The Last Testament. Translated and Edited by Strobe Talbott. With a Foreword by Edward Crankshaw and an Introduction by Jerrold L. Schechter.London 1974.

Lindblom, Charles E., The Policy-Making Process, Englewood Cliffs 1968.

Lindblom, Charles E., Toward a Theory of Economic and Political Decision-Making, Edinburgh 1976 (Xth IPSA Congress paper).

Lipset, S. M., and R. B. Dobson, 'The Intellectuals as Critic and Rebel. With Special Reference to the United States and the Soviet Union', Daedalus Vol. 101, No. 3 (Summer 1972), pp. 137-198.

Macridis, Roy, 'Interest Groups in Comparative Analysis', Journal of Politics Vol. XXIII (February 1961), pp. 25-45.

Mayer, Lawrence C., Comparative Political Inquiry. A Methodological Survey, Homewood Ill. 1972.

Meyer, Alfred, The Soviet Political System. An Interpretation, New York 1965.

Rieber, Alfred J., 'The Moscow Entrepreneurial Group: The Emergence of a New Form in Autocratic Politics', Jahrbücher für Geschichte Osteuropas Band 25, Heft 1 (1977), pp. 1-20.

Schattschneider, E. E., The Semisovereign People. A Realist's View of Democracy in America, New York 1960.

Sidjanski, Dusan (Ed.), Political Decision-Making Processes. Studies in National, Comparative and International Politics, Amsterdam etc. 1973.

Taubman, William, Governing Soviet Cities. Bureaucratic Politics and Urban Development in the USSR, New York & London 1973.

Truman, David, The Governmental Process. Political Interests and Public Opinion, New York 1951 & (2nd edition) 1971.

Wilson, James Q., Political Organizations, New York 1973.

Wootton, Graham, Interest Groups, Englewood Cliffs N.J. 1970.

Decision making in Soviet politics

Azrael, Jeremy R., 'Decision-Making in the USSR', in Richard Cornell (Ed.), The Soviet Political System: A Book of Readings, Englewood Cliffs N.J. 1970.

Brown, A. H., 'Policy Making in the Soviet Union', Soviet Studies Vol. XXIII, No. 1 (July 1971), pp. 120-148.

Brown, A. H., 'Problems of Interest Articulation and Group Influence in the Soviet Union', Government and Opposition Vol. 7, No. 2 (Spring 1972).

Buchholz, Arnold, Die Rolle der Naturwissenschaftler im Sowjetischen Entscheidungsprozess, Cologne 1973 (Berichte des Bundesinstituts für Ostwissenschaftliche und Internationale Studien, No. 44, 1973).

Bunce, Valerie, and John M. Echols III, 'From Soviet Studies to Comparative Politics: The Unfinished Revolution', Soviet Studies Vol. XXXI, No. 1 (January 1979), pp. 43-55.

Castles, Francis G., 'Interest Articulation: A Totalitarian Paradox', Survey 73 (Autumn 1969), pp. 116-132.

Cocks, Paul, 'The Policy Process and Bureaucratic Politics', in Paul Cocks, Robert V. Daniels and Nancy W. Heer (Eds.), The Dynamics of Soviet Politics, Cambridge Mass. 1976, pp. 156-178.

Conyngham, William J., Industrial Management in the Soviet Union. The Role of the CPSU in Industrial Decision-making, 1917 - 1970, Stanford Calif. 1973.

Frolic, B. Michael, 'Decision-Making in Soviet Cities', American Political Science Review 1972:1, pp. 38-52.

Graham, Loren R., 'Science Policy and Planning in the USSR', Survey 64 (July 1967), pp. 61-79.

Hough, Jerry F., 'The Soviet Experience and the Measurement of Power', Journal of Politics 1975:3, pp. 685-710.

Hough, Jerry F., 'The Soviet System: Petrification or Pluralism?', Problems of Communism March-April 1972, pp. 25-45.

Janos, Andrew C., 'Group Politics in Communist Society: A Second Look at the Pluralistic Model', in Samuel P. Huntington and Clement H. Moore (Eds.), Authoritarian Politics in Modern Society. The Dynamics of Established One-Party Systems, New York & London 1970, pp. 437-50.

Juviler, Peter H., and Henry W. Morton (Eds.), Soviet Policy-Making. Studies of Communism in Transition, London 1967.

Kelley, Donald R., 'Toward a Model of Soviet Decision Making: A Research Note', American Political Science Review 1974:2, pp. 701-06.

Kneen, P. N., Group Conflict Approach to Soviet Union. Theories and Approaches to Soviet Politics. The Totalitarian Perspective, Birmingham 1971 (CREES Discussion Paper, No. 7).

Leonard, Wolfgang, 'Politics and Ideology in the Post-Khrushchev Era', in Alexander Dallin and Thomas B. Larson (Eds.), Soviet Politics Since Khrushchev, Englewood Cliffs N.J. 1968, pp. 41-71.

Linden, Carl A., Khrushchev and the Soviet Leadership, 1957 - 1964, Baltimore 1966.

Löwenhardt, John, Het Russische Politburo. Geschiedenis, profiel en werkwijze, Assen 1978; English edition: The Soviet Politburo, Edinburgh (Canongate Publishing) 1981.

Meissner, Boris, and Georg Brunner (Hrsg.), Gruppeninteressen und Entscheidungsprozess in der Sowjetunion, Cologne 1975.

Parrott, Bruce, The Dynamics of Development in the USSR: The Interaction of Politics, Science and Ideology, 1917 - 1941, New York (PhD Thesis, Columbia University).

Ploss, Sidney I., 'Interest Groups', in Allen Kassof (Ed.), Prospects for Soviet Society, New York etc. 1968, pp. 76-103.

Ploss, Sidney I. (Ed.), The Soviet Political Process. Aims, Techniques and Examples of Analysis, Toronto & London 1971.

Remnek, Richard B. (Ed.), Social Scientists and Policy Making in the USSR, New York 1977.

Rigby, T. H., 'The De-concentration of Power in the U.S.S.R., 1953 - 1964', in J. D. B. Miller and T. H. Rigby (Eds.), The Disintegrating Monolith. Pluralist Trends in the Communist World, Canberra 1965, pp. 17-45.

Rigby, T. H., and L. G. Churchward, Policy-making in the USSR, 1953 - 1961: Two Views, Melbourne 1962.

Skilling, H. Gordon, and Franklyn Griffiths (Eds.), Interest Groups in Soviet Politics, Princeton N.J. 1971.

Stewart, Philip D., Political Power in the Soviet Union. A Study of Decision-Making in Stalingrad, Indianapolis 1968.

Tatu, Michel, Le pouvoir en U.R.S.S. Du déclin de Khruchtchev à la direction collective, Paris 1967.

Case studies in Soviet decision making

Armstrong, Marianne, 'The Campaign Against Parasites', in Juviler & Morton, pp. 163-182.

Barry, Donald D., 'The Specialist in Soviet Policy-making: The Adoption of A Law', Soviet Studies Vol. XVI, No. 2 (October 1964), pp. 152-65.

Beermann, Rene, 'A discussion on the draft law against parasites, tramps and beggars', Soviet Studies Vol. IX, No. 2 (October 1957), pp. 214-222.

Beermann, Rene, 'The law against parasites, tramps and beggars', Soviet Studies Vol. XI, No. 4 (April 1960), pp. 453-455.

Beermann, Rene, 'The Parasite Law', Soviet Studies Vol. XIII, No. 2 (October 1961), pp. 191-205.

Beermann, Rene, 'The "Anti-Parasite Law" of the RSFSR Modified', Soviet Studies Vol. XVII, No. 3 (January 1966), pp. 387-388.

Berman, H. J., 'Law Reform in the Soviet Union', American Slavic and East European Review Vol. XV (1956), pp. 179-189.

Bilinsky, Andreas, 'Zu den "Grundlagen der Gesetzgebung der UdSSR und der Unionsrepubliken über Ehe und Familie"', Jahrbuch für Ostrecht Band IX, 1. Halbjahresheft (September 1968), pp. 181-208.

Conquest, Robert, Power and Policy in the USSR. The Study of Soviet Dynastics, London 1961.

De Witt, Nicholas, Education and Professional Employment in the USSR, Washington D. C. 1961.

De Witt, Nicholas, 'Recent Changes in Soviet Educational Policy', in Denis Dirscherl, S. J. (Ed.), The New Russia. Communism in Evolution, Dayton Ohio 1968, pp. 73-85.

Friedgut, Theodore H., 'Interest and Groups in Soviet Policy-Making: the MTS Reforms', Soviet Studies Vol. XXVIII, No. 4 (October 1976), pp. 524-547.

Graham, Loren R., 'Reorganization of the U.S.S.R. Academy of Sciences', in Juviler & Morton, pp. 133-161.

Gray, Whitmore, 'Soviet Tort Law: The New Principles Annotated', in Wayne R. LaFave (Ed.), Law in the Soviet Society, Urbana Ill. 1965, pp. 180-211.

Hastrich, Aloys, 'Die Öffentliche diskussion um die gestaltung der Grundlagen der Zivilgesetzgebung der UdSSR', Osteuropa Recht 1962:3, pp. 242-256.

Juviler, Peter H., 'Family Reforms on the Road to Communism', in Juviler & Morton, pp. 29-60.

Kelley, Donald R., 'Environmental Policy-Making in the USSR: the Role of Industrial and Environmental Interest Groups', Soviet Studies Vol. XXVIII, No. 4 (October 1976), pp. 570-589.

Kelley, Donald R., 'Interest Groups in the USSR: The Impact of Political Sensitivity on Group Influence', Journal of Politics Vol. 34, No. 3 (August 1972), pp. 860-888.

Komarov, Boris, Unichtozhenie prirody. Obostrenie ėkologicheskogo krizisa v SSSR, Frankfurt a.M. 1978, pp. 5-30 on Lake Baikal. English edition: The Destruction of Nature in the Soviet Union, White Plains N.Y. & London 1980.

Korey, William, 'Soviet Decision-Making and the Problems of Jewish Emigration Policy', Survey Vol. 22, No. 1 (Winter 1976), pp. 112-131.

Löwenhardt, John, 'De vervuiling van het Bajkalmeer, De prijs van departementale koppigheid', Internationale Spectator Vol. XXVI, No. 2 (January 22, 1972), pp. 146-174.

Lubrano Greenberg, Linda, 'Policy-making in the USSR Academy of Sciences', Journal of Contemporary History Vol. 8, No. 4 (1973), pp. 67-80.

McCauley, Martin, Khrushchev and the Development of Soviet Agriculture. The Virgin Land Programme, 1953 - 1964, London 1976.

Miller, Robert F., One Hundred Thousand Tractors. The MTS and the Development of Controls in Soviet Agriculture, Cambridge Mass. 1970.

Mills, Richard M., 'The Formation of the Virgin Lands Policy', Slavic Review Vol. 29, No. 1 (March 1970), pp. 58-69.

Mills, Richard M., 'The Virgin Lands since Khrushchev: Choices and Decisions in Soviet Policy Making', in Cocks, Daniels & Heer, pp. 179-192.

Morgan, Glenn G., 'People's Justice: The anti-parasite laws, people's volunteer militia, and comrades' courts', in Z. Szirmai (Ed.), Law in Eastern Europe No. 7, Leyden 1963, pp. 49-81.

Ploss, Sidney, Conflict and Decision-Making in Soviet Russia. A Case Study of Agricultural Policy 1953 - 1963, Princeton N.J. 1965.

Schmidt, Gerlind, Die polytechnische Bildung in der Sowjetunion und in der DDR. Didaktische Konzeptionen und Losungsversuche, Berlin 1973.

Schwartz, Joel, and William R. Keech, 'Group Influence on the Policy Process in the Soviet Union', APSR 62 (September 1968), pp. 840-851

Schwartz, Joel, and William R. Keech, 'Public Influence and Educational Policy in the Soviet Union', in Roger E. Kanet (Ed.), The Behavioral Revolution and Communist Studies, New York 1971, pp. 151-186.

Solomon Jr., Peter H., Soviet Criminologists and Criminal Policy. Specialists in Policy-Making, New York 1978.

Stewart, Philip D., 'Soviet Interest Groups and the Policy Process. The Repeal of Production Education', World Politics Vol. XXII (October 1969), pp. 29-50.

Reorganization of the USSR Academy of Sciences

Newspapers: Izvestia, Komsomol'skaia Pravda, Literaturnaia Gazeta, Pravda, Uchitel'skaia Gazeta.

Journals: Kommunist, Vestnik Akademii Nauk SSSR (VAN), Vestnik Statistiki, Znamia.

In a number of quotations the translation of the Current Digest of the Soviet Press (CDSP) was used.

Bibliografiia Izdanii Akademii Nauk SSSR. Ezhegodnik. t. I - VII, Moscow-Leningrad 1956-1964.

Buchholz, Arnold, Neue Wege Sowjetischer Bildung und Wissenschaft. Methodische und organisatorische Probleme, Cologne 1963.

Deiatel'nost' Akademii Nauk SSSR 1917 - 1972. Ukazatel' literatury, Moscow 1974.

Directory of Selected Scientific Institutions in the USSR, Columbus Ohio 1963.

220 Let Akademii Nauk SSSR. Spravochnaia kniga, Moscow-Leningrad 1945.

Graham, Loren R., The Soviet Academy of Sciences and the Communist Party 1927 - 1932, Princeton N.J. 1967.

Joravsky, David, Soviet Marxism and Natural Science 1917 - 1932, New York 1961.

Kapitsa, Petr L., Ėksperiment, teoriia, praktika. Stat'i, vystupleniia, Izd. 2e, Moscow 1977.

Kasack, Wolfgang, Die Akademie der Wissenschaften der UdSSR. Überblick *über Geschichte und Struktur. Verzeichnis der Institute*. 2e. stark erweiterte Auflage, Wiesbaden 1972.

Komkov, G. D., O. M. Karpenko, B. V. Levshin, L. K. Semenov, *Akademiia Nauk SSSR. Shtab sovetskoi nauki*, Moscow 1968.

Komkov, G. D., B. V. Levshin, L. K. Semenov, *Akademiia Nauk SSSR 1724 - 1974. Kratkii istoricheskii ocherk*, Moscow 1974.

Korol, Alexander, *Soviet Research and Development: its Organization, Personnel and Funds*, Cambridge Mass. 1965.

Levshin, B. V., *Akademiia Nauk SSSR v gody Velikoi Otechestvennoi Voiny (1941 - 1945 gg.)*, Moscow 1966.

Nauka Soiuza SSSR. Sbornik statei, Sostavitel' G. D. Komkov, Moscow 1972.

Nesmeianov, Aleksandr Nikolaevich, Moscow 1974.

Science Policy and Organization of Research in the USSR, Paris (UNESCO) 1967.

Science Policy in the USSR, Paris (OECD) 1969.

Shcherbakov, D. I., 'Akademik K. I. Satpaev i otdelenie geologo-geograficheskikh nauk AN SSSR', in *Akademik K. I. Satpaev, Sbornik posviashchenny vydaiushchegosia sovetskogo uchenogo*, Alma Ata 1965, pp. 50-56.

Sovetskaia nauka i tekhnika za 50 let, tom VIII, *Puti razvitiia tekhniki v SSSR*, Moscow 1967.

Turkevich, John, *Soviet Men of Science. Academicians and Corresponding Members of the Academy of Sciences of the USSR*, Princeton N.J. 1963.

Urban, Paul K., and Andrew J. Lebed (Eds.), *Soviet Science 1917 - 1970. Part I, The Academy of Sciences of the USSR*, Metuchen N.J. 1971.

Ustavy Akademii Nauk SSSR, Moscow 1975.

Vucinich, Alexander, *The Soviet Academy of Sciences*, Stanford Cal. 1956.

Index

Stress is marked in Russian surnames